DUNCAN FISH

ENGAGE

A practical guide to understanding, influencing and connecting with people

ACKNOWLEDGEMENTS

I would like to thank the people who have inspired, influenced or supported me in the writing of this book. To quote the well-used phrase, I have stood on the shoulders of giants in learning and using the practical tips written about in this book.

I would like to thank the following friends, colleagues and clients for devoting the time and effort to making this book the best it can be: Dr Christian Pitsopoulos, Ted Surrette, Peter Gates, Owen Cooper, Dr Tim Payne, Fernanda Afonso, Kate van Hilst and Carly Fisher. I would also like to thank my researcher, Maja Jovelic, for her tireless assistance.

Two special mentions are also necessary. Firstly, John Honey, the man who changed the course of my life in one conversation. I will be eternally thankful to you. Secondly, Damien Diecke, a man wise beyond his years, who put the cherry on the cake of my social skills. Thank you for sharing your many wisdoms and insights into human nature.

Project management and text design by Michael Hanrahan Publishing
Cover design by Peter Reardon

Disclaimer

CONTENTS

PART I: INTRODUCTION

PART II: EN-TRANCE

PART III: NETWORK

PART VI: GUIDE

PART V: ACKNOWLEDGE

PART VI: GLOW

PART VII: ENLIGHTEN

PART VIII: CONCLUSION

INTRODUCTION

Part 1

Chapter 1

WHY YOU NEED TO ENGAGE

An Engaging Executive is not a title but a concept, a way of seeing the world, and a methodology for making the kind of impact that gets results.

If you're reading this book, the chances are you have come to a turning point in your life or career. You have most likely decided that now is the time to invest in balancing your skills as a manager or leader. I wouldn't be surprised if your technical ability to do your job is exceptional and you are a highly intelligent man or woman. You may even be the subject matter expert in your field. Yet there has been something eluding you for a while. Something which, up until now, you may have put in the 'too hard' pile. That something is your ability to understand, influence and connect with people. If this is the case, this book is for you.

THE IMPORTANCE OF ENGAGEMENT

Certain professions have evolved to be ultra-reliant on the quality of their acquired knowledge. People entering these professions have been conditioned from an early age to study hard and focus on their grades. Some have been so heavily conditioned that the attainment of educational prowess became all important, but at a cost. You see, at some point in their careers these people realise that there is a certain kind of person who is making progress in the world: those who can blend technical skills with people skills. These are people who can capture both hearts and minds, and who know that getting ahead is more than just about being able to do the job.

These people are called *Engaging Executives*.

An *Engaging Executive* is not a title but a concept, a way of seeing the world, and a methodology for making the kind of impact that gets results. An *Engaging Executive* is someone who appreciates both tasks and people in equal measure. This could be anybody who is working in a professional capacity and who needs to get results through other people. *Engaging Executives* go by many job titles, such as Accountants, Actuaries, Engineers, Medical Practitioners, Lawyers, Public Servants, Military Officers, General Managers, Partners, Senior Managers and so on.

Why is engagement so important? Because essentially all human beings are social animals. We have evolved over 6 million years to rely on each other and to work as a team. It is hard wired into us, and much of our physiology and neurology is designed to understand human interaction. Yet in a world shifting its focus towards knowledge and technology, we are losing our ability to communicate and connect face to face.

At the very core of every human being is the need for connection, the need to feel understood and the need to feel valued. This book will help you to achieve the intersection of technical or task excellence and interpersonal excellence. This book is a pragmatic guide on how to influence people more effectively by understanding others better, being understood by others better, and by being engaging and interesting to others.

If you are already sold on the need to enhance your interpersonal skills and you are keen to get stuck in then feel free to skip ahead to the next chapter. However, if you are sitting on the fence then allow me to share with you some noteworthy reasons why this is so important.

THE TECHNICAL CEILING

One of my professional services clients once wrote to me about a realisation he had regarding his career. He said, 'People like me have spent much of their education and early career in structured institutions working hard in accordance with rigid rules in order to achieve a promised outcome, much the way you might train an athlete. I've reached a point now where I realise following rules doesn't always lead to the promised outcome. Simply doing what you've been asked to do well isn't enough – in fact it can be counterproductive to advancement. Related to this, I've realised I need to develop the finer skills of personal persuasion and negotiation; that is, "street smarts". I need to learn how to ignore the traditional rules or at least bend them, a skill that other people acquired earlier in life. This means re-programming my approach.'

This is a powerful epiphany for many people who have come up through the technical professions. Many people with a purely task or technical bent tend to hit the 'Technical Ceiling'. They are brilliant at all technical or knowledge based parts of the job, but when it comes to the people side, they struggle.

Let's consider the typical journey I have seen so often. A person initially chooses a profession that lends itself to his logical, rational skills. He studies hard and achieves exceptional results at school and university. Then he gets his first job, which is normally a highly analytical role and one that allows him to flex his academic bent in a real-world setting. However, as the years go on, things start to change. As this person gets further into his career and higher up the corporate ladder, things start to shift. All of a sudden he finds himself in a role or at a level where he does not need to be the technical expert anymore. He needs to be the leader of people. This is the moment of culture shock, the moment when he realises that all the things he has ever practised and enjoyed are not the things that are going to get him success in the higher levels of the organisation. Now he has to deal with the feelings and emotions of others, with abstract concepts that don't have an answer, with other people's values, and with differing personalities. None of these things has he ever before focused on or placed much importance on. This is the Technical Ceiling.

THE TYPICAL CHALLENGES

I have coached over 1000 executives who are brilliant technically but struggle with interpersonal skills. As a result they miss out on promotions, they miss out on developing those all-important connections, and they fail to get cut through when their technical knowhow alone isn't enough. And their peers with more polished interpersonal skills tend to get the promotions, they make the important contacts, and are invited to the 'off the record' conversations where the real decisions are made.

Having coached executives of various levels, professions and corporate structures, I have found some similar themes. So what are the common challenges that these technically or task-minded executives face? These include difficulty in:

o   making a great first impression or having a presence in a room

o   making small talk with new or less familiar people and being liked

o   being part of the in-group where the real decisions are made

o   influencing their boss, their peers and subordinates in non-technical matters

o   feeling completely out of their depth when having tough conversations or having to manage conflict

o   demonstrating empathy with emotional people who do not come across as 'logical'

o   being perceived as socially awkward, uninteresting or boring to others when they have to network

o   motivating and empowering those around them when they have to manage them.

THE FIVE REASONS TO INVEST IN YOUR INTERPERSONAL SKILLS

Let's explore this issue from a number of angles, starting with the changing nature of the workplace.

1. The changing face of work

As little as 30 years ago people were recruited solely for their technical ability. The more expertise you had in an area the better you were considered to be as an employee.

Technical knowledge continues to be highly valued, but at the same time you need to be able to wield these skills with tact and diplomacy. Having previously had 15 years' experience working in a company that specialises in the science of selection, I can tell you that the blue chip companies and leading government departments place a very heavy weighting on a candidate's ability to display team and leadership behaviours. The recruiting teams will turn over every stone to ensure that a candidate has the correct cultural fit. They have a fine array of tools and processes with which to investigate. This could be a personality questionnaire that is designed to assess your character and give telling information about how and how much you like to interact with people. It might be a behavioural-based interview in which you will be probed to give answers about tough interpersonal situations you've had to manage in the workplace. It could even be a 'day in the life' assessment centre where you are immersed in a virtual world that uses professional actors to test and provoke you to see how you respond. I have used all of these processes on aspiring Senior Managers, General Managers, Partners and C-Suite contenders.

There is one thing that shines through from almost every assessment I have ever completed: it is never the technical skills that lose people the job. Nine times out of ten it is their inability to demonstrate the softer skills of leadership.

If you are thinking to yourself, 'You would say that, being a Psychologist', then let me share how these decisions, of which I have been a part, are frequently made. Typically in large firms there will be a panel of Senior Executives or Partners who review each application. They will have a look to see if there is a business case to support you as a moneymaking or saving entity in your own right. Clearly, your technical ability serves you well here. Then they will look at the corporate values and behaviours that Senior Executives or Partners are supposed to exhibit. I have lost count of the times I have been in a room where an applicant had the right commercial or operational experience but did not have the leadership and interpersonal skills. What's more, it was the senior corporate stakeholders who were the most adamant about these being at the appropriate level. All of these issues can also apply to promotions within the workplace.

This anecdotal evidence is supported by the work of Zenger and Folkman, two leadership experts who have conducted decades of empirical research. In an article in *Harvard Business Review* they discuss their research on the interaction between task and people skills. Only 14% of leaders who were strong in results but not people focus achieved extraordinary leadership performance, defined as 90% in overall leadership effectiveness. When they looked at it from the opposite angle, only 12% of people-focused leaders achieved extraordinary leadership performance. The magic happened when leaders were at 72nd percentile in both task and people focus. This led to an impressive 90th percentile score on extraordinary leadership.

The need for interpersonal excellence is not going to disappear. This is because of the changing demographics in the workplace.

2. Changing workplace demographics

So if you are reading this book, the chances are you are between 35 and 50 years old. Most of my clients tend to sit within this age group. If you are sitting outside of this age range, don't let my discussions about generational differences deter you. Keep going.

According to the people who categorise us by the date we were born, that would make you a Generation X, like me. That is, you were born between 1963 and 1980. If you were born before that you would be classed as a Baby Boomer, and if you were born after you would be a Gen Y.

So what? Well, you have probably started to notice that there are now more people in your organisation that are younger than you than are older than you. While we cannot and should not generalise too much, we can notice that the younger generation have different ideas about how a workplace should be. In the old days – and I shall refrain from calling them 'good' – we could have expected a teenage or early twenties new employee who started asking about promotions and 'what's my next job' to get a clip round the ear. However, these days that just won't cut it. Gen Y's have such a strong identity and collective culture that articles are being written about how to manage them every day. Research by Intelligence Group on Gen Y's has found that:

o   64% of them say it's a priority for them to make the world a better place

o   72% would like to be their own boss

o   if they do have to work for a boss, 79% of them would want that boss to serve more as a coach or mentor

o   88% prefer a collaborative work culture rather than a competitive one

o   74% want flexible work schedules.

In another study conducted by Ashridge Business School in the UK it was found that over half (56%) of graduates expect to be in a management role within three years of starting work, while 13% of graduates expect a management role within a year. That's a significant change in workplace attitudes. In addition, graduates want their managers to respect and value them (43%); support them with career progression (36%); trust them to get on with things (35%); and communicate well with them (34%). Finally, 75% of managers believe they are fulfilling the role of coach/mentor, but just 26% of graduates agree.

Such statistics confirm the changing nature of workplaces, and why being technically proficient is no longer enough to get you ahead. You also need to be an *Engaging Executive* if you are to connect with the emerging workforce.

3. *The importance of connection*

We can see from the exploration of Gen Y's that there is need for connection, mentoring and relationship. However, it is not just Gen Y's who are in need of relationships. Time after time, studies of mental health and wellbeing come back to the importance of social interaction as a key driver of happiness. We all know the story of Scrooge and how he liked to sit on his own and count his money. Was he a fulfilled person though? I think not. So maybe you won't be visited by the ghosts of Christmas in order for you to reconsider your ways, but perhaps an amazing longitudinal study will suffice.

Robert Waldinger is a Psychiatrist, Psychoanalyst and Zen Priest. In 2015 he delivered a fantastic TEDx lecture which, in my view, made a profound point about the importance of developing soft skills and connecting with others. He talked about a Harvard study which has been running for over 75 years and which he is currently the Director of. At the time of Robert's lecture there were approximately 700 people in the study, and it continues to grow. By just about any standard this is a meaningful sample for a longitudinal study and hence worthy of note. The purpose of the study was to answer the question, 'What leads to ongoing health and happiness?'

The lessons from tens of thousands of research pages were quite surprising if you contrast them with what Western society conditions us to believe will lead to happiness. None of the findings point to wealth or fame or working hard as sources of contentment. The clearest message is that good relationships keep us healthier and happier, period. Now, you are probably not falling off your chair with shock because you know this book is trying to make this very point. However, to summarise the findings of the study, there were three big lessons about relationships.

First, social connections are really good for us and loneliness kills us. People who are more socially connected to friends, family and the community are happier, healthier and live longer than those less connected. The study went on to explain that loneliness leads to less happiness, which leads to a decline in health.

The second big finding from the study was that it is not the *number* of friends you have or whether you are in a relationship, it is the *quality* of the relationships that matters. We can all be lonely in a crowd or in a bad relationship. High-conflict marriages end up being worse for your health and happiness than being alone. The study looked at what predicted the quality of life for subjects from middle age to being an octogenarian. When starting from age 50 it wasn't their cholesterol levels that predicted their quality of life, it was how satisfied they were in their relationships. Those most happy in their relationships at 50 were the healthiest.

The third big lesson learned was that good relationships are better for your brain too. For less connected people, brain function also declines sooner and they live shorter lives. Now think about that for a second. That thing you value the most, your ability to calculate and intellectualise … diminished. It is a humbling thought.

Robert's final message was that you need to replace screen time with people time. This applies equally to the workplace. This is the goal of an *Engaging Executive*.

4. The impact on your career

David Johnson of the University of Minnesota Twin Cities writes that 'the Center for Public Resources published "Basic Skills in the U.S. Workforce," a nationwide survey of businesses, labour unions, and educational institutions. The Center found that 90 percent of the respondents who had been fired from their jobs were fired for poor job attitudes, poor interpersonal relationships, and inappropriate behaviour. Being fired for lack of basic and technical skills was infrequent. Even in high-tech jobs, the ability to work effectively with other personnel is essential, as is the ability to communicate and work with people from other professions to solve interdisciplinary problems.'

When writing this book I interviewed many Senior Managers, Directors and Partners in some of the most prestigious global organisations in both the private and public sectors. I recall one such conversation with a Senior Partner named Bill where he described his turning point. It was a tough pill to swallow for Bill. He was a technically brilliant accountant working his way up in one of the top-tier professional services firms in the world. He always knew the solution to your problem before you even finished telling him about it, and he let you know this through his abrupt communication style. One day, Bill recalls, he was shown into an office by one of the Partners, who said, 'The way you come across is impatient and you just don't listen to others. This is why you are not getting put on the jobs you want.' This moment was so impactful, Bill can still recall the colour of the room and the table he was sitting at as if it were yesterday. He never knew that this was the way he came across to others – he thought he was just being efficient and solution focused. Despite finding this confronting, Bill took on board the feedback and since that time he has fast tracked to Senior Partner. Bill argues that 'in today's professional services, technical skills are a given. You need to be able to create some level of excitement. You need to be able to draw people in through your actions.' He went on to describe how the best Partners in his firm were those who could collaborate, be inclusive, demonstrate great listening and not show off their technical skills but be there to grow others.

5. The impact on your pocket

How about a financial reason? In each and every type of occupation there is a range of salaries. Let's look at the difference getting a promotion could make. I was interviewing the Human Resources Director (HRD) of one the world's top commercial law firms. In the legal profession in Australia, at the time of writing a good Senior Lawyer earned about $300,000 pa. By most people's standard that is a pretty good income. However, do you know what the financial difference is at the next level up, being Partner? In year one a Partner could earn a salary of $400,000 pa. After three years that Partner could be earning in excess of $1,000,000 pa. Speaking to another HRD of a different law firm, the same message was confirmed. I was told that 'there has been a paradigm shift in clients. Now they want to build a relationship, not just technical skills.' She went on to say: 'A lot of Lawyers can get away with technical skills alone until they hit 35. At that point they will hit a technical ceiling.' The HRD said in conclusion, 'I am worried about the issue. It is a huge problem.'

So, are you convinced yet? Whether you are a Lawyer, an Accountant, an Engineer, or any other technical profession, the message is the same.

✳ ✳ ✳ ✳ ✳

Hopefully this chapter has given you some solid reasons to be motivated to enhance your interpersonal skills. But who am I to tell you these skills can be developed? Well allow me to share with you my story – from social misfit to social coach.

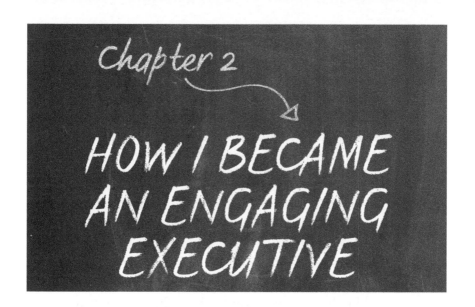

Chapter 2

HOW I BECAME AN ENGAGING EXECUTIVE

To demonstrate that anybody can become an Engaging Executive, allow me to share my story.

If you feel like you might not have what it takes to make this leap, understanding my story could help you on your own journey to becoming an *Engaging Executive*. I have been described as charismatic, charming and engaging, but I wasn't always the person I am today. I was once a quiet, retiring kid. I had to learn how to become outgoing, how to interact with people, and how to do things I was uncomfortable doing. Being sociable didn't come naturally to me at all. To demonstrate that anybody can become an *Engaging Executive*, allow me to share my story.

FROM SOCIAL MISFIT TO SOCIAL COACH

We all have things we naturally gravitate towards. Things that come easily to us. Things we just kind of get. Then there are those other things. The things we don't like to do. The things we don't *want* to do. These are often the things we feel less able to do.

As a child I always admired those people who seemed to be successful at school. There seemed to be two camps: those who were really clever, and those who were really popular. Very rarely did people seem to fit into both camps, although there were people who didn't fit into either group – like me. That being said, sometimes there was that special person who managed to transcend the dichotomy. I remember a boy called Neil. He was in all the top educational streams, and he was also a charming boy, popular with both the guys and the girls.

As a 16-year-old boy I didn't realise it at the time, but that intersection between being clever and being socially skilled was the key to success in the modern world of work. However, it wasn't just that Neil was clever. It was what he was clever in. Neil was brilliant at mathematics and sciences. Now, if he had been into the arts or literature then the contrast wouldn't have been so great. That's almost expected. People who are 'arty' are quite often socially comfortable and expressive. That was what made Neil special. He was a scientifically minded person with social skills – an unusual combination, and a most powerful one.

THE SCHOOL YEARS

Then there was me … academically clueless *and* socially inept. Where did I fit into the land of the 'clever kids' or the 'popular kids'? I guess I fell in the cracks, into the world of the dorks. I didn't consider myself clever enough to be a nerd or interesting enough to be a geek. Most of the time when I was at school I felt lost and deficient. I used to feel overwhelmed in mathematics classes, and on numerous occasions, if you were very observant you would have caught me secretly crying at the back of the class while pretending to work out a calculation.

I was a very, very shy boy with little self-confidence. I didn't mix socially with the other kids in my neighbourhood or at school once I got into my pubescent years. I found it very awkward. I didn't know how to relate to them.

This phobia of talking to people was pervasive in all areas of my life. When relatives visited I would find as many reasons as possible to leave the room. When the phone rang I used to stare at it, afraid of who could be on the other end. I didn't answer it in case I didn't know the caller. If someone knocked on the door of our house, I would creep up and look out the side window. If I didn't know who it was I wouldn't open the door because they might try to sell me something and I didn't know how to refuse.

This problem was still present when I was in my late teens.

When my Mum and Dad got divorced, Mum returned to her working-class roots, which was West London, near Heathrow Airport, and she took my sister and me with her. I ended up in a working class school in the rough part of town.

Given the fact that my self-confidence was at zero and I attended a school that was more a training ground for bullies than an academic institution, I didn't fare too well. I was never great at exams, and back in the 'good' old days everything was about how well you did in the last three hours of a two-year course – there was no ongoing assessment like there is today. You can imagine the feeling of opening your exam results letter as soon as it arrives and seeing that two years of your work had been reviewed and deemed 'unclassifiable'. Not even good enough to be 'poor'. I did retake a couple of courses, but I never managed to get higher than a D. So I left school with little to show.

Once School Performance Tables were introduced the year I left the school, my school only had two stand-out statistics: the lowest amount of exam passes and the highest number of days truancy. It turned out I had gone to the worst school in the area.

MY ENTRY TO THE WORLD OF WORK

As a teenager, I had a neighbour who lived across the road called Pat. Looking back, it was Pat who set me on the long road to where I am today. Pat was working for the Metropolitan Police Service (MPS) as a member of the Civil Staff; in other words, not a Police Officer but a member of the public service who did the behind-the-scenes roles that freed the Police to be out with the public. About once a week Pat would thrust an application form in my face and tell me to go for a job at the Police Station. I kept insisting that I didn't want to work for the Police, and growing up in a working-class neighbourhood that was never going to be a popular choice. Nevertheless, after constant bombardments from Pat, I reluctantly filled in the form. Shock, horror; I was invited to an interview.

I tried really hard not to get the job, but alas, I didn't try hard enough.

So I ended up working for the Police just for a lack of anything better to do. It was an administrative job which was very repetitive and 100% paper based. We didn't get computers for another six years.

By the age of 24 I knew that pushing forms around wasn't for me. I still didn't really know what *was* for me, but after a bit more thought, I considered it was time to learn more about what makes people tick. So I applied for a job in Human Resources (HR), which in those days was known as Personnel. At exactly the same time that I put in an application, the MPS was launching a brand new outplacement facility and they were looking for employees. The MPS had just undergone a review that criticised their organisational structure. So they threw a tonne of money at a state-of-the-art Outplacement Centre and packed it full of self-development gurus, psychologists and career coaches.

That was probably the luckiest break I've ever had.

A TURNING POINT

Now I didn't really have any skills in Career Coaching but what I did have was a strong admin background, so I was hired as the 'admin boy' who could fill out the forms and sign people in and out of the centre. However, when I went there I saw an opportunity. I realised that because it was all unprecedented, there were no clearly defined roles, and managers were making it up as they went along. So, as the expression goes, 'slowly, slowly catch a monkey'; I gradually asked to get involved in more and more aspects of the centre. I effectively did all the same up-skilling as my manager, who was a Chief Inspector. After a while, my manager gained trust in me and allowed me to assist the junior Police Officers who found their way to our centre, usually on the grounds of medical retirement.

I became very interested in what was happening. It was all about helping people to work out what they wanted to do when they left the

Police Service, and I thought to myself, 'Hey, maybe helping people to find out what they want to do is actually what *I* want to do … ?' I was promoted to be Centre Manager and I started to co-run the Outplacement course with one of the external consultants. The more I did that, the more my confidence started to grow.

That's when my first life-changing event occurred.

MY FIRST LIFE-CHANGING EVENT

I'll ask for permission to get a bit teary eyed as I talk about this significant milestone in my life. If ever there was a man to whom I owe career success, it is John; the man who set me free. The man who made me question who I was at the deepest level. The man who showed me how powerful having the right mentor at the right time can be.

I see my life in two halves: before I met John and after I met John. Coming from my past as a poor academic performer and a socially inept person, I was still carrying a lot of baggage and believing I was an academic idiot. I used to feel intimidated by anyone who had a university degree. If someone had a Master's degree then I couldn't even look them in the eye. In fact, as I started to become more friendly with people at the Outplacement Centre, I realised that many of them had Master's degrees. On one occasion I was invited to a party by a friend who was a Psychologist. My first question was, and I kid you not, 'Will there be anyone else there with Master's degrees?' To which she replied, 'Of course'. So I told her I was busy that night. That was how it was in my inner world before I met John.

After co-delivering the Outplacement Courses with me for about a year, John took me to one side and did a Jedi mind trick on me. He could see I was passionate about helping people, and he could see something in me that I couldn't see in myself. He said, 'Duncan, you would make a great Psychologist'. I was shocked, floored, gobsmacked. Unfortunately, at that time the force was not strong enough in me, and so I replied, 'I can't, John. That would mean going to university and I am too old, too dumb, too poor and too scared'. However, John was a Psychologist and a Master Practitioner in Neuro Linguistic Programming (NLP). He could see that I was being held back by my limiting beliefs, and he wasn't about to accept it. So he challenged me on all of these issues; he challenged me until I started to think differently. One by one he questioned my beliefs and probed and disentangled the story I had been telling myself all those years.

That challenging of my beliefs about myself gave me the impetus to turn my whole life around, and that one conversation was the single most important conversation I believe I've ever had in my life. From that moment I realised I wanted to become a Psychologist and I believed I could be a Psychologist, so I applied to university.

Of course, I had to overcome the fact that my academic record was atrocious, so I had a chat to the university entrance panel who told me that on the plus side they did like mature students, and I was 27 at this point. On the down side, I would have to undertake more study to meet their entrance requirements. I think they warmed to my plight, and the challenge was set. So I started studying another 'A' level subject at night school while working full time. I had to finish the course in 26 weeks instead of the normal timeframe of two academic years. It was tough, but I was on a mission and so I threw everything at it.

Then came the day I had to phone up for my result. Now considering the last time I had got my 'A' level results, at the age of 19, I received a D and E and a U (unclassified), you could say that my apprehension was rather high. I remember the call like it was yesterday. I phoned up and said, 'Hello, my name is Duncan Fish and I'm calling about my "A" level results'. 'Yes,' she replied, 'hold on'. So off she went to look them up. Every second felt like a year, and my heart felt like it was going to burst out of my chest. She came back on the phone. 'A,' she said. I replied, 'That's right – "A" level'. 'No,' she responded, 'You got an A'. So I replied, 'Sorry, this is *Duncan Fish* … have you got the right person?'

It turns out she did have the right person, and I was on my way to university.

I ended up finishing in the top 5% out of a class of 100 students. Turns out I wasn't such an idiot after all. I guess your results are a bit different when you start to believe in yourself. So now I was off to change the world.

I wanted to be an Organisational Psychologist, just like John. I wanted to help people change their lives, just like John. That became the narrative that sat behind my drive to get into the psychological profession, and I thought that becoming an Organisational Psychologist would mean doing all of this wonderful life-changing work. But as I went through my two degrees I realised a lot of it was more about statistically proving things, and that very little was actually solidly provable. Even the things we hold on to very dearly as Organisational Psychologists really only have a quite low predictive validity.

WHEN PSYCHOLOGY ISN'T ENOUGH

Once I graduated I got a job at one of the leading global consultancies for Organisational Psychology, based out of the UK. In fact, when I joined it was the second largest employer of Organisational Psychologists in the world after the US Government. I delivered tried and tested processes related to selection, such as psychometric testing, assessment centres, competency-based interviews and a whole range of other tools. I even ran statistics courses, which made me chuckle … me, the boy who used to cry in mathematics classes.

I realised after a while that I wasn't actually very interested in the 'statistically' proven things. What was more interesting were the stories that people told about themselves; that is, what they *believed* about themselves. I guess after about five years on the job I realised that psychology didn't necessarily have all the answers; or not the answers that I wanted, at least. Being a classically trained Psychologist gave me a great ability to label people and describe situations but less ability to effect changes in them.

So I started learning about Neuro Linguistic Programming (NLP). In a nutshell, this is the study of linguistics and how this impacts on our thought processes, which in turn impacts our lives. I read some books, and then I did my NLP Practitioner course in 2006. It was eye opening. I loved studying the subjective, which was far more telling to me than a cold and sterile standardised questionnaire. In fact, I found NLP so enlightening, I went on to complete my Master of NLP and Trainer of NLP certifications. As a Psychologist I was able to cherry pick from the toolkit of NLP and choose those methods that were the most powerful. This was where I found some of the most useful tools and processes to complement my psychological knowledge. What fascinated me was the realisation that everything we experience is subjective and that we are all prisoners of our own beliefs. Once I started delving into what someone believed was possible and impossible, I could see in others that self-doubting man I had once been. It became my purpose to help free others from their self-imposed prisons.

MY SECOND LIFE-CHANGING EVENT

I carried on using a combination of conventional psychology and NLP for a couple of years, and then in 2008 I got my second life-changing opportunity – a secondment to Sydney, Australia. It turned out I would fall in love with Sydney and decide to stay.

In 2012, after working in Australia for a while, I decided to take two months off work to circumnavigate the continent on an adventure-tourer motorbike – a 20,500 km round trip. At the time I thought the trip was going to be about physical endurance, it was going to be about being physically uncomfortable in unusual surroundings, it was going to be about challenging myself to do things that could kill me. However, as in all good stories, there was a twist.

The biggest learning I took out of it, the thing that was most life changing, was actually something that took me right back to being that shy, socially awkward boy again.

After three weeks of being on the road and having relatively little company, I arrived in Darwin. Now Darwin is a small city in the grand scheme of cities but a big city compared to everything else in that part of the world. So when I arrived I was really excited to go out for the night. I checked into a motel that was a pleasant treat after sleeping in a tent for the previous two weeks. I asked the receptionist, 'So, what are the people like here?' She said, 'They're so wonderful, they're so friendly … all you have to do is stand by the bar and they'll literally come up and talk to you'. I responded, 'Wow, that sounds awesome. Just what I need'.

So I found the busiest pub in Darwin and I stood there with a beer in my hand waiting for these friendly locals to ask me about my travels and share a yarn or two. Nothing. For two hours I stood there and not one person spoke to me. This was when my big learning smacked me in the face ... and ouch, did it hurt. As I stood there in a packed pub full of people laughing and joking all around me, I found it completely impossible to cross through this imaginary force field between me and them to start a conversation. I was absolutely rooted to the spot. There was nothing I could do. I felt completely incapacitated. I suddenly realised that after all the work I had done on myself and with all the skills I had learned in business communications and relationships, I was still the scared little boy who didn't want to talk to strangers. No matter what I said to myself I just could not overcome my anxiety about speaking to people. I had all this chatter in my head saying, 'What do I talk about? What value do I bring? Why would they want to speak to me? I'd just be a nuisance', and a thousand other unproductive thoughts. So I stood there, a voyeur of other people's fun.

Despite the fact that I was in the busiest place that I'd been in for the last three weeks, I felt the loneliest I'd felt on the whole trip. In fact, the loneliest I'd felt for a long, long time. It made me realise there was some part of me that wasn't how I wanted it to be. There was some part of me that was still that shy little boy I was many, many years ago, and now I was absolutely determined to fix it. So I vowed that once I got back to Sydney I would find the most extreme way of overcoming that fear.

THE FINAL FRONTIER

So now let's cut to the end of my trip. I arrived back in Sydney all fired up to conquer my fear of talking to strangers. I had given it more attempts during the remainder of my trip, but unless someone came up and initiated a conversation with me, I still struggled. So I looked into training and coaching options to help me. Most seemed to be related to being assertive, or communication skills. This just wasn't my issue. I could stand up in front of a packed room and speak all day, and I had been doing this for 15 years. I needed something that was related to social skills. So I dug deep and I found something that was really eye opening.

Now, as a relevant part of my story, just before commencing on my soul-searching motorbike trip I had found myself, after seven years of being in a relationship, single at the age of 40 on the other side of the world with no friends. How did this happen!?! Everything in my life was going so well. This being said, it was exactly the problem I needed to help me focus on a part of personal development that had eluded me so far.

So how is this relevant to my story, I hear you ask? Well, let me explain.

I did what everyone does these days when they have a problem: I Googled it. I found a man called Damien, and he ran a highly ethical form of dating coaching. Essentially, he taught men and women how to meet each other. His philosophy was based on being someone who speaks their truth, and has purpose, confidence, and charisma, but who is also devoid of ego. It was exactly what I was looking for. It was the art of how to be charming, engaging and confident in social situations, with the intention of projecting your best and genuine qualities. It was more about developing confidence and self-esteem in social situations than it was about dating. It matched with my Psychologist's code of ethics perfectly, and so my next adventure began.

My first big shock was this was a dry course, despite being run in night spots – not dry as in boring but dry as in no alcohol. After the briefing I said to Damien, 'Okay, I'm just off to get a beer'. He responded, 'No, there's no alcohol allowed'. My world was suddenly turned upside down. 'You mean … I have to talk to strangers all weekend … sober? But this is my greatest fear.'

Damien explained that alcohol was just a safety blanket that many people hang on to. He asked, 'What if you are walking down the street and the next love of your life walks past? Are you going to run off to a bottle shop to buy a beer before approaching?' You should have seen the panic on my face. That weekend was hell on earth for me, and I took away a big learning from it: I was appalling at small talk if I wasn't wearing my corporate identity.

After that weekend, I realised that I had a lot of work to do on my social skills in non-work environments. It seemed that I was fine if I was in a business meeting or running a coaching or training session. In these contexts I had bulletproof confidence as I was the technical expert. However, take me out of the suit and put me in an environment where I didn't have a role and I was hopeless. So that is when I decided to approach Damien again and explore my options.

The journey was long and tough, but after a few months a new version of me was emerging. I had found my social skills. It was as if that scared little boy had finally grown up. It was the cherry on the cake and it rounded me off as a person – the new, complete version of me had been born. Damien and I subsequently started to develop such a good relationship that he offered me a position as a Dating Coach, so to add to Psychology and NLP I now had Dating Coaching.

Nowadays, when I coach executives in leadership soft skills, I draw on Psychology, NLP and Dating Coaching. Each has something to add to understanding how best to connect with, influence and engage the people you work with in an ethical manner.

Maybe you have a similar story? Maybe within my story there are struggles of your own you can relate to? Whatever your starting point, if I did it, you can too. Even better news is that you don't need to make 20 years of mistakes in order to learn what I have. This book is a distilled, updated and refined version of everything I have ever learned and applied.

So become the person you have always wanted to be. Become an *Engaging Executive*.

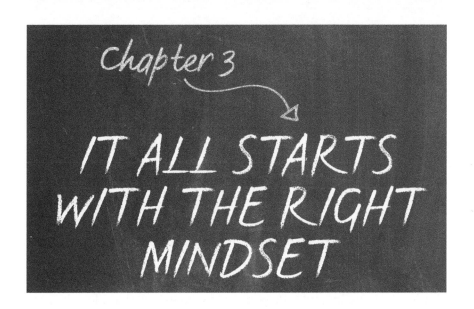

Chapter 3

IT ALL STARTS WITH THE RIGHT MINDSET

*If you start off with the wrong mindset,
nothing in this book will be of any help to you.*

Before we get into some highly useful and practical tips on how to enhance your interpersonal and influencing abilities, it is important to start by looking at your mindset. Undoubtedly, to some degree you will find the process of enhancing your interpersonal skills a challenge. As such, let's deal with the elephant in the room: at first, some of the techniques are going to be hard work. You are going to make mistakes, you are going to feel clunky, and you may feel a little lost at points. This is all part of your journey to becoming an *Engaging Executive*.

Welcome to the world of human behaviour.

You may well have chosen your current profession because of a logical and linear argument. This makes it easy to predict and model things. Unfortunately, the human brain does not work in such a linear fashion. This being said, although there are no absolutes, there are many principles of human behaviour that will get you a result more often than not, if you take the time to understand them. The key thing to remember is that interpersonal skills are an art form and not a science. So this chapter is dedicated to acknowledging this and giving you some frameworks and techniques to put this into perspective and guide you down the right path – especially when it all seems to be going wrong and you feel like giving up.

HOW PEOPLE LEARN

We all have preferences for the way in which we learn things, but reassuringly we all follow the same overarching process. 'The Four Stages of Learning' model is a fantastic place to start. I have been using this model for over 20 years and it still resonates. Interestingly, no-one can quite pin down the originator of this model. Some say it was Maslow, some Herzberg, and some say it was developed by Noel Burch from the Gordon Training Institute. Regardless of who invented it, I love it. I use it to help participants understand what lies ahead just about every time I begin one of my training programs. The process of learning is slightly less confronting if you consider that everyone has to pass through the same four stages, which we'll have a look at now.

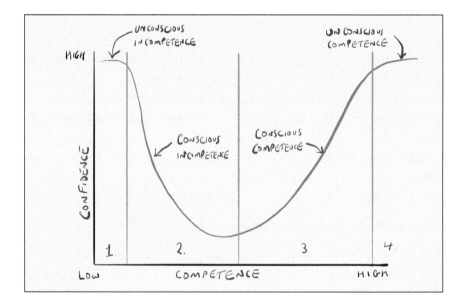

Unconscious Incompetence

At the beginning we all start in this beautiful place of blissful ignorance where we don't know what we don't know. You are going about your career being a technical expert and loving what you do, blissfully ignorant of the fact that you may not be getting the traction you need with the people around you. This is called *Unconscious Incompetence*. This is a bittersweet place where you can exist with a false sense of competence, as the realisation of your ignorance has not yet hit you. At this point your confidence is fairly high.

Conscious Incompetence

Then something happens and it all changes. This is the moment of realisation that you need to enhance your interpersonal and influential skills. This can come in many different forms. For some it is missing out on a promotion. For others it is receiving feedback from a manager, peers or staff. It may even be that a change of role forces you to have to network more or differently and you just don't know how. Whatever the catalyst, you are suddenly aware that there is a gap that you need to fill or a skill you need to improve. This is called *Conscious Incompetence*. So begins the journey of learning the new skill, which in this case will be something connected with influencing or interpersonal skills. This stage is the toughest, and you will have small wins and then failures. You will feel you are making progress, and then you will feel it slipping away again. This can be damaging to your confidence levels but this is completely normal. This is the time when you need to persevere.

Conscious Competence

As you progress through this book I will set you practice exercises that you are strongly advised to complete. These will help you get to the next stage, which is called *Conscious Competence*. This is a satisfying stage, but it is not the end of the journey. As the name suggests, there is still a conscious process in that you still have to think about what you are doing. For example, you might go into a networking situation during which you can apply some of the techniques from this book: you will still need to think about the techniques in a considered way while you are in the Conscious Competence stage. It will be like applying a formula rather doing it intuitively or naturally.

Unconscious Competence

However, one day, which will be sooner or later depending on how much you practise, you will reach the wonderful state of *Unconscious Competence*. This is where you just do what you want to do without thinking about it.

GOING BEYOND YOUR COMFORT ZONE

There is going to be a level of discomfort when learning any new skill. I like to talk to my clients about three levels of 'stretch' when it comes to pushing themselves to learn new interpersonal skills.

Let's have a look.

The Comfort Zone

The first level is called the Comfort Zone. This is, as the name suggests, a pleasant, familiar and comfortable place where you are doing what you know and acting how you normally act. This is a great place to be if you just want to cruise and do what you can already do. In this zone you don't really learn that much as it is quite a passive state.

The Stretch Zone

The next level is called the Stretch Zone, and this is the sweet spot for learning interpersonal and influencing skills. This level is where you are actively pushing yourself to do something new, and with it may come some discomfort, some confusion, some self-doubt and some reluctance. This is, however, the optimum state for learning. The more you act outside your Comfort Zone, the bigger your Comfort Zone becomes. Let's say, for example, that I set you a task of going up to and starting a conversation with a random stranger every day for a month. On day one you will probably be a bit embarrassed, uncomfortable and clunky. However, by the thirtieth day I am pretty sure you would be able to do it much more comfortably without giving it too much thought. In psychology we call this 'habituation'. To quote the *Oxford*

Dictionary, this means, 'the diminishing of an innate response to a frequently repeated stimulus'. In more simple terms, you just get over it. What used to cause a reaction no longer causes a reaction.

The Overwhelm Zone

Finally, we have the Overwhelm Zone. This is when you have taken things too far. This is not a good place to learn as by this stage your brain has gone into fight or flight mode. Your sympathetic nervous system kicks in and pumps your body full of hormones and neurotransmitters. As a consequence, the rational part of your brain, the cerebral cortex, becomes less able to function as your body is being prepared to defend against physical attack.

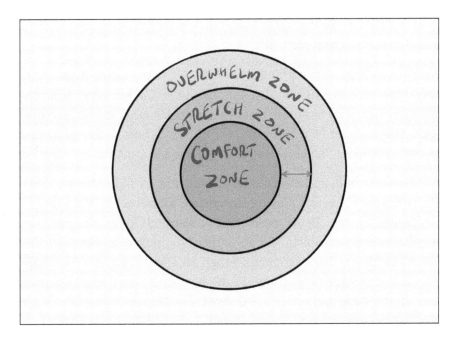

So if you are to learn effectively from this book you need to find the sweet spot of the Stretch Zone. If you are cruising along you are not pushing yourself enough, and nothing will change. If you are overwhelmed to the point of going blank, you are pushing yourself too much, and nothing will change.

ARE YOUR BELIEFS HELPING OR HINDERING?

Let's now talk about another common problem I encounter when coaching executives which interferes with their learning: your belief system.

Take the red pill

Let me first set the scene.

Deep within us all lie our beliefs and values. Beliefs are like a computer program in that they are the rules by which we live our lives, and they can be both a blessing and a curse. Some people have a very powerful program that assists them to achieve great things. Others have a program full of bugs which derails them. The key point to remember is, your beliefs are not the truth. However, we act as if they are the truth and that makes them *our* truth.

Many of us believe something so strongly we refuse to see it any other way. Now, this is fantastic if it gets us the result we want. Unfortunately, many of us continue to hold onto beliefs that do not serve us well. Beliefs about how the world should be. Beliefs about how other people should be. Beliefs about what we can and can't do.

I am a movie buff, and I am always looking out for films that are beautiful metaphors for this. One of my all-time favourites is *The Matrix*. I frequently ask my clients to watch it or re-watch it and imagine they are the main protagonist, Neo. I ask them to think of all the ways that Neo's situation is similar to theirs. I then ask them to ponder what happened that enabled Neo to change the situation. I am going to suggest you do the same and watch or re-watch *The Matrix*. If you can accept the assumption that your beliefs about the world are not actually how the world works then you can start to go deeper.

'But … what has this got to do with developing my interpersonal skills?', I hear you ask?

The answer is: 'Everything'.

Are you at cause or at the effect?

One of the principles that really resonated with me when I first learned Neuro Linguistic Programming (NLP) was the concept of 'being at cause'. Allow me to unpack what this means. It was quite a confronting concept, but at the same time life changing. Essentially, you are either 'at cause' or you're 'at the effect'. To be 'at cause' means that for everything you have in your life – the good, the bad and the indifferent – you take full accountability. So everything good is your doing and everything bad is your doing. Everything has happened as a consequence of a decision that you made or didn't make, or an action you took or didn't take, or something you said or didn't say. Everything in your world happened because of you. Don't confuse this with being self-centred or having delusions of grandeur. I mean that ultimately you are the master of your own destiny. Remember, this is a philosophy and a mindset. I am not saying this is reality because we all create our own reality through what we believe. One side of this equation happens to be a mindset of highly successful people, and the other, well … I think you know where I'm going with this. This can be a tough pill to swallow for most people. With it comes great responsibility, as it means you have no-one to blame when something goes wrong. Ouch. That is a bit scary, right? No-one to blame means blaming yourself, right? Not exactly – it means seeing the world for what it is: a series of choices. The empowering part of being 'at cause' is that if you got yourself into something you can get yourself out of something.

On the other side of the fence sit the majority of people who are 'at the effect'. This is a wonderfully easy place to be because it requires no action or effort whatsoever. The additional good news is that you can blame everyone else for your problems. People who are 'at the effect' will often be caught saying such things as, 'I would have been all right if it wasn't for my boss', or 'my peers', or 'my staff', or 'my spouse', or 'my kids', or 'the government', or … the list is endless. Don't get me wrong: we all enjoy a bit of a whinge occasionally, and there's nothing wrong with that. In fact, it can be a good stress reliever. Unfortunately, if that is where you place most of your effort then you become a victim. Whinging doesn't move a situation forward – it just makes you feel sorry for yourself.

Attack of the Ego

So why am I being all philosophical when it comes to developing interpersonal skills? It is because if you start off with the wrong mind-set, nothing in this book will be of any help to you. You must start by believing that you are 'at cause' to change your situation.

Many people become upset when others do not understand them. Sometimes we blame other people for being 'stupid' or inarticulate. But the fact of the matter is, it is *your* responsibility to change your communication, not the other way around. I was coaching a highly intellectual lawyer once and he was explaining how he had been trying out some of my methodologies but he had been getting annoyed by the behaviour of others. In other words, he had come to me to help him enhance his communication skills, yet he was annoyed by the fact that other people were not communicating with him in a way he appreciated. This is what I call an Ego Attack. It is when your beliefs and values about how people *should* communicate or behave around you make you choose to feel annoyed. This is being 'at the effect'.

If you were to truly be 'at cause' then you would adopt another useful mindset from NLP, which is, 'the meaning of your communication is the response you get'. This is absolutely the only way to think about communication.

Let's consider an example. Say you have a favourite joke, and you tell it to someone but she doesn't laugh. You might think to yourself, 'Idiot … clearly you have no sense of humour'. The truth of the matter is, your joke wasn't funny. Not to this person, anyway.

Let's consider another example from business. Let's say you pitch an idea to a client, who subsequently goes with someone else who has an 'inferior' product or service. The fact of the matter is, you did not communicate to that client in a way that was right for him, and someone else did. This is why great communicators are flexible communicators, which brings us to another useful NLP mindset, 'the law of requisite variety'. This essentially means that the individual with the highest amount of flexibility of behaviour will have the most influence on the system. Those who can adapt the most will always win.

If you look at any environment on Earth, the dominant species is the one that can adapt the most to the changing environment. A species that can't adapt to environmental changes becomes extinct. Out of all the creatures on the planet, which species is the most adaptive? Humans, of course. So, therefore, out of the human race, those that can adapt the most will also be the most successful.

So coming full circle on the Ego Attack, your way of communicating is not automatically the right way. It is only the right way if it gets you the results you want. This book is designed to help you get more of the results you want more of the time.

Let's begin by taking a look at the ENGAGE model, which is the framework outlined in this book.

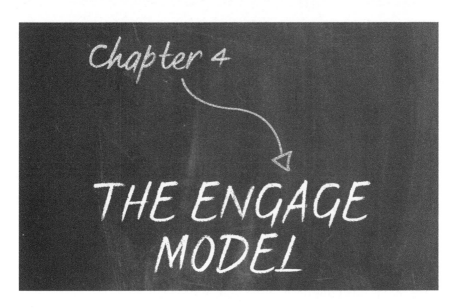

Chapter 4

THE ENGAGE MODEL

My absolute belief is that the greatest leaders are those who are technically brilliant and who have a mastery of connecting with people.

When coaching people from highly technical and knowledge-based professions I often find that they really like to work with coaching models that have steps. This is where I find the rubber hits the road. So, in the spirit of 'the meaning of your communication is the response you get', I have created an overarching model which is very pragmatic. I call it the ENGAGE model, and it represents, broadly speaking, the order in which I coach executives how to become an *Engaging Executive*. This book is an eclectic collection of powerful tips, each related to a specific stage of the model. Some of the stages may already be a strength for you while others can be used to complement your existing strengths.

Let's have a look at an overview of each stage so I can give you a sense of what each is about.

E IS FOR EN-TRANCE

The first step to being engaging is to make a noticeable entrance, but that alone does not make you engaging. It is, however, a vital first step.

In fact, so much rests on the first 30 seconds that this part alone can make or break an interaction with someone. Therefore, this stage of the model is going to cover everything you need to do when you first meet someone in order to 'en-trance' them.

Now here is the interesting part. This first stage does not even touch on what to say. 'Huh?' you may be thinking. That's right, this stage is all about the elements of communication that happen before you even get into the content of your message; in other words, your expressions, your posture, your walk, how you use your voice, your gesticulations and, most importantly, your eyes.

En-trance is all about developing your presence.

N IS FOR NETWORK

Once you have a clear understanding of how to hold yourself and how to make use of nature's most powerful assets, we will move on to a practical application. This stage of the model is about how to network effectively. When I talk about networking, what I am really saying is 'how to build connection' with people. This may be in an actual networking event, it could be by the water cooler, it could be one to one with a peer, it could be standing on a train platform talking to a complete stranger. The purpose of this stage is to help you build relationships with just about anyone. This section will have some great tips on how to introduce yourself to strangers, how to master small talk, how to develop meaningful rapport and then how to disengage gracefully.

G IS FOR GUIDE

Once you have learned how to connect with someone you can move to the next stage, which is to guide the conversation.

This stage is often what people want to get to first. The problem is, if you make a bad first impression or fail to develop rapport with someone, the chances of you influencing them without positional power is minimal. In this section you will learn how to marry your physiology with your voice and words to create maximum impact. You will learn how to influence by asking questions. Yes, questions can be more powerful than statements. You will learn how to insert yourself into conversations dominated by others. You will learn how to use the language of influence artfully by controlling the level of abstraction or specificity used. You will also learn how to resolve conflict and get a win–win outcome.

A IS FOR ACKNOWLEDGE

After you have mastered the art of influence we can start rounding you off with some skills that will make you more approachable and an all round better leader of people. This section is all about how to develop empathy, thereby acknowledging the needs of others. By this I mean really understanding people and what is important to them. If all you ever do is influence people for your own gain, your success will be short lived. You may not want to get 'touchy feely' all the time but being able to go there in appropriate moments is what makes you stand out as a people manager. This section is all about winning hearts and minds.

G IS FOR GLOW

So by this stage you would have learned how to connect with people, influence them more successfully and understand them in a much more meaningful way. You may start getting invited to more networking events, business lunches or social events. How are you going to make sure that you are the person in the room that everyone remembers fondly? Well, this stage is all about lighting up the room and leaving a lasting impression. You will be able to tell engaging stories and use humour appropriately. This stage is about how to add the secret sauce to how you deliver content. It will also ensure you never run out of things to say in social settings.

E IS FOR ENLIGHTEN

Having worked on yourself for the majority of this book, in this section we will turn to how to help others flourish. For many technical or task-focused people their pride and joy is the intellectual knowledge they have in their head. This, however, is the realm of the technical expert and not the *Engaging Executive*. The best people leaders are those who can inspire others to greater heights, who can shape and mould the talent around them in a way that is not teaching but coaching. So this section is dedicated to how you give feedback in a way that is constructive and positively received. Finally, we look at how to coach and mentor others to greatness.

* * * * *

The ENGAGE model is all about how to become more interpersonally skilled. My absolute belief is that the greatest leaders are those who are technically brilliant and who have a mastery of connecting with people. My goal for this book is to help you raise your interpersonal skills up to the same level as your technical skills. My goal is for you to become an *Engaging Executive*.

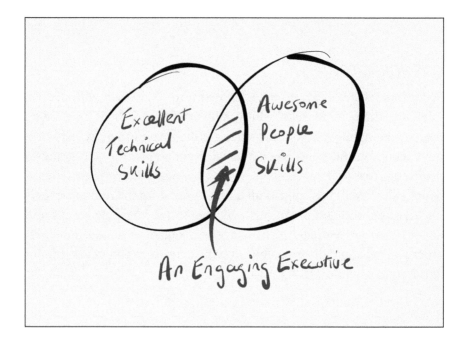

If you would like to get a sense of how you stack up against the ENGAGE Model then take the free questionnaire on our website: www.engagingexec.com.au.

HOW TO GET THE MOST FROM THIS BOOK

This book is best used interactively. It is more like a manual than a novel. Therefore, it is not a 'cover to cover' read. I would suggest you read one chapter at a time and then put the book down and practise the techniques. Some of these sections may be more relevant to your particular goals than others. While the model holds together as a process, you can also dip in and out of specific sections to get what you need immediately.

You'll notice throughout the book that I alternate between using male and female examples. This is to avoid the awkward use of 'he or she' and 'him or her'. Of course, with the exception of just one technique, everything in this book can be applied equally to males and females.

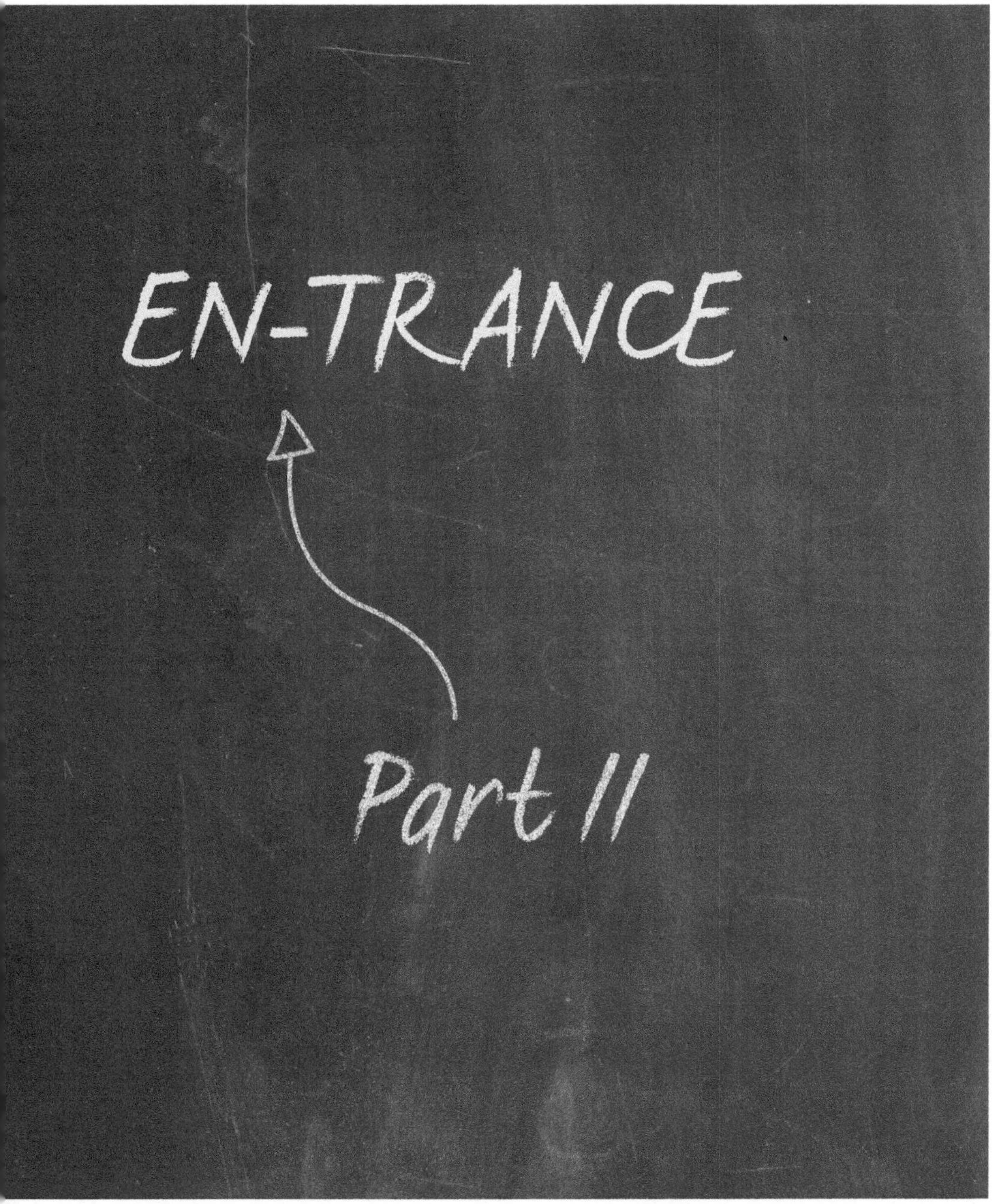
EN-TRANCE
Part II

Chapter 5

THE EYES HAVE IT

There is a special connection when you look someone directly in the eye.

It has been appreciated for thousands of years that the eyes are very telling. You have probably heard the expression that 'the eyes are the window to the soul'. According to Dr Paul Ekman, a renowned body language expert, the human face is capable of 10,000 micro expressions. However, ask yourself, which part of the face do you tend to notice first? For most people, when they are talking to someone they tend to look that person in the eye. It would be pretty odd to talk to someone's nose or ear.

There is a connection that is made when you look someone directly in the eye. You can tell so much from looking people in the eye, and that means they can tell just as much when they look at you. So this chapter is dedicated to the power of eye contact. It is right at the beginning of the ENGAGE model as I believe this is a make-or-break communication skill you need to get right in the first five seconds of an interaction.

THE POWER OF EYE CONTACT

There is a joke I have heard about eye contact that has been told to me by people in a number of different professions. Funnily enough, I seem to hear a different profession mentioned depending on the one I am working with at the time, so I will pick one at random for the purposes of the joke, but feel free to insert your own profession if you think it fits. So after that massive build up, the joke goes, 'How can you tell if you are dealing with an extroverted Accountant? He looks at *your* shoes as he talks to you.' Boom, boom.

Okay, it's a terrible joke, but it has a very serious message. For some professions, and typically the ones that attract the more introverted and technically minded people, eye contact can be a massive issue. Many introverted people feel uncomfortable holding someone else's gaze. As a consequence, they are not picking up on the other person's non-verbal communications, and equally they are communicating a lack of confidence or a social awkwardness.

Have you ever met someone who just seemed to hold your gaze? I don't mean in a leery or manic way but in a way that made you feel you had her undivided attention. As she spoke or listened, you could just feel her presence. There was a weight behind her eye contact that projected certainty and strength. This is most certainly part of the armoury you need to make a powerful impression.

PORTRAYING CONFIDENCE

I once attended a course on presence where we had to do eye gazing exercises; that is, you stood opposite another person and you stared at the person's left eye. We would do this for up to five minutes without speaking. Why the left eye? Research suggests that about 80% of people have a dominant right eye. This means that when you look at someone, most people will look from their right eye to a person's left eye, if directly in front of them. We might think we are looking at both eyes but in reality we can only ever look at one. Research has also found that the left side of the face displays slightly more emotion than the right due to lateralisation of brain function. So for most of us, our brains are conditioned to focus more on the left side of the face.

If you want to find out which eye is dominant for you, look at an object in the distance, and point to it with your finger so that your finger is on the same spot. Close one eye at a time, and whichever eye is lined up with the finger is your dominant eye.

By having a focus on just one eye you are able to have a single point of attention. If you swap between both eyes as you look at someone it breaks the connection momentarily and it looks less solid.

It is actually very challenging to stare at someone in the eye and not laugh or smile or talk. However, what starts to happen is a connection and a calmness develop, where you just look into the person and you start to feel them. I don't mean with your hands but with your connection. This is actually a very powerful exercise to try if you want to increase intimacy and connection with someone. Numerous studies have shown that people who make higher levels of eye contact with others are perceived as being:

o   more dominant and powerful

o   more warm and personable

o   more attractive and likeable

o   more qualified, skilled, competent and valuable

o   more trustworthy, honest and sincere

o   more confident and emotionally stable.

For our purposes though, I am not going to ask you to start staring into the eyes of other people for five minutes without speaking. You might come across as a bit weird.

So how do we use this in a business and social context?

Think for a second about an actor or actress who has presence. Ensure it is a person who projects confidence and authority; for example, Cate Blanchett, George Clooney, Christoph Waltz or Helen Mirren. Find a clip of this person on YouTube and observe how he or she holds someone's gaze.

Yes, it is quite normal for your eyes to move around as you speak (more on that later), but I want you to focus on keeping your gaze on the left eye of whoever you are talking to. Two things will happen when you do this. First, you will notice so much more about what the other person is saying and how they are reacting to you. Secondly, you will inspire within the other person a sense of confidence and certainty in what you say.

There is more to this, which again we will come back to, but if your eye contact is weak and you cannot hold someone's gaze it is a massive clue to that person that you are not confident.

USING YOUR EYES LIKE A SPOTLIGHT

You can use your eyes in many ways when communicating with others. We have focused on using your eyes to demonstrate strength and confidence, but what if you do not want to be the person who is the focus of attention? Sometimes you need to give the floor to someone else and step out of the limelight. This is particularly important if you are trying to build respect for or raise the profile of someone else in the room.

Let me give you an example. As I have moved through my career and have become one of the more seasoned veterans in my area, I frequently work with more junior colleagues. As I normally open the client sessions, and as many of my clients are more my age than the age of my more junior colleagues, it is not unusual for my clients to mostly speak to me. I really want my colleagues to be valued by our clients, yet sometimes my junior colleagues will ask a brilliant question to the group but the clients will still address their answers to me.

Rather than be rude and ask the client to address my colleague and not me, I use my eyes. So as the client looks at me and starts to speak, I look at them and then deliberately and purposefully turn my eyes and head to my colleague. I hold it there for five seconds, and then I look back to see if the client has followed my direction. Sometimes it will take two or three attempts until the direction is followed.

Think of it like a mirror that is deflecting the sun from one direction to another. Your eyes can be a very powerful tool for diverting attention away from you when you do not want it.

THE EYES DON'T LIE

I mentioned earlier that people tend to move their eyes around as they talk. Have you ever noticed this? If not, next time you are talking to someone I want you to watch what their eyes do. You will notice that they look up, down or sideways. According to Bandler and Grinder, the founders of Neuro Liguistic Programming (NLP), eye patterns are telling of how someone is processing information at that given moment.

Think about this for a minute. I want you to visualise a cartoon character that is having a bright idea. Imagine what the eyes of the character are doing. What direction are they looking? As you picture this, look away from this book and just imagine it for five seconds. Really, do this exercise … as a little experiment.

Did you notice your eyes looking upwards? I bet you did. Interesting, eh? What Bandler and Grinder discovered was that each direction has a meaning: each time you look in a particular direction it means you are processing a particular type of information.

Let's look at the diagram below.

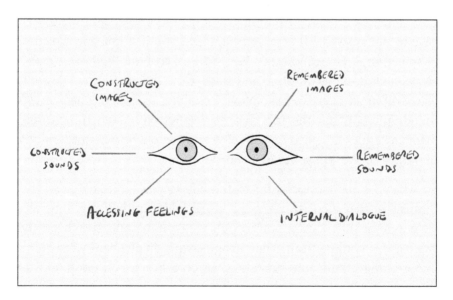

It is most important that you use this chart as if you are looking at someone else. In other words, this is not a diagram for yourself, looking out of your own eyes. As I go through the rest of this explanation it is most important you remember I am describing it as you look at someone else. To see how it looks on yourself, do the exercises by using your phone to take a photo or video.

This eye pattern chart holds true if the person you are looking at is 'normally organised'. In other words, this is the most common way that someone is wired. People can also be 'reverse organised', in which case everything on the horizontal axis swaps sides. The up and down order stays the same though.

If someone is looking upwards they are normally imagining some kind of image. According to the eye chart, if someone you are looking at looks up and to the right they are recalling a picture of something they have seen before. So, for example, if you were to ask someone what the colour of her room was when she was a child, you may find her eyes going up to the right.

I was once speaking to a friend who is a brilliant financial guru. I was asking him about the best types of investments. As I asked him a question, he paused, looked up to the right (as I looked at him), and then gave me an answer. I then asked him, 'Did you just imagine a picture of something?' He responded, 'Yes'. So I asked him, 'Was it a graph?' He looked at me astounded, and said, 'How did you know?' Easy. It was written all over his face. Now, I couldn't *really* tell what he was thinking about, but the fact that he was recalling something visual made my educated guess pay off. How did I know he was not thinking of numbers? We will get to that shortly.

So what if someone looks up to the left as you look at them? This means that they are constructing a visual image in their mind. So let's have a go at this. I want you to pull your phone out, switch on the video and record yourself. Then imagine what an elephant would look like wearing a pink tutu and standing on a beach ball. Stop and do this now.

Did your eyes go up and to the left (if you were recording yourself)? Unfortunately, this eye pattern has been misinterpreted by some people as a lie detector test. There is a rather amusing scene in the movie *The Negotiator*, where Samuel L. Jackson plays a tough cop who is trying to get a confession out of a suspect. He asks the man to tell him exactly what happened. The man looks up and to the left, and Jackson shouts, 'You're lying. The eyes don't lie!' Okay, so could it mean that someone is lying? It is possible. However, what we can really only tell is that someone is constructing a visual image.

What about if someone looks horizontally to their right, as you look at them? This means that they are remembering a sound. It could be a piece of music, a voice or a conversation. Put the book down after you read this next task and have a go. I want you to recall the sound of your pet when you were young. If you had a goldfish then choose another sound from your childhood.

Okay, do this now.

Did you notice your eyes move to the side? If you were looking at someone it would have been their right.

What about if the eyes go to the left as you look at someone? I often notice this eye pattern when I ask a client to imagine a conversation they are going to have. When I ask, 'What exactly would the other person say?', if the eyes go horizontal and to the left as you look at them then they are constructing a sound or a conversation. This would be an external sound and not their own internal dialogue. If I asked you now to imagine what your boss or partner would sound like if they spoke like a pirate, you will probably find your eyes going horizontally to your left, if you were recording yourself.

Stop and do this now.

So then, what about when someone looks downward? This one is slightly more complex as it really does depend on which side the person looks towards. If, as you look at someone, they look down and to the left, they are accessing their feelings. Think about this for a moment. Imagine a scene in a movie where someone is feeling really sad. Where do they look? Always down. This is not to say that a person looking down and to the left is necessarily sad. It is likely to mean that they are feeling some kind of emotion or remembering an emotional event. Think of a time in which you felt some kind of low energy: mild disappointment, for example. Avoid anything too negative as we only want to test the theory. Try this now.

Did your eyes go down and to your left, if you were recording yourself?

So what about down and to the right, as you look at someone? This normally means that someone is having some kind of internal dialogue or processing something analytical. So if you were to ask someone else to calculate a sum in their head, you would most likely see them looking down and to the right. Try this now; say your 7 times table and observe if your eyes want to go down and to your right, as you recorded yourself. If you remember back, this is how I knew my financial guru wasn't thinking of numbers at the time I asked him as his eyes looked up.

TAPPING INTO HOW OTHERS ARE THINKING

Paying attention to the eyes is a very powerful way of understanding how someone is thinking. Of course, it changes moment to moment and we all look in different directions as we speak, if only for a second. This can be used to tap into how a person is thinking in the moment and therefore help you to adjust your message to that person. From this point on, start observing people as they speak and notice how their eyes move.

Let's get started with some practical exercises.

PRACTICAL EXERCISES

EXERCISE ONE: FOCUS ON THE LEFT EYE

- Practise focusing on just the left eye of everyone you speak to. If you find your eyes drifting, bring them back to the other person's left eye.

EXERCISE TWO: REDIRECTING EYE CONTACT

- Practise redirecting the eye contact you are getting onto someone else next time you are in a meeting. See if you can get the other person to shift their gaze from you to another person.

EXERCISE THREE: OBSERVE PEOPLE'S EYE PATTERNS

- Observe people's eye patterns as they talk. Ask them to imagine an image of something and see if their eyes go up. Ask them to imagine a sound and see if they go sideways. Ask them to imagine how they felt about something and see if they go down.

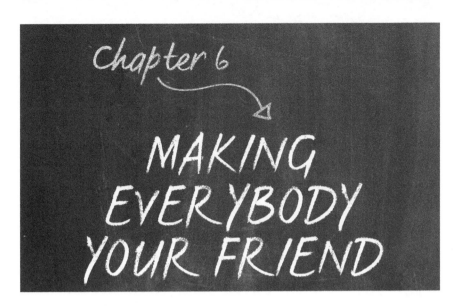

Chapter 6

MAKING
EVERYBODY
YOUR FRIEND

If it comes down to a choice between two equally talented people, it will always be the one who is liked that gets the job, the promotion or the favour.

This chapter is all about being friendly.

Okay, maybe you have another motive, something more career focused. However, you need to remember one thing: if it comes down to a choice between two equally talented people, it will always be the one who is liked that gets the job, promotion or the favour.

Would you like to know something else? Sometimes it is not even the person with the best technical skills. I was having lunch with a Principal Lawyer while writing this book and I was asking him what relevance social skills have in his profession. He said that, absolutely, technical brilliance is of the utmost importance. However, he went on to tell me how he had to fire the most talented young Lawyer he had ever hired. He described, in a rather comical fashion, how this genius Lawyer used to attend meetings with absolutely no clue as to how to present himself. He would sit in meetings scoffing all the biscuits and allow the crumbs to fall down his shirt. This guy didn't know how to meet and greet. His social skill was non-existent. As a consequence, his phenomenal intelligence was seen as arrogance. In the end, the

Principal Lawyer was too embarrassed to keep taking him to clients and he had to let him go.

So you might be thinking to yourself right now, 'Okay, Duncan picked an extreme example and I am not that bad' – and hopefully you are right. Think about it though. If being technically excellent was all that mattered, why would this Principal Lawyer have fired this talented young person?

WHY FIRST IMPRESSIONS MATTER

In psychology this is known as the 'primacy effect'. In other words, the very first impression you have of someone is the one that is most remembered.

As an Outplacement Consultant, I used to find out all sorts of amazing facts about how employers make recruitment decisions. There are many studies on exactly how long it takes a recruiter to make a hiring decision. Some are as generous as four minutes while others are more along the lines of 30 seconds. What happens after the initial impression is a wonderful illustration of human conditioning. You see, when you first meet someone, in those first vital moments your facial expression, your first words, and the way you carry yourself are all assessed in a flash. This largely happens at an unconscious level. Consequently, our own biases and stereotypes kick in. What then happens is we judge people based on this information. This is largely unavoidable, although I have spent years of my life as an Organisational Psychologist training recruiters and managers how to minimise this.

While you can recover from a bad first impression, it is best not to go there at all. A few years back I was running an assessment centre for one of the big four accounting firms. The purpose of the assessment was to help the Senior Partners select potential new Partners in the firm. As you can imagine, there were a lot of potential Partners trying their best to make a good impression.

As part of this assessment there were a number of role-plays. We always used professional actors or existing Partners as the role-players in order to simulate real life as best as possible. One candidate stood out during these role-plays – for all the wrong reasons. In an attempt to build rapport he used a really disingenuous routine that looked more like he was auditioning for a movie than a Partnership position. To give him some credit he was trying to utilise a current event: the bushfires close to Sydney. As a result of the fires, the city had an ominous cloud hanging over it for days. From the office you could see the smoke just hanging there. I walked into the room as the assessor, and the actor followed behind me. The Candidate was standing with his back to us and his hands on his hips looking out the window. As he heard the door click, without even turning around, he said his opening line. Now for the purposes of illustration and a little humour, imagine the voice of Clint Eastwood saying this. He opened with, 'Those God damn bushfires … when will they ever stop'. At which point he turned around and shook the hand of the actor. It was the most odd opening to a meeting I had ever seen.

Later that day I caught up with the other assessors to complete our candidate reviews. One colleague opened up with his evidence on said candidate by stating that in his role-play – which was completely separate to the one I had observed – there was a slightly unusual start. He started to explain how the candidate was facing out the window with his back to the actor – I jumped in and said, 'Let me guess what happened; did he say, "Those God damn bushfires … ?"' With that we both gave each other a knowing look and shook our heads.

So why did I tell you this story? It's because first impressions really matter, and I want to make the right one. So in this chapter we will take a look at how we can build on the power of eye contact with some supporting artists, so that you don't come across like Clint Eastwood doing a weird movie scene next time you meet someone for the first time.

THE POWER OF A SMILE

We are going to start with something so simple its power almost gets forgotten in the grand scheme of things, yet this is something so hardwired into us that if you do not do it you are really missing one of nature's gifts. That, of course, is to smile.

It doesn't sound like much, but there is a lot in a smile. According to research done by University of California, San Francisco there are 19 types of smiles. While I'm not going to cover them all as some types are not relevant to a business context, I will touch on some of the key findings. There are two main categories: polite smiles and genuine smiles. Do you know how to tell the difference? It is actually the eyes. Yes, our friends the eyes have made a guest appearance in this chapter as well.

Berkeley University has also done some great research to define different types of smiles. They describe a polite smile as the corners of the mouth being slightly uplifted but the eye muscles remaining completely relaxed, with no movement. Try doing this now so you can feel it. Smile with your mouth but leave the muscles around your eyes completely relaxed. It might feel a little strange, but try doing this in the mirror. You will see that it does look polite but it does not look like an absolutely genuine smile. It is the sort of smile you give someone if they hold the door open for you, or when you thank someone in a shop for giving you your coffee. Actually, this is the type of smile you tend to see most of the time in the workplace, especially in meetings.

There is only one truly genuine smile and that is technically known as the Duchenne smile. This was named after Guillaume-Benjamin Duchenne, a contemporary of Darwin specialising in neurology. He conducted experiments where he would zap single muscles of the face with electricity and then look at the changes. He postulated that there was a difference between smiles that came from the soul and the ones put there consciously. A true Duchenne smile activates a lot of muscles in the face. For a start, the cheek muscles are raised in addition to the sides of the mouth. Most importantly, the muscles around the eyes contract and you get crows feet. Try this kind of smile now. If you can, do it in front of a mirror or even take a photo on your phone. See how wide you can get your smile and how high you can make your cheek muscles go. Notice how it looks and feels around the eyes. Notice I said, 'how it feels'. I want you to start focusing on how your facial muscles feel as you pull different expressions. In this way we have more awareness of what expressions we are making and how to make different ones.

A good smile is contagious

Have you ever had the following experience? You are walking along the street and a memory of something funny pops in your head. As a reaction you break into a smile just as you walk past someone, and he catches your eye. Guess what happens? He smiles right back at you, doesn't he? It is an amazing thing to watch.

There is something very contagious about a good smile. It is almost impossible not to smile back at someone if they give you a full Duchenne smile. You can feel a bit indifferent about a polite smile but a full smile just seems to trigger something automatic.

Do you want to know the best part? Smiling makes you feel good. You might be thinking to yourself, 'Hold on, no … feeling good makes you smile'. That also happens, but the act of smiling is something that causes you to feel happy as well. There is a famous experiment by Dr Fritz Strack and his colleagues at the University of Mannheim in Germany that proved the power of smiling. Volunteers were divided into two groups. Some were asked to hold a pencil between their teeth, and the rest were asked to hold it between their lips. Participants were then asked to read a series of comics and rate the degree of humour. The findings, published in the *Journal of Personality and Social Psychology*, suggested that a forced smile can indeed boost humour, as participants who held the pencil between their teeth found the comics funnier than those who held it between their lips. Therefore even a contrived smile can lead to good feelings. But, a true Duchenne smile given to someone else and then returned is actually doing them a public service. What did it cost you? Nothing.

Adding light to every interaction

As a Dating Coach, one of the first things I learned was the power of a smile. The first 10 seconds of meeting someone are so important, and an overwhelmingly friendly smile is really disarming. Having seen literally hundreds of men and women meet each other, I can tell you that a huge amount of the initial reaction came down to the smile. A large Duchenne smile had a positive impact, while a polite smile was less well received. If the smile was non-existent then the person was frequently met with animosity.

Now, don't think this only applies to dating. This is a life skill. I love to smile. In fact, I often go out of my way to smile at people that I don't need to. Why? Because it adds a little light to every interaction. For example, I grab a coffee at the same café a few times a week. Every time a new staff member starts I go out of my way to give this person a massive smile and then have a little joke. I do this every time. It always starts with a smile, and I often do it through the glass door before I even enter the café. Every time I do this I get a really warm welcome, even if I join the back of the coffee queue. You may be thinking to yourself that it's just because I go so often. Well, so do many of the other customers – the staff know them by name too. However, none of them get the warm welcome I do.

It's not just cafés either. I do this routinely with my colleagues and my clients. As a consequence I'm regularly told how easy I am to be around. When someone feels comfortable with you, they are far more likely to open up to you and trust you.

The art of smiling

You can do this too, so let's dig a little deeper into the art of smiling.

Smiling eyes

Have you ever noticed how some people just look eternally playful? It's not that you can't take them seriously, it is the fact that there is a glint in their eye that just suggests they ooze cheekiness and fun. I have done a lot of work at a certain Defence institution in Australia. There is an Officer there who always has a cheeky look in his eye. Whenever I walk past him I just know there will be a playful comment that comes my way. It puts a smile on my face every time. I also work very hard on doing this myself. I am not suggesting that I do not take things seriously. However, when I meet people I like to have a playful glint in my eye. I had a boss in the UK many moons ago who once said to me, 'Duncan, you seem to have this ability to be playful one minute and then switch to serious when you need to. I really admire that in you.' That comment stuck with me. I do believe it genuinely helps people relate to me more easily and to like me.

So let's practise this now. Relax your face so that there is no tension in your muscles at all. I want you to imagine you are just about to prank somebody and you are imagining their reaction to the prank. See if you can feel that cheekiness in your eyes. You should start to feel them changing shape, and you may notice a slight pull on your cheek muscles as well. Find a mirror or use your phone to see if the smile in your eyes gives off a sense of playfulness. Keep practising until you can do it on command.

The sunrise smile

Okay, so what I am not suggesting is that you walk around with a permanent grin on your face. People may think you have been on the happy pills. I am talking about smiling deliberately and with purpose. It is a powerful tool, and as such you must use it to gain the maximum advantage at the most appropriate times.

I once had a client I was coaching who found it difficult to smile. He was a good-looking man and had a very artistic, hipster look about him. The problem was, he never smiled. He always had this intense look about him. As a result, whenever he approached someone, that person would think he was going to have a serious word. When I asked him to smile he said it felt false as he wasn't the smiling kind. When I pressed him, it was more to do with the fact that he felt silly going from intense to smiling in a flash. So I taught him the 'sunrise smile'. This is where you break into a smile slowly. Remember for a moment the image of the sun coming up in the morning. How it gradually breaks over the horizon, a little at first and then the light floods the landscape. This is just like the sunrise smile. You start with the eyes by squeezing the muscles around them, then you allow your cheek muscles to rise, and the corners of your mouth start to follow. Finally, you allow your lips to part and reveal your pearly whites. The whole movement only takes two seconds. It looks really natural and it creates the perfect Duchenne smile. Try it now, and again do it in front of the mirror or record it on your phone using the video function. This time it needs to be the dynamic motion that is observed, not just the end state.

Have a go now.

BUILDING THE SOCIAL FABRIC

By now you should have learned the perfect smile. Don't be concerned if it still feels a little false and mechanical. It will do until you develop muscle memory around the movements. I would strongly suggest that you keep practising regularly so that it does become a habit.

So now let's talk about a general principle of building the social fabric. This is one of my personal hot topics and one that I live and breathe every day. Really, this is the very essence of everything in this book that relates to the social skill elements. As pointed out in the research in the Introduction to this book, there is strong evidence to suggest that relationships are good for us. Well, in order for us to have relationships we have to make them happen.

I was coaching a corporate client in how to develop his social connection with other people and we got about five sessions through the coaching when he asked me an interesting question. He asked, 'Duncan, I have been making lots of effort now for several weeks but it always seems to be me who has to make the first move to be social. When are people going to start initiating it with me?' The fact of the matter was this client was in negative equity when it came to the social piggy bank. For years he had just focused on being technically brilliant, which he was. He had locked himself away in his office and kept his head down. So I explained to him how building the social fabric really works. It is not a transaction, it is more organic. First you have to sow the seeds, then you have to tend to them, and then you can harvest them later. It is a process that takes time and investment.

Why is this important in a workplace? In just about every study I have ever seen of why people leave their job it nearly always comes down to two reasons. First, they do not like their manager, and secondly, they do not like the culture of the workplace. I have never heard of one person who left an organisation because the people were too friendly towards each other. I have heard of plenty of folk who have left because they felt alienated or felt like a cog in the machine and not valued as a human being.

So how do we change this? Simple: interact with people who you do not need anything from, just for the sake of it. You don't need to take hours, just a couple of minutes here and there. Stop by someone's desk, catch someone at the photocopier or by the coffee machine and have a chat. Pull out the sunrise smile and just shoot the breeze. This is how we begin to stitch the social fabric.

In later chapters I will provide you with a structure you can use to skillfully develop small talk. For now though, just get into the habit of being social and smiling via some exercises. A journey of a thousand miles starts with but a single step.

Let's get into some exercises that will help you on this journey.

PRACTICAL EXERCISES

EXERCISE ONE: SUNRISE SMILE

o Every day for the next week, practise the sunrise smile in the mirror before you go to work. See if you can get it from zero to Duchenne in two full seconds. Don't rush to the smile, make it graceful and smooth.

EXERCISE TWO: SMILING AT STRANGERS

o Every day, go out of your way to smile at people you don't need to. Start with staff in cafés, bars, or restaurants as these people will be naturally receptive. Then graduate to smiling at people who are not paid to respond to your smiles. Smile at people you walk past in the street or the postman or whoever comes your way.

EXERCISE THREE: SMILING AT COLLEAGUES

o Next, start smiling at the people you work with. If you work on your own or in a small office then smile at those who share your building. Remember, to reap the benefits you need to sow the seeds within your own field.

EXERCISE FOUR: HAVING A CHAT

o Finally, start dropping by on people in your office who you don't need anything from at that particular time. Give them a sunrise smile and have a couple of minutes of non-task-related chit chat, and then bid them a good day and leave them feeling happy that someone took the time to chat when they didn't need to.

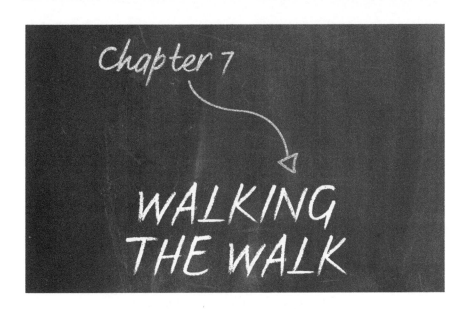

WALKING THE WALK

Remember, you are always communicating with your body language.

In this chapter I am going to be talking about posture and how to move your body for maximum presence and impact. This chapter will be short and sweet, however it is an important one if you want to become an *Engaging Executive*. Sometimes an impression is formed of you before you even open your mouth. Be mindful of how you hold yourself; as we all know by now, first impressions matter.

STANDING TALL

Some might say I am gifted with natural height, as I am 6'5" (196 cm). Some might not, especially when it comes to finding a pair of jeans off the rack. However, much more important than your height is how you hold yourself. Your posture is of utmost importance.

When I was a child I was always about the 70th percentile when it came to height among the other boys. That was, until everyone hit puberty. For some reason I seemed to go through it later than everyone else, and so I actually became average height for a while. Then, in a miraculous act of catching up, I suddenly hit a growth spurt over the six-week summer holidays – my legs seemed to grow like Mr Fantastic in the Fantastic Five. However, the rest of my body stayed the same size. It took years for my body and arms to catch up. This meant that for a couple of years I felt massively disproportioned.

I had also become the tallest boy in the class. Kids being kids, they saw me as an easy target and took the mickey out of me for looking like a stork. As you may recall, there is this weird mindset when you become a teenager: you want to be the same as everyone else and yet you want to be different at the same time. There are the fashion items you all need to have, such as the 'in' trainers, or shirts, or jeans, or logos. If you don't have those then you get placed in the out-group. Well, as previously discussed in the Introduction to this book, I squarely sat in the out-group, and this just made things worse.

At that stage of my life I was ashamed of my height and so I used to stoop. I had terrible posture with a slouchy back and rounded shoulders. In this way I was lessening my height so as not to stick out. Now if you have ever seen anyone who slouches, what does it normally project to you? That's right: someone who is lacking confidence. He does not have confidence in his own body and appearance, as he is not using what he has to the full. This isn't just a problem faced by tall people. I am forever coaching people of different heights who do not use their posture properly. So let's address how we can make the most of our presence through our posture.

The oak in the wind

First, we will talk about how to stand. Sounds simple, right? And it is. Saying that, how conscious are you of the way you stand? How much attention do you actually give to your posture as you stand and talk to people? I'm not talking just formal presentations but every time you address someone. When people are nervous it often shows. This is the concept of 'leakage' (see chapter 8). Your words might be saying one thing but your body language is saying something else. Often, what happens when someone is nervous is his torso goes rigid and so do his arms. He also starts to shuffle around on his feet. (I call this the 'Michael Flatley' look, from River Dance. If you have ever seen traditional Irish dancing there is a distinct style of having a deadpan expression, a stiff torso and vertical arms, and then the feet are flying all over the place. It is an impressive dance, but not one you need to be doing when you meet someone.)

One of the movements I teach men I call the 'oak in the wind'. Let's start with the feet. Imagine yourself standing with your feet shoulder-width apart with your feet facing forwards, and your weight evenly distributed. Now imagine this is the trunk of a mighty oak tree. The roots are deep and solid and the trunk is thick and immovable. This is your power base. People who stand still and hold their ground have presence. Those that shuffle their feet or stand with their legs wrapped around each other look nervous. Those that stand with their weight unevenly balanced, which raises one hip higher than the other, may even look awkward.

As I said earlier, when a person is nervous the torso tends to lock up. So if we want to look confident then the torso must be loose and relaxed. Imagine again the mighty oak. The trunk is solid, and the strong boughs are too, but there is still a gentle flow of movement as the wind passes through the leaves. Confident executives can use their hands in a controlled and expressive manner. As they do this their head is still and their eye contact is solid, as discussed earlier. It is also perfectly fine to smile if that is appropriate for the tone of the conversation. Yet their hands move freely and with purpose.

Try this now. Stand with your feet shoulder-width apart and plant them evenly on the floor. Stand with your back straight and shoulders back, keeping your head relatively stable. Now, practise just talking and using your hands in a deliberate yet not overly excitable way. (We will come back to specific types of hand gestures in later chapters.)

WALK LIKE SEAN CONNERY (A TIP FOR MEN)

Maybe it's because I'm English but I just adore James Bond. I have read all of the original Fleming books and seen all the movies more times than I can count. And yes, everyone has their favourite Bond actor. However, for the purposes of this topic I am going to discuss the first Bond actor, Sean Connery. As Bond, he brought the character to life.

Interestingly, Connery's portrayal of James Bond is not that similar to the characters in the books. Connery's interpretation was much more charming and light-hearted. However, Sean Connery did have to be groomed for the part as he was a rough and ready, relatively unknown actor from the streets of Edinburgh. This was not the look Cubby Broccoli was going for, and neither was Bond's creator, Ian Fleming.

Sean Connery was well down the list of choices for the part but the other actors rejected the role. One of the main qualities that won Connery the part was when he was spied out the window walking across the road to the audition: someone commented, 'He moves like a panther'. Think about that for a second. Sean Connery was being compared to actors such as Cary Grant and David Niven, and yet what opened the door for him was the way he moved. How powerful is that?

So I would like you to go online and have a look at a YouTube clip of Sean Connery as James Bond. Make sure it shows him walking side on. You will notice how he leads with his shoulders in a smooth rotational fashion with a very slight tilt to the centre. If we think about how he does it in an exaggerated manner, it is as if he is rowing through a river with his shoulders. It is constant movement and yet his head stays level and solid. Have a go now. Walk across the room and imagine you are a panther on two legs. Imagine that sleek shoulder movement slowly rowing you across the room. See if you can catch yourself in the mirror or in a reflection in a window.

Remember, you are always communicating with your body language. Be like Sean Connery and make an impression before you even open your mouth.

MOVE LIKE CATE BLANCHETT (A TIP FOR WOMEN)

As the last tip was exclusively for men, this tip is for women. While a man can get away with a bit of swagger in his stride, a woman needs to pull this off in a slightly different way. One of my actor friends was trained in how to walk with presence and command the attention of a crowd. She told me that one of the techniques actress Cate Blanchett uses is to imagine she is wearing a crown. Apparently, just before she enters a room she visualises herself putting a crown on her head.

Imagine this right now. Imagine the weight of a crown made of solid gold and encrusted with jewels. Imagine how stable you would need to keep your head so that it didn't slip off. Now imagine the look and feel of nobility as you enter a room, walking purposefully but with perfect posture, turning your head slowly to observe the room. Imagine the grace and confidence that wearing a crown would give you.

THE FIRST TOUCH MATTERS

For most situations, the first time you ever touch someone, at least in a business context, will be with a handshake.

Have you ever reacted aversely to a handshake? I know I have. You get a few different types. There is the 'vice grip' which crushes every bone in your hand in an act of macho dominance. This is not a good look. There is nothing impressive about you showing how strong you are with your hands. Unless you are applying for a job as a Bouncer or a Labourer there is no call for displays of physical strength. In fact, it is often a sign of insecurity if someone feels the need to intimidate you in order to make himself feel better. Then you get the opposite – the classic 'dead fish' handshake. You know the one; it feels like someone laying a cold, dead fish in your hand. This has absolutely no authority whatsoever. This projects a sense of low self-esteem. The final type of unwelcome handshake is the 'finger grabber' – when you put out your hand and someone grabs the end of your finger tips prematurely and insists on shaking them. This projects nervousness in the rush to get it over and done with.

So, what is a good handshake? There are all kinds of theories on this. Some say you need to have your hand on top in order to show dominance; some say at the bottom to show openness. I suggest a solid vertical handshake that is firmly but not forcefully pushed into the hand of the other person with a light squeeze. The squeeze should last about three seconds, and it should not be too tight or too light. It should be like the strength required to pick up a can of drink.

One addition I often do is to cup my other hand underneath the person's forearm; so, if I was to shake a person's right hand, which is the norm, I would cup my left hand under the forearm of their right hand.

So why would I do that? It is simple biology. When you touch someone it releases a hormone called oxytocin, which is a bonding hormone. It is actually the same hormone that is released when a mother first holds her newborn baby. The more points of contact, the more oxytocin is released and, in theory, the more the person feels connected to you. The famous Psychologist Robert Cialdini in his book *Influence* (2008) even talks about studies showing how touching someone at the same time as asking for something improves your chances of getting it. There is something to be said for oxytocin.

Okay, so let us practise this via some exercises. Remember, practice makes perfect.

PRACTICAL EXERCISES

EXERCISE ONE: PLANTING YOUR FEET

o Stand in front of a mirror and plant your feet shoulder-width apart. Make your legs strong, and from your waist up make your body loose and flexible but not floppy. Keep your head upright and your eyes level.

EXERCISE TWO: TALKING TO YOURSELF

o Try talking to yourself in the mirror and using your hands in a deliberate way while standing with your feet planted.

EXERCISE THREE (FOR MEN): WALK LIKE SEAN CONNERY

o Walk across the room in view of a mirror or a reflection in a window. See if you can walk like a panther. Start by over-exaggerating the movement, even though it might feel silly. Then back off until it looks like a smooth and graceful motion akin to Sean Connery.

EXERCISE FOUR (FOR WOMEN): WALK LIKE CATE BLANCHETT

o Walk across the room in view of a mirror or a reflection in a window. Pretend to put a heavy crown on your head before you move. Then walk towards the mirror keeping your head as stable and as smooth as you can. Observe how the rest of your body follows suit.

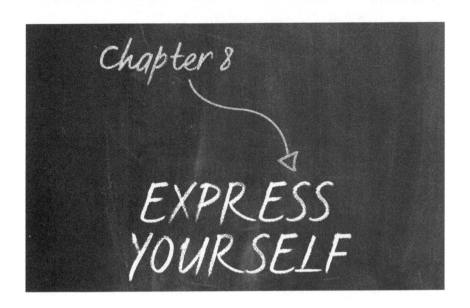

Chapter 8

EXPRESS YOURSELF

People with an analytical bent often focus exclusively on the content of what they say and not how they say it.

Up to this stage of the ENGAGE model it has been all about your physiology. We are now going to switch to focusing on expressing yourself more fully, which is vital for an *Engaging Executive*.

IT'S NOT JUST WHAT YOU SAY …

Often people with an analytical bent focus exclusively on the content of what they say and not how they say it. This is a great waste of a good message, as it has been shown in studies of communication that the words you use only make up part of your message. The other two really important factors are how you say it using the various qualities of your voice, and also your body language, which is frequently referred to as non-verbal communication (NVC). Ray Birdwhistell was an American Anthropologist who was a pioneer in the study of non-verbal communication. He conducted numerous studies in the 1950s to show just how much of our day-to-day communication was made up of NVC. He estimated that 'no more than 30 to 35 percent of the social meaning of a conversation or an interaction is carried by the words'.

Now this may be a shock to you, especially if you have the belief that everyone is hanging purely on the intellectual gravitas of what you have to say, but Birdwhistell was not alone in his assumptions about communication and its balance. Albert Mehrabian, Professor Emeritus of Psychology, UCLA, also did multiple studies around the make up of communication. Unfortunately, this is one of the most misquoted communication studies in psychology. You may have heard of the 55–38–7 rule of communication? The grossly overstated version suggests that 55% of your message is communicated by your body language, 38% by your voice qualities and only 7% by your actual words. This is incorrect. However, when you understand what the true meaning of the study was, it is still incredibly useful. The actual research was all about how trustworthy someone was perceived to be when communicating a message with emotional content. What Professor Mehrabian found was it becomes more likely that the receiver will trust the predominant form of communication, which to Mehrabian's findings is the non-verbal impact of tone and gestures (38% + 55%), rather than the literal meaning of the words (7%). So if you communicate something with your words but your tone and body language do not line up then you are unlikely to have a congruent message.

In psychology this is known as 'leakage'. I know, it doesn't sound very pleasant, right? Think about this for a minute. Have you ever spoken to someone and not believed him for reasons that you could not put down to logic? I bet you have. It was most probably something to do with either his voice or NVC. This is why you must always focus on the words, voice and NVC together.

So why am I telling you this? Because this chapter is dedicated to helping you fully tap into your words, voice and body language. When you combine this with later chapters in the *Guide* part of the book it will form a powerful combination of delivery and content. For now, we will focus on your delivery.

CHOOSING YOUR WORDS WISELY

Okay, so we just considered how words are not the only important part of a message, and now I'm starting discuss how to use words. Have I contradicted myself? The fact is, you can't communicate all that well without them, and so your choice of words is going to matter.

Technical vs social

There is a difference between having a technical conversation and a more social conversation. If you are discussing a fact of law then there are precise terms and phrases and legalese that you must stick to. If you are discussing an engineering problem then there are expressions and terminology that are essential to create understanding. However, you are not always having these types of conversations. If you are, we are about to change this. Later in the *Network* and *Glow* parts of the book we will focus on how to structure small talk and storytelling. For now, though, we are going to focus on enriching your vocabulary with some words that just delight the ears.

'How are you today?'

My uncle is a bit of a character. He was telling me once how he was frequently asked throughout his working day, 'How are you today?' Most people would respond in a very banal way with words such as 'fine', 'okay', or 'good thanks'. What a wasted opportunity to put a smile on somebody's face. What my uncle told me made me chuckle so much I started doing it myself. He replied with words that were playful and silly but still answered the question; for example, he would say, 'Glorious', 'Magnificent', 'Glowing', 'Effervescent' or 'Wondiferous'.

I too have found that this type of response immediately puts a smile on people's faces. Of course, I wouldn't do this at a new client meeting or in a tense situation. It is, however, great to do with people you have daily contact with, such as people in a regular café, or receptionists, or those who you don't normally have any deep and meaningfuls with but who you can practise being light-hearted with.

Another man who is absolutely wonderful with his words is Russell Brand. I have seen him perform live several times, and he is all over the media for good and bad reasons. Whatever you think of him as a person, put that to one side and just listen to his language. Go to YouTube and find one of his stand-up shows and give it five minutes.

You will see how he pulls quirky, rarely used words from the English language and makes his sentences pop with novelty, but not in a way that is ridiculous or nonsensical.

Have a think about the types of words you could incorporate into your lexicon to add just a bit of sparkle to your language.

YOUR VOICE IS LIKE AN ORCHESTRA – USE ALL OF THE INSTRUMENTS

Have you ever noticed how some people seem to be easier to listen to than others? How some people seem to capture your attention while others tend to bore you? This is not just a random effect. It is to do with the way people use their voice and whether they use it purposefully.

Of course, there is a time for being serious and monotone and a time for being more colourful in the use of your voice. However, many people tend to stay in the grey in just about every conversation. Let's look at the qualities of the voice that you can play with. These are not in any specific order. You have:

o   volume

o   intonation

o   tonality

o   tempo

o   timbre

o   rhythm.

A lot of men and women that I coach, particularly if they are shy, tend to speak quite softly. As a consequence they are sometimes hard to hear. The problem is that if people are struggling to hear you then your message is falling on deaf ears. You need to ensure that you project your voice from the abdomen. On the other hand, some people speak way too loud for the proximity they are to others. This is much rarer. I did have a client once who worked in IT. He was a very big man. Sometimes when we sat opposite each other he would just boom sentences out at me and my ears would feel like they were bleeding. I used to give him feedback to soften his voice.

The most powerful use of volume is when you modulate your volume up and down within a conversation to place emphasis on particular words or feelings. I like to think of a good conversation as a little like a symphony compared to modern dance music. Often modern dance music has a constant beat that goes through it and it is very repetitive. This is designed to put you in a trance while you dance. Have you noticed how some people have a voice that seems to be constantly at the same level and tone? After a while you start to go into a trance. Now think of a piece of classical music. Some of the best classical music is where the listener is taken on an emotional journey. Take the *Four Seasons, Summer Allegro Non Molto*, by Vivaldi. This is one of my favourite pieces – it starts off quietly and gently, then it picks up speed, before softening again for a while, until a massive uplift in tempo and volume. This is also the secret of being a powerful communicator. Use your voice to do the same thing. Don't do this within the context of a very short sentence, as you don't want to come across as erratic. However, if you are delivering a reasonable chunk of content, and I'm talking minutes not hours, then take people on a journey. Imagine you are a storyteller, using your voice to project your emotions and the gravitas of the story or message.

YOUR HANDS AND FACE ARE LIKE THE SOUNDTRACK TO A MOVIE

One day I was sitting in a bar when I noticed a man in front of me having a conversation with a woman. Being a bit of a nosy parker and unabashed people watcher, I suspected they were on a first date. They were out of earshot but they were close enough that I could see their expressions and hand gestures. The man was telling a story so well that, although I could not hear his words, just his expressions and hand gestures were almost enough for me to imagine he was talking about being on a boat. I imagined he was telling a story of going on a boat trip in a small fishing boat. I could see that at some point he had engine trouble, and had to desperately get the engine started again. The lady he was with seemed to revel in the story.

So how did he have this effect on his listener? He used a full range of expressions to match the mood of the story. When he was talking about something spectacular he raised his eyebrows and opened his eyes wide. When he was expressing concentration he furrowed his eyebrows and squinted his eyes. When he was expressing dismay he looked down and shook his head.

His hands were also supporting the story. He would put his hands up, palm forward to indicate stopping. He would show the relative size of something between his hands. He would denote the passage of time by making his hands go off to his right.

To watch him was like listening to poetry. Now imagine how good that story would have been if I had actually heard his colourful words too.

Let us now turn to some exercises, which will help you to express your message with some more pizazz.

For more information and resources on the EN-TRANCE stage, go to www.engagingexec.com.au

PRACTICAL EXERCISES

EXERCISE ONE: WORDS

- Draw a line down a page and write down a list of normal words and phrases you tend to use when meeting and responding to everyday folk; for example, 'Fine', 'Good thanks', 'I'm well', 'All good'.

- Write down as many ways as you can think of to make those phrases have a bit of a sparkle to them. If needed, use a thesaurus (you can easily find them online) and find as many ways of saying something similar as you can but with a bit of colour to it.

EXERCISE TWO: VOICE

- Take any passage of text, say a paragraph, from a fictional book or lifestyle magazine and read it out five times and record it onto your smartphone voice memo app.

- With each reading, experiment by putting the emphasis on different parts of the sentence and by making your voice change speed and tempo.

- Play each back and get a feel for which one sounds the most engaging.

EXERCISE THREE: EXPRESSIONS AND GESTURES

- Find a mirror in a quiet place where you can speak freely and you do not feel self-conscious.

- Read the same paragraph that you were practising before, but this time focus on your facial expressions and hand gestures as you tell the story. Make sure to keep the voice expressive as well, as in the previous exercise.

NETWORK

Part III

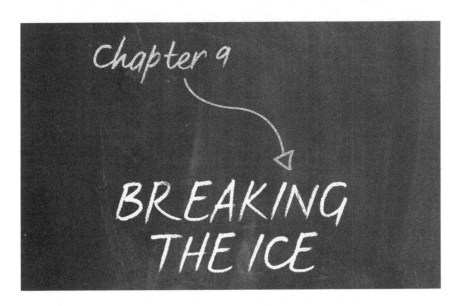

Chapter 9

BREAKING THE ICE

If you cannot bring yourself to speak to new people then you will only ever be able to influence those you already know or who introduce themselves to you.

One of the most common nightmare scenarios for my clients is to find themselves in a room where they know absolutely no-one. This could be at a networking event, a social gathering, a formal dinner or even a corporate training event, to list just a few. This is actually a very common fear, and one that used to plague me too. So this chapter is dedicated to 'breaking the ice', getting yourself motivated and on the move towards meeting new people. We'll examine the psychological and practical aspects of getting through the first and most difficult part: first contact. Then we will look at what to do once you get there.

As the old Chinese proverb says, 'a journey of a thousand miles starts with a single step'. Never has a saying been so apt to meeting new people.

YOU ARE NOT ALONE

Let me be clear: *it's not just you*. This is a problem that almost everyone experiences at some time. However, some people are really great at 'faking it'.

There are actually some people who do genuinely enjoy meeting new people. I once dated a very extroverted woman in London; she absolutely adored going to her hip and trendy friends' parties. To her it was heaven. For me, it was a living hell. I always found this a little strange, as when I was at work I would regularly give presentations and run events in front of strangers. Yet, for some reason, when you put me in a room full of people I didn't know and I didn't have a role to perform, I felt naked. On the days of these parties I would start feeling uneasy. I would try to talk my girlfriend out of going, or make 'deals' about how long we would stay so I could control the level of agony I was anticipating.

Does any of this sound familiar to you? If so, you and I are soulmates. And the events were often as bad as I was expecting. My girlfriend normally knew more people at the events than I did. I used to trail behind her and wait for her to introduce me. Then I would fumble my way through a really awkward conversation before the person I was speaking to moved on. I just wanted the floor to open up and swallow me.

I recall a birthday party in Central London. There was a young man there who still sticks out in my mind. I was standing with my girlfriend who was having one of those 'why do you have to be so anti-social' conversations with me when this guy floated over and introduced himself. He didn't know either of us, yet he seemed so comfortable in his own skin. He actually seemed to be enjoying meeting new people. I remember him like it was yesterday, yet that incident was over a decade ago. I thought to myself, 'I wish I could work a room like him'.

So, why couldn't I?

THE FEAR OF REJECTION

It all boils down to the fear of feeling rejected. That's right. At our core we have a little kid who doesn't want to be rejected. So how do you manage this fear?

Managing the fear

There is no tougher place to learn this than in the world of dating. You have to get used to one thing very quickly: rejection.

While coaching hundreds of men and women on how to start a conversation, I have seen a common pattern. Before someone approaches someone else, he is concerned about everything that can go wrong. This person dramatises in his head all the possible terrible outcomes. But believe me: what you imagine is *always* worse than what actually happens. As each person starts to approach other people more they soon realise they won't get screamed at, slapped in the face or laughed at. In fact, they start to become habituated to the feeling of what is called Approach Anxiety. I find that men and women both suffer equally from Approach Anxiety in a business context.

That doesn't mean that everyone will always want to talk to you. Sometimes it will not be the right moment. So what? There are a few million more people you can find to speak to.

The barrier

However, before I was a Dating Coach I was a student on the course. Now, if you remember how concerned I was about chatting to random strangers at a party, you can only imagine how terrified I was about walking up to random women and trying to be interesting. I knew there was a pain barrier I had to pass through. It was the 'Fear of Rejection Barrier'. To do this, for three nights a week, for three months, I had to face my fears and approach women until the act of starting a conversation became the norm.

Not only did it become the norm: it became fun.

At this point you might be thinking, 'Oh, this is interesting, but I have no intention of walking around a nightclub for three months to get over my fear of talking to strangers'. No problem. The great news is, you don't have to. Everything I am talking about can be practised every day, at work and in your social life. It just requires you to do something you don't normally do: talk to strangers. Now, I appreciate your mum told you not to talk to strangers when you were younger, but you are a grown up now. It is in your best interests.

The homework I give my clients after the first few sessions is always the same: go and talk to strangers. For you, it is going to be no different. At the end of this chapter I will suggest tasks for you. These will more than likely require you to go way outside your comfort zone. However, this is the first step to becoming engaging and influential. If you cannot bring yourself to speak to new people then you will only ever be able to influence those you already know or who introduce themselves to you. If you follow that logic, those people who are already more social than you are likely to be introducing themselves to many other new people and therefore will be able to influence many more people than you can. So it's time to toughen up and get out there.

GETTING INTO A SOCIAL MINDSET

Before I let you loose on the world, I will share with you some techniques for breaking the ice.

The inner game of approaching

Many of the tips in this segment were inspired by my learning from Damien on the dating course. Please remember though, I am not teaching you how to meet a romantic partner. I am teaching you the fundamentals of meeting strangers, male or female. But the skills are universal and can be used socially or for business.

The first thing you have to do before being social is get into a 'social mood'. This is your 'inner game'. This is when you get yourself into the mindset of being social by thinking and behaving in a social way, before going out to a social event. Instead of sitting there feeling the dread creeping up from your feet to your head, you can do the exact opposite and start 'getting in the mood'. Some great techniques to help you do this are:

o   uplifting personal soundtrack

o   creating a happy button

o   chatting on the way

o   giving yourself a role or a goal.

We'll look at each of these below.

The uplifting personal soundtrack

Have you ever noticed how music can be like a time machine? A song can take you right back to the past in a heartbeat. Some songs can put a grin on your face as you think back to a time in your life that was sheer magic. Other songs can take you to a sad place and remind you of things you don't wish to remember.

Do you have certain songs that inspire you with different moods? Some that make you feel really happy? Some that make you feel pumped up? Some that make you feel confident? I do, and I'm sure you do too. For example, when I played a lot of tennis I would listen to ... wait for it ... the *Star Wars* theme to get me psyched up. I know, right. But it really helped me get into a positive state and made me feel confident before a match.

What songs get you fired up and feeling social and upbeat? My suggestion would be to create a playlist on your phone and fill it full of those handpicked songs that make you feel motivated and uplifted. Once you have this list on your phone, play it before you have that 'dreaded' social event and get into a great social mood.

Creating a happy button

This is a tool taken from NLP. Technically it is known as resource anchoring and it is a manufactured association between a stimulus and response. In the music playlist above you were asked to find songs that made you feel social and uplifted. These are naturally occurring resource anchors. You didn't need to sit down at the time you heard the song and say, 'Right, I'm going to feel great whenever I hear this song'. It just kinda happened. But in resource anchoring you *do* consciously decide to link a stimulus to the response you desire.

Lots of professional sportspeople have resource anchors that they use at big moments. Tiger Woods always wears a red shirt on the big days of a tournament. Rafa Nadal does a fist pump to get himself going.

These are simple examples of resource anchors. I went to an Anthony Robbins seminar a few years back, and for four days and nights Tony (as he likes to be called) got us to dance around, chant, challenge our own limiting beliefs, and generally keep the energy up over some very intense sessions. Periodically, after getting the audience in a peak state, he would tell us to 'make our move'. This was a physical, whole-body movement of our own choice, which Tony asked us to create on day one. (Mine, for example, was a fist pump diagonally down across my body, requiring a twist and slight crouching movement.)

The 'move' itself was not important. It was what Tony did with it that was clever. Once the audience was feeling pumped up and the energy in the room was palpable, Tony would shout, 'Make your move!' On his command, we would all do our unique move, and he would make us do this three times in a row. We did this multiple times a day, every day. What Tony was actually doing was creating a powerful resource anchor that was being 'stacked' every time we repeated the process.

After the four days, whenever I made my 'move' I felt unstoppable. This resource anchor lasted for months after the seminar, and each time I needed a 'pick me up' I would 'make my move'. It only faded as I went through a bit of a purple patch in my life and forgot to use it. Resource anchors need constant reinforcement to remain strong.

Does that mean you must spend four days dancing around and being screamed at by a seven-foot-tall American? No, of course not. There is a much simpler way of creating resource anchors, or as I like to call them, 'happy buttons':

1 **Decide on the emotional state you want to feel** – pick an emotional state or feeling that you would like to feel when socialising; for example, confident, sociable, talkative, curious.

2 **Decide on a physical button that will act as your trigger** – for example, pinching your ear, pressing the side of your temple, squeezing a finger. It can be anything you like, as long as it is something that you do not normally do. For example, if you normally pinch your ears then don't pick that as it will not be unique. Your trigger needs to be distinctive, accurate (you are only touching this specific place), and sensitive (you need to be able to physically feel it).

3 **Remember a specific time that you felt the desired emotional state intensely** – this is a key step. Find a time in your life that you can remember vividly the same desired behaviour. For example, there may have been a time at a party when your conversational skills were on fire. Or a moment at work when you were giving the speech of a lifetime and had the crowd in your hand. It needs to be a memory so full and rich that you can take yourself back to that place and time in your head and feel what you felt, see what you saw, and hear what you heard.

4 **Associate the button (trigger) to the memory** – once you have this great memory of the desired emotion you want to capture, bring it back as fully as you can. Notice how you start to feel the same emotion that was present in your body. As you sense the feeling is about to peak, but before it has actually peaked, press your button from step 2. Hold this down for as long as it takes to ride the emotional memory to the top of the curve. As soon as you feel it start to reduce in intensity, let go of the trigger (see the diagram below). Generally speaking, the pressing of the button tends to last 5 to 10 seconds.

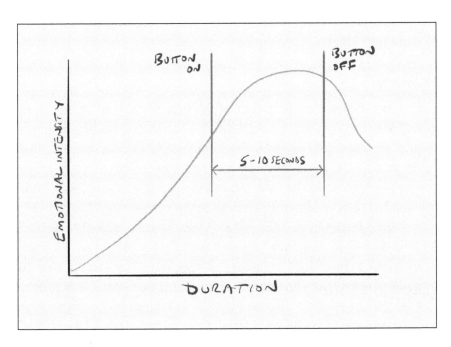

5 **Repeat the above step to strengthen the button** – if you have multiple memories for an emotion you wish to associate with the button then you can use these too. To do this, as soon as step 4 is finished, start immediately again with the new memory and repeat the whole of step 4. Do this for as many memories as you can that get you into that state. If you can come up with five separate memories then this will give you a lot of juice.

6 **Test the button** – once you have set it up, you need to test it. Make sure you have a short break between steps 5 and 6, and distract yourself with other thoughts during this time. Once you have done this, settle again, press the button, and observe the positive emotion coming back. As you touch the button the emotion should be instantaneous. For most people you will be surprised at how great you suddenly feel. (If the feeling is not very strong then you may need to come up with some more potent examples in step 3 and repeat the process.) You have now created a 'happy button' you can use whenever you need to get into a social mood.

7 **Reinforce the button** – this process works best the more times you rehearse it. As I have no doubt you would have heard before: 'use it or lose it'.

Power poses

I am a firm believer in the power of resource anchors to change your emotional state. While I would strongly recommend putting a 'happy button' in place, perhaps you need something more immediate and easier to pull off, while you wait for the event to start. This is where power poses come in. No, I'm not talking about standing like a body builder, but there is something inbuilt in your physiology that can help you. I am a huge fan of TED Talks. If you have not already done so, look up the talk by Associate Professor Amy Cuddy of Harvard Business School called 'Your Body Language Shapes Who You Are'. In this 20 minutes of excellence she describes how scientific research has proven that adopting a number of power poses can temporarily increase your testosterone and decrease your cortisol, giving you a confidence boost.

While the video describes about five different poses, the easiest to pull off in public is to stand with your hands on your hips. It is as simple as that. Stand up straight, bend you elbows, put your hands on your hips and stick your elbows out sideways. The net effect is your body becomes larger and your brain is fooled into feeling more dominant. Amy's recommended dose is two minutes in this pose before you need the confidence boost.

Chatting on the way

This next step will be a walk in the park. And it could be … literally.

Let's say you have to go to a networking event. For whatever reason, you didn't have a chance to use the above techniques before you left but you still need to get into a social mood. On your way to the event you will have to pass numerous other people, so you can use this opportunity. The next best thing to the first two techniques is to have random chats with random people. It may be people you pass in the office; stop and shoot the breeze with them for five minutes. It might be the taxi driver; they always like a chat. It might be someone you stand next to at the train station. It could even be the receptionist at the venue you are going to. Who it is doesn't matter – what is important is the act of being social. Once you start chatting you will find you begin to get into a social mood.

Give yourself a role or a goal

One of the toughest parts of social events is that they can take away your comfort zone. For some, wearing business attire is like wearing a suit of armour. It protects us by giving us our workplace identity. Once in it, you put on your, 'I'm an Accountant / Engineer / Lawyer / Whatever' persona. The problem is, when you go to social events you often have to talk about things that sit outside this role, and suddenly you can feel exposed. It's as if you suddenly have to find your identity again.

One trick I have found really helps is to set yourself a role. For example, you could imagine that your role for the event is to help the other uncomfortable people feel more comfortable. You will always find someone standing alone or someone looking a little lost. Be that person who takes the initiative and goes over and starts a conversation. In this way, you become someone who is doing a public service. This becomes your role.

You can also set yourself a goal. Back in the day, when I was an employee, the company I was working for was acquired by another company. We had our first joint event together in a private function room. If you had been a fly on the wall you would have thought it was hilarious. As soon as a new person walked into the room, they looked around and immediately went over to the people they already knew. Before long we had a scene reminiscent of a school disco, but instead of boys on one side and girls on another, it was the two companies. So in that moment I set myself a goal to meet as many people as I could from the new company. I simply strolled over to the other side of the room and started speaking to the first friendly face I met. From that point on I started to work my way around the room, and before long the two sides started to chat.

PRACTICAL TIPS ON HOW TO BREAK THE ICE

Let's discuss some really hands-on ways of breaking the ice. It does work better if you have already gotten into a social mood by completing the processes above before trying the techniques below. I am going to focus on the context of a networking or business social function, but these methods can be applied in just about any circumstance. (These tips are really only covering the first 30 seconds of an interaction. The deeper conversational tips come in the following chapter, 'The overlooked art of small talk'.)

Arrive early

Have you ever rocked up late to a social function or networking event? What did you notice? That's right: everyone is already talking to each other. This makes your job more daunting, and it also means you will have to interject into other people's conversations. This is not impossible of course, but it is more of a challenge.

Now imagine you arrive early. You might be among the first two or three people. How much easier is it to talk to two or three people who are all there early and probably looking to get a foot in the door before anyone else? As Australian's like to say, 'Too easy'. As more and more people arrive you will already be in the 'in-group', and the law of social proof will make you look like someone worth talking to.

The lost and the lonely

At any networking event there are going to be other people who are socially uncomfortable. This is a blessing in disguise. These are the sort of people who are desperately hoping someone will save them from being a 'Billy No Mates'. (Clearly they haven't read this book!) That hero could be you.

These people are usually easy to spot. They take a lot of time getting a beverage or looking at the catering. They will be looking at their phone in a quiet corner of the room. They may even be looking around as if to scout out the event. This is your moment to take the conversation to them. You can wander over and use a 'situational opener' by looking at the environment you are in and making a comment or asking a question. For example, if you are standing by the catering, you could ask, 'Have you tried any of the food yet? Do you have any recommendations?' Or if they already have food on their plate, 'That food looks great … where did you get it?' At this point you will probably get their attention and they will most probably answer your question directly. Whatever you do, don't rush off to grab a sandwich at that point. You have just done the hardest part: opening the conversation. Instead, say something like, 'Thanks, I will go and grab some. Hello, by the way … My name is … ' Remember, the purpose of the question is to get an introduction.

Coffee queue question

An extension of the above tactic works very well in the coffee queue of a networking event. This is especially easy to do in networking settings that happen in the morning. In Australia, and I am sure where you live, people absolutely adore their coffee in the morning. We will form a massive queue in order to wait for the barista-made coffee rather than the brown water from the flasks. This means you have a few all-important minutes with someone directly in front and behind you. This is a great chance to introduce yourself by making use of the fact you are already there.

Who's who in the zoo

Depending on the types of events you go to, there may be some high-profile people there or some other types of people you would like to connect with for business purposes. However, if you don't know who they are you are going to have to find out. This is another great excuse to use when starting a conversation with a stranger. You can pick the first person you see or a small group of people and use the following excuse to start a conversation: 'Excuse me, do you happen to know who is running this event? I've just arrived and I am looking for the organiser.' At that point you will either get a 'yes' or 'no' answer. You may even get a pointer in the right direction. Remember, this was not the point of the question in the first place – you just wanted an excuse to start a conversation. So once you get the answer, go straight into your introduction and build on that by saying, 'So, how did you hear about this event?'

Something caught my eye

There may be a time when you notice something about someone that really catches your attention. For example, someone may be wearing a really stunning coat, be carrying a great looking bag or briefcase, or the latest phone or tablet. In fact, any item is a great excuse for you to give that person a compliment or show interest in the item. For example, 'Excuse me. Is that the latest iPad? It looks amazing. What is it like to use?' Most people who have the latest technology love nothing more than explaining it to other enthusiasts. Once you have found out a bit about the item, introduce yourself. For example, 'Thanks for showing me that. By the way, my name is … '

You caught my eye

You need to remember back to part II of this book, *En-trance*. Keep a half-cocked smile on and be ready to launch as you walk around the room looking for your next conversation. It really helps if you also use smiling eyes, as mentioned in chapter 6, 'Making everybody your friend'. A half smile and some solid eye contact can be all you need to catch someone else's attention. As you move around the room, smile with an expression like you have just been released from prison after several years and the world is an exciting place to be. This relaxed and positive expression caught by a passer-by is often enough to get a smile coming back at you. Once this happens, seize the moment and ask, 'Hi, how are you? How are you enjoying the event?'

Two is company, three is a networking opportunity

In my experience of networking events I often find there is a magic number when it comes to introducing yourself. We have already talked about how to approach the lost and the lonely. The other magic number is three. Frequently, if two people are speaking they are intensely focused on each other. There may be a good reason why the two of them have broken away from a group. As a simple rule of thumb, two is company so leave them alone. Three, however, is the sweet spot. This number of people is less likely to be having a deep and meaningful and they are already having to spread their eye contact around the group. So adding another person to this gathering is a lot less intrusive. Typically, as people are talking in a group of three there will be one side of the triangle that is more open. In other words, you need to consider where to stand as you approach them. Go for the side of the triangle that has the biggest gap. Once you have identified the gap, move towards it but stop one step away from the gap. Address the group with your eyes, and have your smile half-cocked and ready to go. As the group turns to look at you, go into your introduction by asking, 'Do you mind if I join you?'

Name, same and fame

In the lead up to writing this book I attended a fantastic business acceleration programme called Key Person of Influence (KPI). It was a game-changing experience. One of the first tips we were given was around how to do a social pitch about who you are. The KPI course have a great system that they call 'Name, Same and Fame', which works like this:

o 'Name' is your first and second name. For example, 'Hi, I'm Duncan Fish'.

o 'Same' is the generic job title you do which people can relate to. For example, 'I'm an Executive Coach … '

o 'Fame' is what differentiates you or what you are known for (famous for) in your field. For example, ' … and I'm known for helping to bring out the people person within'.

The great thing about this form of introduction is that it helps people immediately have something to hook into. I often get, 'Wow, that sounds interesting. So how does that work?'

Most people just say their name, or at best their name and job title: 'Hi, I'm Dave and I'm an Accountant'. Unfortunately, when faced with this type of introduction most people are not socially curious enough to dig deeper. By adding the 'fame' element you will often find that people do want to know more and it kick starts the conversation.

So, let's have a look at some exercises that can help your master the first 30 seconds of meeting someone.

PRACTICAL EXERCISES

EXERCISE ONE: CREATE YOUR OWN UPLIFTING PERSONAL SOUNDTRACK

- Dig through your music collection or trawl the internet and find three to five songs that really get you in a social mood.

- Save them as a playlist on your phone and listen to them before going into any social setting.

EXERCISE TWO: SET UP A HAPPY BUTTON

- Follow the six steps to create a happy button, listed in this chapter. Consider some social moods or states you would like to be in and create buttons for them. You can stack them — that is, create them — on the same physical spot (button).

- Keep rehearsing these — as in step 7 on page 88 — twice a day for a week until the button becomes instantaneous and powerful.

EXERCISE THREE: CHATTING TO STRANGERS

- On your way to or from work, or during your break, go and find yourself a complete stranger and start chatting to them. Nothing deep and meaningful, just shoot the breeze or ask how their day is going so far.

- Talk to three new people every day. Do this at least five days a week so that the act of talking to strangers becomes easy. This could be people in the office you have never spoken to before or people you meet out on the street. The goal is to talk to three people you have never met before. Remember to smile with your eyes to project playfulness.

EXERCISE FOUR: GIVE YOURSELF A GOAL OR A ROLE

○ Next time you go to a social event, be it a networking event or other social gathering, give yourself the role of 'Saviour of the Lost and Lonely'. Walk around the event and find people who are on their own or looking a little socially awkward and introduce yourself.

○ Set yourself a goal of meeting a minimum of five new people at the event. These only count if you make the introduction yourself, not if you just stand there like a plum and other people introduce people to you.

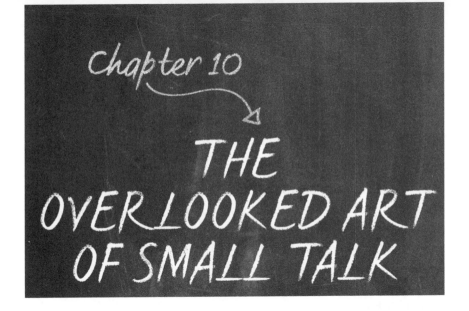

Chapter 10

THE OVERLOOKED ART OF SMALL TALK

If you think that small talk is just about idle chit chat, you are missing the point.

Having read the previous chapter you should now know how to get yourself into a social mood and how to approach others and introduce yourself. So, having got yourself across the floor and in front of someone, and started the conversation, what do you do next? This chapter is all about the art of small talk, and how to escalate from small talk to big talk; in other words, the more serious and deeper issues. These are essential skills for the *Engaging Executive*.

A MEANINGLESS EXCHANGE OF TRIVIA OR A VITAL RITUAL?

The concept of small talk is intriguing to me as when I speak to most executives about it they seem to grimace. Many see it as a waste of time, a meaningless exchange of trivia. In fact, I was recently running a seminar, and when I asked the group what the purpose of small talk was, someone responded, 'It is just something that enables my mouth to go blah, blah, blah'.

If you think that small talk is just about idle chit chat, you are missing the point. It is, in fact, an essential stepping-stone to deeper rapport and a more meaningful exchange. It is part of a societal ritual, and not honouring this ritual can lead to a much-diminished conversation and, possibly, relationship.

This chapter will explain the secret structure of conversation. Yes, there is a secret structure to all small talk, and once I explain it you will see just how obvious it is. If you follow the formula you will soon become a master of small talk. For me it was the cherry on the cake of my own social skills. Once I had internalised this model I have subsequently been able to master the one area of my social skills that had always been a bit hit and miss.

So, let's see how you too can become a master of small talk.

THE FIRST FIVE MINUTES

It is surprising how little time and effort people put into planning and practising their small talk. Considering it is the one thing you need to do almost every time you meet someone new, I would have imagined that being good at it was quite a useful skill. What's more surprising is that whenever you have small talk with someone you can practically predict at least the first five minutes of conversation. It is a no-brainer. So let's start with the first five minutes.

Business conversations

I want you to do a quick exercise for me right now. Make a list mentally or on paper of all the types of questions you normally ask or get asked within the first five minutes of meeting someone in a business setting. Please put the book down and do this now. I'll wait.

Okay, so what did you come up with? Let me see if I can read your mind. While there will undoubtedly be some variation and regional differences, I would be surprised if your list differed too much from this:

o   'Hi, how are you?' Or, 'How are you going/doing?'

o   'My name is … What's yours?'

o   'What do you do for a living?'

o   'So who do you work for?'

o   'Where are you based?'

o   'Where are you from?'

o   'So how are things at the moment/how is business at the moment?'

Was I close? Remember, I was putting this in the context of a business setting.

Social conversations

So what about the first five minutes in a social setting? Let's have a look:

o   'Hi, how are you?' Or, 'How are you going/doing?'

o   'My name is … What's yours?'

o   'So how's your day/weekend going?'

o   'What have you been up to?'

o   'So where do you live?'

o   'What do you do for work?'

A safe haven

It seems the question about career is pretty inevitable, unless you are talking to someone who is actually very good at small talk. Then it may never come up at all. It is a bit of a safe haven for first conversations as it gives people the ability to categorise you. This in turn gives them something to relate to you about. When it comes to purely social chit chat I tend to steer away from discussing jobs unless I am really feeling in the mood to talk about it or I get asked first. There are so many other wonderful topics to discuss when you first meet someone. In a business context it makes much more sense, as after all you are trying to get some business out of the conversation and it will only help to credentialise yourself.

USING CONTEXTUAL HOOKS

You may be thinking right now, 'Wow, how insightful … *not*. Isn't this all a bit obvious?' The fact is, yes, it is. Yet so many people *do absolutely nothing with it*. They come up with the same vanilla answers each time, even though they are given the perfect canvas to come up with something that will really get a conversation started. I am not saying my introduction to these predictable questions is going to blow anyone's mind, but it does normally give people enough context and flavour to continue an interesting conversation with me. At the end of the day, that is part of the process of small talk. Try to make it as easy as possible for the other person to engage with you. Throw them some 'Contextual Hooks' that they can use to generate their own questions.

My personal introduction and responses to questions go something like this. (I have only given my side of the dialogue, so please remember I am not suggesting a five-minute monologue … that would be enough to get anyone looking at their watch.)

Question to me: 'How are you?'

Response: 'Pretty good, as it happens. So far I am having a very productive day. How about you?'

Question to me: 'So what do you do for a living?'

Response: 'That's a good question. While I have a background as an Organisational Psychologist, I am actually an Executive Coach. I specialise in helping task-focused people understand, influence and connect with non-technical people. I absolutely love it. What about you?'

Question to me: 'So who do you work for?'

Response: 'Actually, I am a bit of a portfolio worker. I have a company called The *Engaging Executive*, which runs programmes on what I just spoke about. I also have a training company that teaches Neuro Linguistic Programming. Occasionally, I do a bit of contract work for some of my favourite clients around leadership development. What about yourself?'

Question to me: 'So where are you based?'

Response: 'I live in Sydney but I work between Sydney, Canberra and Melbourne mostly. Saying that, I have clients all over the Asia Pacific region so I get to travel a bit. How about yourself?'

Question to me: 'So where are you from?'

Response: 'Well, I'm originally from the UK. I came to Sydney, Australia for a one-week business trip back in 2008. Having delivered work in 24 countries I always made the most of it but normally looked forward to going home. But after three days in Sydney I never wanted to go back, and I have been here ever since ... I'm still on the run from the Department of Immigration.'

The above is all completely true (except for the bit about being on the run ... maybe ...), and while not that remarkable in any way, I wanted to demonstrate how giving people Contextual Hooks can help to stimulate a conversation. Most people tend to give one-word answers to most of these questions and move on. It is very transactional. I often find that how you introduce yourself to people is how they will respond to you. If you give a brief answer to a question you will get a brief answer back. Give them a little bit more and you will get a little bit more back.

Follow-up questions to Contextual Hooks

So let's have a think about some of the follow-up questions that my introduction could stimulate. These are based on my experiences to date and represent the typical questions that my introduction provokes:

o 'Productive day? So what have you been up to?'

o 'An Organisational Psychologist; that sounds interesting. What does that entail?'

o 'You coach executives how to connect? How do you go about that?'

o 'You sound like you love what you do. How did you get into that profession?'

o 'You run two companies and you do contract work? Wow, that must keep you busy. Who do you contract to?'

o 'Neuro Linguistic Programming? What is that?'

o 'You certainly get around a bit. Which is your favourite city?'

o 'You used to live in the UK? Where abouts?'

o '24 countries? Which was your favourite?'

o 'Sydney, eh? What do you like most about Sydney?'

Any of these questions could nicely lead into a conversational topic that would fit perfectly into the category of small talk. What I am consciously doing with my introduction is giving people something to drill into to make the conversation easier for them. In return, I ask questions back that help them share a similar level of information.

HAVING A TWO-WAY CONVERSATION

The art of having a two-way conversation is not always as easy as it seems, especially if you are feeling socially anxious. When people become nervous they tend to run out of things to say. As a consequence, they default to asking questions.

Most people are taught to ask questions as a way to show interest in other people. However, this only works up to a point. If you only ask questions, a conversation starts to feel more like the Spanish Inquisition, and as Monty Python once said, 'Nobody expects the Spanish Inquisition'. Nor should they. A conversation is supposed to be fun.

So, let's see how you can avoid such tedious conversations using the Question Validate Reciprocate Model.

QUESTION, VALIDATE, RECIPROCATE

There is a simple three-step process for making just about any social encounter an easy two-way conversation. It is inspired by a model my friend and mentor Damien created. I have been astounded by how powerfully such a simple model can completely change the dynamics of a conversation. It helps avoid the Spanish Inquisition by forcing the conversation to be far more interactive and by fully acknowledging the answers you are receiving.

Let's break it down.

Question

This is as simple as asking just about any type of open question to get the conversation rolling, such as what, why, when, where, who or how. For example, 'So, what do you do for work?', 'Where do you live?', 'Who do you work for?', 'Who else do you know here?' You are likely to get back some useful information.

Validate

This is the stage of the model that avoids the Spanish Inquisition. This is where you need to really listen to the response and find something, anything, that validates the answer you have just heard. This could be an opinion you have on the topic, it could be something you have read in the news, it could be an experience you have had, or even an admittance that you have absolutely no knowledge of the topic but that you are intrigued to find out more. For example, if someone tells you she is an Accountant, how could you relate to that? What could you draw from your own experience of the world to connect with that specific role? Given my background, I might say, 'I like working with Accountants. I actually do a lot of work with Accountants, and some of my biggest clients work in Insurance and Professional Services. And I have to admit, I am completely reliant on mine. I am clueless in such things, and without him I would be lost.'

Your answer does not need to be an in-depth showcase of how much you know about a topic. The purpose is to personalise your response to the information you have just been given, which shows respect and appreciation for the answer. In this way the person you are speaking with feels valued.

Reciprocate

Once you have explored the other person's response and validated it, you may be asked the same question in return. If not, a good trick is to reciprocate by adding some content of your own. In this way you complete the cycle and you are giving information as well as receiving. You are building a reciprocal database of information about each other and avoiding the Spanish Inquisition. Your response needs to share something interesting about yourself. This information should be something that the listener can do something with. In other words, it should provide some Contextual Hooks that help the listener to form a question back to you. In this example, I would speak about my profession in the same way I did above in the Contextual Hooks segment.

THE RAPPORT TRIANGLE

Once you have mastered the art of Contextual Hooks and Question Validate Reciprocate, you are ready to implant them in a broader model of developing small talk. This model is called the Rapport Triangle, and for love or money I can't find the originator of it. Whoever you are, *thank you*. It is one of the most powerful and simple frameworks I have ever seen for building a conversation from scratch. It is insightful and easy to learn, and I have tweaked it a little to simplify it. Having discovered it, I have both used it myself and taught it to hundreds of people, so I can vouch for the profound impact this can have in any given small talk scenario.

The Rapport Triangle works on the principle that a conversation has five levels. Each level becomes a little more intimate and therefore brings you closer to building rapport. You will notice the triangle is inverted and this denotes spending longer at each level to deepen rapport. In this chapter we are going to talk about the concept of rapport building as developed by the Rapport Triangle. This will enable you to generate the content you need to start building rapport. In chapter 12, 'Creating rapport', we will talk further about how to build really deep rapport at an unconscious level.

Let's look now at the five levels, as depicted in the diagram following.

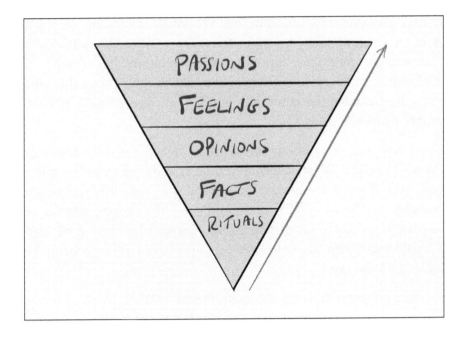

Rituals

Rituals are the very beginnings of any conversation. They are the comments or questions we direct towards each other when we first meet, and these do not actually do much in the way of developing rapport. However, skip them and you run the risk of not honouring the ritual of small talk.

When people do not honour the ritual they tend to move into the higher levels prematurely, and other people can find this disconcerting. For example, imagine if someone randomly walked up to you on the street and asked you, 'What do you want to achieve most in life?' How would you respond? Unless you are a *very* open person, I imagine you would be taken aback. You may even suspect that they were trying to sell you something or convert you to a religion. That is because this question is a deep social interaction, and something you are only likely to reveal to someone if you feel very comfortable. If someone asks that question much deeper into a conversation you may be more likely to answer it.

Rituals are apparently meaningless yet vitally important stepping stones to the more involved aspects of a conversation. In each society there are different rituals, but they exist in all cultures. For example, in the UK it is quite common for people to say 'Alright?' when they first meet. In Australia, the equivalent is, 'How are you going?', or often simply, 'How you going?'

The interesting thing about this ritual is nobody actually wants or expects the truth. When someone you don't know asks you this question, even if you were having the worst day of your life, you would probably say, 'Yeah, good thanks. And you?' If you were actually to respond truthfully to the question with, 'Oh, not that good at all. Had a terrible row with my wife', the person asking would probably be looking for the exit.

Another common ritual is the topic of the weather. In most of the countries I have been to the topic of weather is nearly always a ritual. It does nothing to build deep rapport but it is something that everyone can relate to. No-one is going to walk away from the conversation thinking, 'That Duncan. Hell of guy. He was all over the weather situation.' However, it gets you to the next step.

From working with and speaking to many Indians I have deduced that talking about cricket is one of their rituals. And when I was working in Singapore, people kept asking me, 'Have you eaten?'

Each country has its own rituals, so look out for them and honour them. This will open the door to the next level … facts.

Facts

The second level of the Rapport Triangle is where the conversation moves beyond customs and into useful information. Have a think about a typical conversation with someone you do not know. After the pleasantries, what sort of questions do you tend to ask each other? Normally things like, 'What is your name?', 'Who do you work for?', 'What do you do for work?' and 'Where are you from?' All of these types of questions reveal factual information that allows us to categorise people and make generalisations. These then steer us in the questions we ask next or the information we share of ourselves.

At this stage of the Rapport Triangle it is merely a factual exchange. People often ask me 'Where are you from?' due to my accent. I will tell them about my journey from the UK, and then I will return the question. Facts are useful, but they do not really help you connect with people in depth. This is why you need to get stuck into the next level … opinions.

Opinions

This is where you start to exchange your views and opinions on a topic. It is the first level of the Rapport Triangle where you actually understand how somebody thinks about the world. For example, having asked someone what he does for a living, you may then ask, 'So what made you choose that profession?' This would start to give you an insight into his values and beliefs.

At this level of the Rapport Triangle the exchange you are having is on a cognitive and cerebral level. It uses language like, 'So what did you think of that?', 'What is your view on this?' or 'What is your opinion?'

For many, this is as far as they are willing to take a conversation. These are the people who are not going to master small talk or develop deep rapport. To achieve this, you need to transcend an invisible barrier: the emotional barrier. This is the next level.

Emotions

On this level of the Rapport Triangle you start to tap into the emotions of the person you are speaking to as well as starting to share your own. Once you transcend into feelings and emotions you are getting closer to the top of the triangle.

When people are ready to share feelings and emotions, it means they are starting to share more intimate information. For example, if I was to ask you, 'What do you think about that?', or, 'How does that make you feel?', which do you believe will yield the most intimate information? The latter of course.

I do want to caution you here though. At this level you do not turn into a caricature of a 'Shrink'. You are not going to have an entire Q&A

session, just asking 'How does that make you feel?' You could ask that type of question, but you could also use language that has an emotional component to it. For example, 'You sound excited about that?', or, 'Wow, you seem fired up about this?' Using emotional words such as 'happy', 'excited', 'motivated', 'concerned', 'worried', 'down' and so on is at this level of the Rapport Triangle.

Once you are having these types of conversations, you are one step closer to the top of the triangle … passions.

Passions

At the very top of the Rapport Triangle sits your passions. These are the topics or the interests that you feel most strongly about. You know when you have triggered someone's passions because her eyes light up and her speech becomes animated, and all you have to do is show interest and ask questions in order to fan the flames.

At this level you can ask the most revealing questions. If you can connect with the other person's passions you are on the fast track to deep and meaningful rapport.

Often you may find that what you are passionate about is not exactly the same as somebody else. This is where you need to look for the similarities and focus on these. For example, let's imagine I was talking to a Civil Engineer about her passion for building bridges. I might ask her, 'So what is it about building bridges that you love so much?' She might tell me how she loves the technical challenge of working through the problem. She may also talk about trying to find the most efficient way of building the structure, or the immense satisfaction she feels when it is complete and it is now helping the community reach new destinations.

Now, my career is very different to this, so how could I possibly connect with what I have just been told about building a bridge? Well, I could speak about how I like to make transformations of my own, and that I too like to help people get from one place in their life to another. How what I love most about my career is designing processes that enable people to make massive changes in their lives, which take them on a journey and enable them to achieve things that were out of reach before.

At this point we would both be feeling pretty good about the world, as we would both be sharing our passions. Imagine if I then asked the question, 'What do you want to achieve most in life?' Do you think she is more likely to answer now that we have worked our way to the top of the Rapport Triangle? Of course she is.

Let's now turn to some exercises that will help you to master small talk.

PRACTICAL EXERCISES

EXERCISE ONE: ANTICIPATING THE FIRST FIVE MINUTES

o Sit down and write a list of all the questions you may be asked within the first five minutes of meeting someone. Consider each question and write your responses, remembering to load them full of Contextual Hooks.

o Each time you are asked a question within the first five minutes that is not on your list, write it down and add a response to it for next time.

EXERCISE TWO: QUESTION VALIDATE RECIPROCATE

o Next time you meet someone new and you are practising your small talk, remember to use the Question Validate Reciprocate model. Once you have asked each question, ensure that you relate something back to the answer from your own experience. Make sure that for every question you ask you also have your own response ready, and that you give that as well.

o Keep practising this until the Question Validate Reciprocate model comes with ease. Then you can move onto the next exercise.

EXERCISE THREE: RAPPORT TRIANGLE

o Memorise the five levels of the Rapport Triangle.
   Next time you are engaging in small talk, remember
   to start at the bottom and work your way up. See
   how far up the triangle you can get, remembering to
   honour each level and not skip any.

o Once you become proficient at the Rapport Triangle,
   see how quickly you can move through the levels with
   a new acquaintance and get to the top.

Chapter 11

GETTING COMFORTABLE

Rapport can happen naturally and spontaneously, but the great news is that the process for assisting in its creation can also be learned.

A TALE OF TWO DOCTORS

During the period I was writing this book, I pulled a muscle in my back while exercising. The pain was excruciating, and after hobbling around for a day and a sleepless night I took myself to the emergency ward of the local hospital. Eventually I got to see a Doctor, who I'll refer to as Dr Young. He was very professional and clearly knew his stuff. He asked me numerous questions about the types of pain I was experiencing, which were mostly questions that generated a yes or no. He was getting me to move about and tell him when it was most painful, and at all times he was polite and respectful. He was also firing questions at me to do with my lifestyle. He asked how much alcohol I consumed each week. He asked me if I consumed recreational drugs, which he followed up with, 'It's confidential, so be honest'. I replied, 'No ... I can't find any good ones', and laughed at my own joke.

I was met with a wall of silence. Not so much as a smile. Once he had finished his tests I was taken back to the waiting room while he consulted with his 'boss', who I'll refer to as Dr Elder. I sat there in great agony for nearly three hours before Dr Elder came to chat to me. Once in his consulting room he asked how I was feeling. I repeated exactly what I had said to Dr Young, but as I said it I was panting and grimacing due to the pain. I then said, 'Sorry, I can't speak very clearly due to the pain', to which he responded, 'I see it has given you an English accent, too'. I laughed out loud, which hurt my ribs, but it lightened the moment and changed the dynamic between us.

He then repeated what Dr Young had told me, with a sense of genuine curiosity. It was notable how his language was much more inclusive than Dr Young's. For example, he said, 'Hhhhmmm … we need to work out what's going on together'. He then asked me a series of open-ended questions, and then empathised with me whenever I winced at the pain. Dr Elder was also very professional and knew his stuff, however his 'bedside manner' was much more comforting and engaging than his colleague, Dr Young.

So what was the difference between the two Doctors? Both of them knew their stuff, both of them needed to isolate the problem, but only one of them made me feel comforted and connected. In an unexplainable way this made me trust Dr Elder's advice more.

This is the power of good rapport.

WHY IS GOOD RAPPORT SO IMPORTANT?

Interestingly, Dr Jeffrey Mogil, a Neuroscientist at McGill University in Montreal, has discovered that stress is actually a blocker to feeling empathy. In his experiments he has discovered that when two people meet for the first time there is a degree of stress present. Going back to evolutionary psychology this makes sense, as any stranger would be considered a threat and part of the out-group. In evolutionary terms, it is far more likely that someone from the out-group would be willing to attack you than someone from your in-group. In Dr Mogil's experiments it became clear that this social anxiety leads to a lack of empathy. When he conducted experiments in which he gave participants a drug called metyrapone, which blocks the formation of the stress hormone cortisol, he found that their level of empathy increased. Therefore, it stands to reason that if you can do something – anything – that speeds up the process of feeling comfortable then the stress hormone will subside and you will be able to connect on a human level much more quickly. This is why developing the skill of rapport building is so useful.

I am a strong believer in rapport, and I use the techniques in the following chapters each and every time I meet someone new. As such, this chapter is all about building the argument for rapport. The next chapter will begin the journey of how to foster it.

As you could probably guess, the ability to connect with new people is a skill I hold very dear. Some people are just naturally very good at it, and some people have to work really hard to learn how to be good at it. I was the latter. The key point to remember is that *everyone* can get better at it. It is just a process with a number of steps and components. Then practice is all that is needed. When it comes to the application of the skills, you only need to use the techniques with people you do not naturally have rapport with or people you are meeting for the first time. Once you have rapport with someone you can just let the magic happen. For example, when you catch up with old friends, rapport is just there. You don't need to work on it with them.

WHAT IS RAPPORT?

I often ask people what they think is meant by rapport. There are a few terms that seem to come up time and time again: trust, connection, comfort and commonality are words I hear frequently. One of my favourite definitions of the word 'rapport' was once expressed to me as a formula. I thought it captured the meaning perfectly. It was as simple as:

$$Rapport = Trust + Comfort$$

Think about this for a second. Have you ever noticed how when you meet certain people you just feel instantly comfortable? You may even take an immediate liking to them. There is something about them you just trust, and it makes you feel very open and willing to connect. Now contrast that with someone you first meet who makes you feel on edge. The former is having instant rapport, and the latter is not.

Rapport can happen naturally and spontaneously, but the great news is that the process for assisting in its creation can also be learned. The art of building rapport works on both a conscious and unconscious level. There are the things that you say and how you structure a conversation. There are also the non-verbal communication elements that often happen outside of conscious awareness.

We looked at the Rapport Triangle in the previous chapter. However, that is just the tip of the iceberg. If you want to truly get into rapport then you need to tap into the rest of the iceberg, which sits below the waterline: these are the unconscious elements of rapport.

PEOPLE LIKE PEOPLE LIKE THEMSELVES

If you are questioning this assumption, imagine you are about to walk into a room full of strangers. In one corner there is a small group of people dressed outrageously, as if they are going to be performing on stage. In another corner there is a small group of people twice your age, and in the third corner a group half your age. However, in the fourth corner there is a small group of people who are your age, who are dressed like you and seem to act with the same level of energy as you. Which group do you feel most comfortable joining?

If you said the stage performers, there is probably a thespian in you trying to get out. But most likely, you would feel most comfortable going to the group most like you. In the next chapter we will talk about how to use the unconscious process of building rapport, consciously.

A TALE OF TWO MEETINGS

To end this chapter I'll tell two more tales to exemplify the stark differences between those who understand the power of rapport and those who do not.

I have had two memorable client meetings that illustrate this topic perfectly. Both meetings were with senior organisational leaders with similar budgets and responsibilities, to whom I was prospecting for professional services work. Each had very different styles. The first leader, who I'll call David, I had never met before. We had arranged to meet and discuss a possible project. Upon walking into his office he instructed me to sit down without shaking my hand or introducing himself – not so much as a 'hello'. He didn't ask me a single question, and instead launched into a one-sided narrative starting with, 'I already know what I want so you don't need to ask me any questions'. He spoke at me for 20 minutes before I was allowed to say anything. It turned out this man ruled with an iron fist, and everyone who reported to him was terrified of him. When he eventually moved on people were relieved.

The second meeting was with a leader I'll call Peter. We had never met, but upon meeting he smiled warmly and shook my hand. He asked about my weekend with genuine interest, and I told him about a motorbike ride I had been on. He explained that he used to ride, and how he missed it. He noticed my English accent, and he talked about a couple of fantastic years he had spent there during his career. It seemed this man had a gift for relating his own experiences back to mine. It made me feel very connected to him. It turned out that this man was someone who was adored and respected by everyone who worked with him, and he achieved great organisational results. When he moved on, those who worked for him were very upset, as they knew he was a very special person.

He was an *Engaging Executive*.

✻ ✻ ✻ ✻ ✻

Now that we have built a solid case for the importance of developing rapport, in the next chapter we'll look at how to build it using the process of Matching.

Chapter 12

CREATING RAPPORT

Energy matching is the 'master key' to creating rapport.

We have now built the case for the importance of good rapport, and we have looked at how we can utilise the Rapport Triangle. I have also introduced the concept of Matching. In this chapter we will explore in detail how to develop the skill of Matching, and I will end with some practical exercises that will help you to perfect it.

HOW TO MATCH

In the world of NLP this process is formally known as Matching and Mirroring. Psychologist Dr Robert Cialdini, in his book *Influence: science and practice* (2008), verifies the power of this process. In fact, many of you would be familiar with this term, and like many of the concepts in this book, that is probably about as far as you have taken it. In other academic circles the topic is often referred to as Postural Echo. Drs Brinkman and Kirschner also talk about this concept as 'blending' in their book *Dealing with People You Can't Stand* (2012). So, to simplify things I am going to call this technique 'Matching'. Once we break it down into its component parts you will find it is about much more than just posture; in fact, we use our entire body, including our voice.

There are a number of very granular aspects of Matching, but they all fit under the three broader categories of body language, voice and words. The broad category of 'words' refers to the type of words and structure, not so much the content of what you say. This will come later.

So let's start by looking at body language.

MATCHING BODY LANGUAGE

In body language I am including all things that are outward elements of communication that your body displays every second of the day. A really powerful quote I heard once is: 'You cannot, not communicate'. Ponder on this a moment. Everything you do is communication. Everything. Even if you were to just sit looking catatonic you are communicating something, especially if someone is trying to interact with you.

I was running a workshop once and there was a participant who had clearly been 'volun-told' to participate. It was apparent from the first moment that he didn't want to be there. At a break in the course I asked him what was going on. I pointed out that he had been sitting there all day with his legs wide apart, his arms folded across his body, with a piercing stare that could have melted ice. He looked at me totally aghast and said, 'I don't know what you're talking about. I've been trying very hard not to communicate anything.' Well … it hadn't worked. So we need to be especially conscious of our body language, and we will focus very heavily on this when we look at the *Guide* stage of the book, as it is a big part of influencing. It is also a big part of rapport building, so let's have a look at the ingredients before breaking each down further.

Before we look at the list, let's just have a quick conversation about how to match body language. The idea is to make yourself as similar to the other person as you can in the way he holds himself. This may mean making some big changes or just slight changes.

To understand this better, I would like you to imagine that your behaviour has its own baseline against the list below. From this baseline you may have to move up or down to match the other person. If you move towards the other person's behaviour and away from your baseline, this will be a good start.

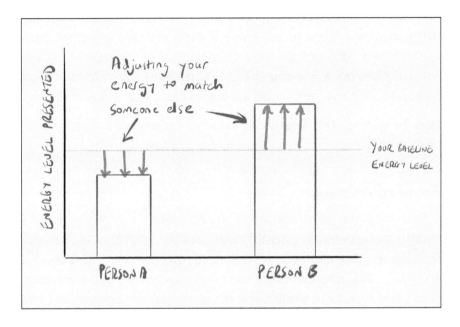

Below is a list of body language that you can match. This list is by no means exhaustive, however it covers the most important aspects of body language:

o   eye contact

o   facial expressions

o   posture of your back and arms

o   gesticulations

o   leg position

o   level of energy.

Let's explore each of these.

Eye contact

When building rapport with someone new it is important to observe his eyes as this can be the first indication of his general state of mind and personality in that moment. What I mean by this is the emotional signals the eyes present. Does this person look like he is full of excitement to meet you? Or does he look a little low key? These are just the two polarities – it can be anywhere in between. (We will come back to this when we touch on level of energy.) How constant is his eye contact? Does he look at you and hold your gaze or does he look away quite often? Is there seriousness in his eyes or are they soft and smiling?

How he is projecting from his eyes is how you should be projecting back at him.

Facial expressions

This is very similar to the rules of eye contact except you have a broader range of more noticeable variations to observe. Is this person's face relaxed, friendly, serious, frustrated, shy, nervous? And the list goes on … It is important that you gauge this quickly and then adapt your expression to be similar. If someone is looking deadpan and you greet her with an over-the-top smile, you are immediately in a different headspace to her. Equally, if someone is smiling ear to ear and you look back at her as if you are at a funeral, that is a rapport killer right there.

Posture of your back and arms

As you are standing or sitting, you can observe how the other person is holding himself. How is the line of his back? Is it straight or hunched? Are the shoulders back or rounded? Is the person leaning to one side or bolt upright? Are his arms by his side or resting on something like his hips or the table? However this person is standing or sitting, this is how you need to make your body shape.

Gesticulations

Some people use their hands vibrantly when they speak. Think of the stereotypical Mediterranean person telling a passionate story. Other people have hands that seem to be glued to their sides. If you are speaking to someone who is flapping her hands around wildly and you are more of a steady-handed person then it is your responsibility to move from your baseline and gesticulate more. Clearly, you only gesticulate when you are speaking, otherwise you will just look bonkers. The same is true if you are speaking to someone who is more stoic and you are naturally a wild gesticulator: you will need to tone your movements down.

Leg position

This is similar to posture, as mentioned above. Have a look at the position of his feet, if he is standing up. Are his feet shoulder-width apart or very close together? If he is sitting down, are his feet planted squarely on the floor or are they crossed? Are his legs crossed? Again, you will need to do the same or similar. Some men find it uncomfortable to do what I refer to as a European leg cross, which is one knee over the other knee. If this is the case, you may want to cross your feet at the ankles. I would suggest not doing what I refer to as an American leg cross, which is an ankle over the opposing knee. This can look a little too informal or even defensive as the leg forms a barrier.

Level of energy

This is probably the most important of them all. This is about the general level of energy that the other person brings to the interaction. Is she a high, medium or low energy person? Is this person a screaming extrovert or a reclusive introvert? You will need to come up or drop down from your baseline to match this.

A few years ago I was doing a feedback session with an Accountant. I had never met this person before, and so I marched into the room full of energy and engaged him with a massive smile and loads of enthusiasm. As I spoke to him I could see him recoiling – he looked overwhelmed by my energy. He was one of the most introverted people I had ever met. I certainly have no issue with introverts and I have a strong element of introversion in me, but this man was so introverted it felt like he was sucking all the light in the room into himself like a black hole. Once I noticed this I backed my energy right off. When I asked him a question it felt like I had to wait 30 seconds for a response. So, I started to leave big gaps between my own responses to his statements and my questions. It wasn't long before he started to settle down and slowly relax into the session.

If you remember to practise only one thing from this chapter, make sure it is energy matching. This is the 'master key' to rapport.

CROSS-OVER MATCHING

Cross-over Matching is when, for whatever reason, it is difficult or inappropriate to copy the position or movement of the other party. For example, let's say you found it uncomfortable to do the European leg cross. What you would do instead would be to cross your feet at the ankles. Another example is when someone who is high energy communicates, he might wave his hands around. You could match the energy when listening by nodding more energetically than you normally would, thereby Cross-over Matching his movement. This is a useful technique when what the other person is doing seems difficult to imitate.

DON'T GET CAUGHT!

Another rule of Matching is 'don't get caught'. It is a game of subtlety. When I was five years old, my sister was three. As cute as she was, she went through this really annoying stage of copying everything I did. She would say exactly what I had said right back at me. When I got up, she got up. When I sat down, she sat down. It drove me bonkers. Okay, so she was only three years old, however being consciously aware of her copying me was really off putting.

The same is true for Matching.

When you do it, do it gradually. Be subtle about it. Do not attempt to match abrupt or sudden gestures such as someone rubbing her nose. Only match the elements we have discussed above. If someone is seated and shifts position, should you follow them? The answer is yes, but leave it five seconds before doing this. If you get busted it will become a rapport killer. Saying that, I have never, ever been caught out – well, that I know of – in over a decade of using this technique. Have I had comments that I am very easy to like and easy to open up to? All the time.

WHEN IT WORKS IT REALLY WORKS

There is one occasion that I employed Matching that will always stand out in my mind as a unique and beautiful moment. I was part of a corporate charity day and the company I was working for at the time volunteered to sponsor and assist a special needs school with a day of games and activities. The place was an explosion of energy as the kids were being treated to all sorts of amazing activities such as mural painting, patting puppies, jumping castles, pizza making and much more. The kids were really enjoying the day, with one exception. There was a little boy who just wanted to lie on the grass. He was five years old and had a permanent Carer with him. With all the action going on around him he chose to lay on his tummy, rest on his elbows and pick at the grass. He would pick it up in his hand, twist it in his fingers and drop it. Then he would do exactly the same thing again.

I was fascinated by him, and at the same time felt his loneliness as he lay alone as the other kids had the time of their life. I wandered over to his Carer and enquired about him. She told me he was heavily autistic. I felt a real urge to connect with this little fella, so I lay down on the grass with my tummy on the ground and I rested on my elbows. I lay about two feet from the boy and didn't look at him directly. He did not look at me either. So I stared at the ground and starting picking the grass. I twisted it in my fingers and dropped it, before picking another bit up and repeating the process. I did this for about five minutes, side by side with the boy, him in his world and me in mine. Then the most beautiful thing happened. The boy picked a piece of grass out of the ground, turned his head and looked at me for the first time. He put out his hand and gave me the piece of grass.

In that moment we connected. All I did was act like him. It is a memory I will cherish forever.

MATCHING VOICE AND WORDS

Just as with body language, there is a whole set of voice qualities and words that you can match. Now when I say *match*, I am not talking about 'doing an impression' of the other person's voice – that is the last thing you want to do. I am not suggesting you mimic people. In the same way as copying body language movements too closely or obviously, 'doing an impression' can be a rapport killer. It is about adjusting yourself up or down from your baseline to get closer to the level of the other person.

Let's have a look at the list of main voice and word qualities you can match:

o pitch and intonation

o volume

o speed

o chunk size.

Again, let's consider each and understand how to utilise them.

Pitch and intonation

Some people have deeper voices than others. Some people have high sounding voices and some have low sounding voices. Of course, men typically have deeper voices than women. When voice matching, we are trying to get closer to the pitch of someone else's voice. Now, if someone talks like Mickey Mouse and you sound closer to Barry White then clearly you are not going to come up that far in your pitch. However, see if you can move towards the pitch you are hearing.

This also applies to intonation. Some people have a very flat tone, a monotone, when they speak, with few inflections. Others are much more likely to vary their voice, and for there to be highs and lows. You should attempt to match the pattern of this to build rapport.

Volume

Some people seem to have their voice box switched to 'loud' and some to 'quiet'. One of my friends quite possibly has the loudest voice in the world. Even when we are sitting in a small café he will boom out as if we are at opposite ends of a football field. I love him to bits, but he does have a very loud voice.

At the other end of the scale, recently I was working with a client who I could barely hear at all. When I asked him to speak up a little, he whispered, 'I feel like I'm shouting now'.

So we all speak at different volumes. Just as with pitch, you need to raise your baseline up or down to get closer to theirs.

Speed

This variant of voice is normally matched to energy level. Some people speak really fast – they sound like the rapper Ludacris after drinking a litre of Red Bull. Others seem to have a slow-motion voice with very drawn out words. Try to get into the same rhythm as the person you are talking to, as someone who speaks fast normally thinks fast so you don't want to keep them waiting. Equally, someone who talks slow may be a deep thinker, so don't overwhelm them with too much information at once.

Chunk size

This relates to the amount of information people tend to give you in one go. Have you ever noticed that some people speak in short, simple bursts? I tend to find that more senior people in organisations tend to speak like this. These people want the big picture, and they want it quickly. Then there are those who love to take a metaphorical ramble through the woods. They speak in rich and detailed passages, and often give you a lot of information in one hit.

If you speak to a 'big picture' person then only give her the outline. Allow her to ask questions to drill down further. If talking to a 'rambler' then put a bit more meat on the bones and give him something to sink his teeth into.

A TALE OF TWO TENNIS BOOKINGS

I have an example of voice matching that has become somewhat legendary on the training programmes I run. It is a story I tell whenever I run a session on rapport building. Unfortunately, it relies on me doing an impression of this person's actual voice to get the full effect. However, I'll do my best to relay the story in written form. It is an example of when I used voice matching to help someone remember me.

I used to play a lot of tennis when I first arrived in Australia. I played at the same local court about three times a week. The court did not have a clubhouse, so if you wanted to play you had to call up a number, speak to someone in the admin office, and make a booking. As I phoned up so many times a week it started to niggle me that the same guy I spoke to every time never ever remembered me or my requests, which were always the same. So each time I had to give him the same instructions and all my contact details. I was thinking to myself that if only he could remember me and my preferences we could cut the entire process down. Considering I had a distinctive 'fresh off the boat' English accent, it made it even more bizarre that I had to keep reintroducing myself.

A normal conversation would go something like this. 'Helllllloooo … this is Aaaaaronnn speakinnnnng … how can I heeeelp yoooou?' He had a completely monotone voice, which was really drawn out – he sounded like he was an old vinyl record running at half speed. We would have a conversation about my court choice, which was always the same, my time of booking, which was always the same, and my contact details, which were always the same. It was at this point one day that I remembered voice matching, so I decided to put it to use to see if it would work. I called up and I went through our entire conversation as per usual, except this time I did it all in pace with his voice. I slowed down my speech and I dragged my words out. I was similar but not the same as him. We went through the conversation all the way to the end, and then I was curious to see what would happen the next time I called up.

A few days went past and I made my normal call. I let him do his introduction. When I introduced myself using the same words as usual,

I did it in the same slow pace I had used previously. This is when the miracle happened: he suddenly said, 'Hellllllllo Duncan ... how are yooooou todaaaay?' He then said, 'Saaaame court?' I said, 'Yes, please'. I then asked him if he wanted my details. He said, 'Noooo ... I stilllll have them frooooooom the otherrrrrr day'.

I nearly fainted.

Let's have a go at some exercises that take your Matching to the next level.

PRACTICAL EXERCISES

EXERCISE ONE: BODY MATCHING

- Pick a person who you do not already have good rapport with. As you talk to them, match as many parts of their body posture as you can. Use cross-over matching if necessary. Do this for the entire conversation.

- Repeat this every day until you feel you can do it naturally, and then move onto the next exercise.

EXERCISE TWO: VOICE MATCHING

- Pick someone who speaks at a different pitch or speed to you. In the same way as the last exercise, see if you can move closer to the qualities of their voice without taking it to extremes. Only focus on matching the voice.

- Repeat this every day until you feel you can do it naturally, and then move onto the next exercise.

EXERCISE THREE: ENERGY MATCHING

- Find someone who is a totally different energy to you — either higher or lower. Match this person's energy in terms of movement and speech.

- Repeat this every day until you feel you can do it naturally, and then move onto the next exercise.

EXERCISE FOUR: PUTTING IT ALL TOGETHER

- Put together all of your Matching skills from the above exercises and see if you can Match every person you meet for a day. Notice how you need to change in order to Match each person.

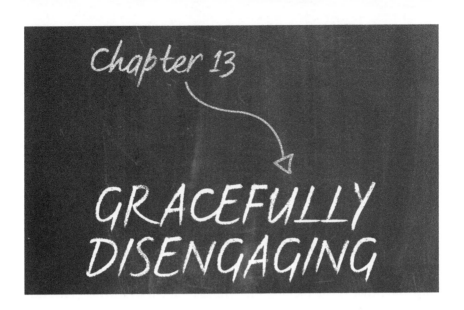

Chapter 13

GRACEFULLY DISENGAGING

Having put in the hard work to make a good impression, you don't want to blow it all at the end.

As we have examined the art of making an approach and developing small talk, it makes sense to also discuss the art of disengaging gracefully. Having put in the hard work to make a good impression, you don't want to blow it all at the end. That's not being an *Engaging Executive*.

We are going to imagine a few different scenarios whereby you don't know how to exit a conversation. Let's set up the scenarios with a common start point. You have made a fantastic entrance, you have worked your way skillfully up the Rapport Triangle, and you have now been talking for a sufficient amount of time and you want to move on. Scenario number one is that you fumble the ball by looking awkwardly around, clearly demonstrating that you want to talk to someone else, leaving your conversational partner feeling like she has bored you. Scenario number two is that you completely run out of things to say and just stop talking. All of a sudden there is a deathly silence, which hangs between you until your conversational partner makes his excuses and leaves. Scenario number three is that you really wanted to leave but you have been left with someone who can talk for hours and who has no sense that you want to wind it up, so you politely stand there nodding and listening and hoping that someone will come and save you, and the minutes and hours tick on.

How on earth do you manage such situations while not damaging the great connection you have just made? This is what we'll deal with in this brief yet important chapter.

PICKING YOUR MOMENT TO EXIT

If you are anything like me, you would have learned about this the hard way; that is, by picking the wrong moment to leave a conversation, especially if it is a first meeting and a purely social one.

Unlike formal business meetings, there is no structure or clear purpose to social meetings. In a formal meeting you would introduce, explore, solve, action plan and then wrap up. It is clear when you are at the end. So how does this work during informal or social meetings? The answer is, you have to take the lead and pick your moment. This is something I learned as a Dating Coach. I have had hundreds, if not thousands, of random social interactions with people as a consequence of this role. Therefore, I have had a lot of practice at getting myself into conversations and an equal amount of practice getting myself out of conversations. I found that the skill is just as applicable to the business world and to the informal conversations that happen there. The key to timing your exit is to leave at the peak of the conversation. 'What?' I hear you ask. 'You mean the best bit?' Yes, that is exactly what I mean.

It sounds counterintuitive, yet it is absolutely the best time to leave. It goes back to that old question, 'when is the best time to leave a party?' The answer is, 'before it ends'. Why is this? Well, if you leave a party while it is still raging you will always remember it as an awesome party. But if you try to hold onto the moment too long and you are the last one to leave, what are your last memories of the party? It is a bit like watching a really good stand-up comedian. Have you ever noticed that a really good comedian never leaves a set on a bad joke? A great comedian will always work the audience up to a frenzy, and just as the audience hits the peak, it's, 'Thank you. You have been a wonderful audience.' Why? The comedian wants you to remember the feeling she left you with, not, 'The start was good but it went a bit flat at the end'.

This is exactly what you need to consider when leaving your first impression on someone.

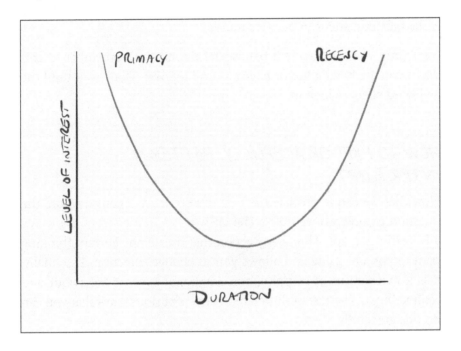

The above diagram is something I was taught back in the 1990s. Back then I was an Outplacement Consultant helping retired Police Officers find their second career. I used to coach them on how to go for job interviews, and it has stuck with me ever since as a powerful model of how human attention works. The model works via two important principles in Psychology: *Primacy* and *Recency*.

Primacy is a documented phenomenon which states that people are far more likely to remember the first thing they experience than what comes after. This is where the concept of making a good first impression comes from. This is also why we have focused so heavily in the first two stages of the ENGAGE model on making a good first impression. As you can see in the diagram, the first couple of minutes of an interaction are where there is the most interest and attention given.

Then, just as people get into their stride, everything becomes more relaxed and the attention drops.

This continues until people can sense the end is near. Then the attention comes back up and the last part of the interaction is remembered. This effect is called Recency. This is why you need to end on a high. It is the part that sticks in people's minds.

Next time you are having a new social interaction, remember to end when you are having fun or have aroused interest. Don't wait until the awkward silences kick in.

HOW TO EXIT GRACEFULLY: PATTERN INTERRUPTS

Now that we can appreciate the best time to leave a conversation, the question is, how do we do it? The answer lies in a concept known as a Pattern Interrupt. This is any action that breaks the current thinking pattern you are using and allows you to change direction. Essentially, it is a mechanism of stopping one emotional state or behaviour and redirecting it. The rest of this chapter covers various ways that you can do this gracefully.

End on a compliment

One way of ending on a high is to end on a compliment. If you have made a reasonable stab at getting up the Rapport Triangle, you should have uncovered at least something that the other person is interested in. Let's say, for example, you have been talking about hobbies and the person has declared that he likes to sail. He may have even talked a little about the type of sailing he does and whether it is competitive. This is all good fuel for your strong close.

If you feel the need to wrap up the conversation, end it by relating back to something the person was passionate about. In that way you leave him feeling good. You could say something like, 'I'm going circulate now, but I have to say, you have given me a lot to think about with the sailing. I never knew that much about it. You have made it sound very rewarding. Best of luck with the competition. I hope to see you around soon.' This is my default technique for ending a conversation. At the very least, it shows you have been paying attention to what the person has been saying, and that in itself can be very powerful.

Two's company, three's an exit

Sometimes there has not been enough time to climb up the Rapport Triangle, or maybe you just see an opportune moment to leave. At most social gatherings there will be people wandering past. Some of them may stop and join you, or they may walk past and smile at you as they go. One way of exiting a conversation is to invite someone else into the conversation. This is a Pattern Interrupt because as soon as someone else joins the conversation the dynamics change. There is a new energy in the group and a new set of introductions to be made. This is a great time to take your leave. Seize the moment by introducing the new person to the existing person or group and then saying, 'Excuse me, it was lovely to meet you. I will leave you to get to know each other'. Like a magician you will disappear in a puff of smoke, and the conversation will take new life with the replacement person.

'Oh you must meet' tactic

I have observed lots of people in networking scenarios and how they exit conversations. There are some very smooth operators if you study attentively enough. One such trick is similar to the above tactic except it is more deliberate, rather than waiting for a passer-by. It involves using the Rapport Triangle until you have enough information to form a hypothesis about who else at the event may have a common interest as the person you are speaking to. For example, you find out that someone has a passion for classic cars and then you think about who else might have the same interest. At that point you say, 'Classic cars … Oh, you must meet Dave. He loves classic cars with a passion!' At which point you escort this person over to Dave and introduce them via their shared passion. At which point, you exit stage left.

BREAKING RAPPORT GENTLY

Just as we have focused on how to create rapport in this *Network* part of this book, we also need to focus on how to break rapport gently.

Rapport is easy to break badly. This is not what we want to do. We can use some subtle body language instead that can help people recognise in a very discreet way that it is time to finish the conversation. The trick here is to do as little as possible to get the job done. We are only looking for the minimum effective dose and nothing more.

Let's have a look at some of the different methods you can use.

The sneak peak at the watch

This may seem rude but it is all about how you pull it off. Let's say you are standing at someone's desk and you have an urgent meeting to go to, but your colleague seems determined to give you the intricate details of her seven-course meal from last night. One escape technique is to pretend to be looking at your watch. What I mean by 'pretend' is that you *do* want her to notice you are looking at your watch but you want to be pretending that you *do not* want her to notice. This is because if you blatantly look at your watch in the middle of a conversation you will come across as rude. However, if the person you are speaking to thinks you are trying to look discreetly without them noticing, they are likely to assume you don't want to be rude yet you must have something important to do. You therefore get released from the conversation with their blessing.

What time is it?

This is a slight variant on the above technique except you use a question as a break state. If you find yourself in a long conversation and you spot a gap in the dialogue, instead of looking at your own watch, ask 'Oh, do you have the time?' You should deliver this line with a slight sense of urgency, as if you have just remembered something. When you get the response you will notice there is a pause in the conversation. Your conversational partner may even ask you if you have to go. This is the time to make your excuses and leave.

Talking with your feet

Having observed hundreds of men and women chatting in my former role as a Dating Coach I have become somewhat of a body language expert. In most situations the woman and man speaking to each other are too far away for me to hear what they are saying, yet I can almost always pick when a woman is keen and interested to speak to the man. It all comes down to the direction of her feet.

What a person does with her feet can be an accurate clue to her level of interest. The more distant a body part is from the brain, the less aware we are of its movements, and hence the less we are able to manipulate it. Our feet often give away our true feelings without us being aware of it. The direction in which a person's foot points reveals the actual direction in which the person wants to go, even if they're engaged in conversation.

I have often seen a woman smiling and being polite with a man, and if you were only to look at her face you would imagine she was very content. But, within 30 seconds she makes her excuses and leaves. If you had been looking at the direction of her feet, it would have been obvious. This happens for both genders.

If we want to leave a meeting or a conversation, our foot will point in the direction of the nearest exit.

If you notice a foot pointing elsewhere with a person you are talking to, it can mean a lot of things, such as he is not interested in you or what you have to say, he is late for an appointment, or that he wants to go to the bathroom. Interestingly, most people will pick up on this at a subconscious level. So, if you want to leave a situation, all you need to do is clearly point your feet away from the person you are speaking to. Hopefully, he will pick up on this, albeit subconsciously, and wind up the conversation.

Okay, let's get practical and focus on some exercises to develop these skills.

For more information and resources on the NETWORK stage, go to www.engagingexec.com.au

PRACTICAL EXERCISES

EXERCISE ONE: OBSERVING THE HIGH POINT IN CONVERSATIONS

- Next time you are having a social interaction, look out for the highs and lows of the conversation. See if you can time your exit on a peak.

- Repeat this until you can master leaving a conversation at its peak. Then move on to the next exercise.

EXERCISE TWO: END ON A COMPLIMENT

- Pick a social interaction that is going well and one in which you have gotten quite far up the Rapport Triangle. Look for the peak, and at the appropriate moment end on a compliment.

EXERCISE THREE: BREAKING RAPPORT GENTLY

- Next time you are talking to someone who never seems to stop, try using one of the rapport-breaking moves. Try the sneak peak at the watch or change the angle of your feet to point towards the door. Make sure you do this subtly, and observe if the conversation starts to wind up.

GUIDE

Part IV

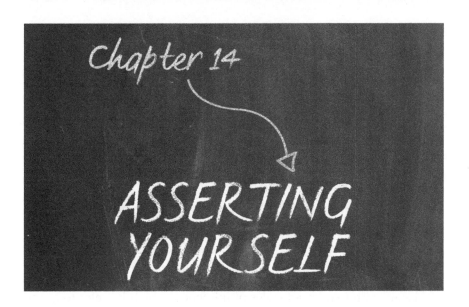

Chapter 14

ASSERTING YOURSELF

The Push style is about being confident and assertive, never aggressive.

In part IV we are going to move on to the ways in which you can *Guide* a conversation. That's right, this section is all about influencing skills. Part of being an *Engaging Executive* is being able to influence others.

It is important to remember that this part builds on the work we have done so far, so we will be referencing some of the topics covered in previous chapters. We will look at some of the key ingredients of influence, and break them down into the specifics of words, voice and non-verbal communication (NVC).

The brilliant part about the learning points in this chapter is that you have already been developing an awareness of the voice and NVC elements in previous chapters. We will examine how to bring together patterns of words, voice and NVC combinations to project different styles of influence. This chapter on how to guide a conversation focuses on assertiveness. The remaining chapters will look at other aspects of influence, and by putting these together your ability to influence will go through the roof.

Of course, with great power comes great responsibility. I am not writing a chapter about how to manipulate people for evil intent. The processes I share with you are very powerful – you must be responsible in their use.

Execute your powers wisely.

AN OVERVIEW OF PUSH AND PULL

Influencing is a massive subject. There have been so many articles and books written on influencing that it is enough to overwhelm you, so I am going to cherry pick from the many sources I have used as a Psychologist and NLP Master Coach over the last 15 years.

We'll start with two broad styles of influence, which I'll refer to as the Push and Pull styles. They are like the Yin and Yang of influence. I first came across these broad definitions about 15 years ago and yet I am still unable to pin down an official source for them. If you plunder Google you will find many similar versions of the same model, each with a slight variation. This is my version of the model based on my vast experience of using it and teaching others how to use it.

Push is a style you would use when it is imperative that you get people on board with your agenda and that you influence them towards the things that are important to you – you are pushing what is important to you onto other people.

The *Pull* style is the opposite. It is where you influence people by finding out what is important to them and then drawing on that. It requires that you ask a lot of questions, and is a much more subtle and gentle style of influencing, yet it is especially useful for longer lasting influence.

Both styles are incredibly powerful, and once you have become accomplished you can flip between them in a single interaction. However, I do find that they are easier to learn if you consider one at a time. So let's begin our journey with the Push style. We will cover Pull in chapter 16.

THE PUSH STYLE

Before we go any further, I want to be very clear that the Push style is not about being aggressive. If you are imagining a screaming, red-faced person pounding the table with his fist, think again. The Push style is a far stretch from the bully. The Push style is a deliberate and controlled use of power, not an uncontrolled use of it in which you are channelling your anger. This is not the way of the *Engaging Executive*. The Push style is about being confident and assertive, never aggressive. Aggression is a sign you have lost control, and *Engaging Executives* remain in control of their emotions at all times.

Getting what you want

The Push style is about getting what you want.

Some people are very good at this. Some people are not. Those who are not often get talked over, ignored, or feel unable to express their own needs. If this happens for too long it can be damaging to self-esteem. This chapter is for those of you who need to toughen up. Those of you who need to develop your assertiveness and command more respect. So let's focus on those who are good at being assertive. These are people who always seem to get what they want, but without being bullying, confrontational or aggressive. Can you think of anyone you know like this? Stop and think about this for a minute. What do you notice about this person's behaviour? What kind of language does this person use? What voice qualities? What is the body language when this person is pushing for what she wants? Stop reading for a moment and consider this now. I'll wait.

I bet you I can list some of the qualities that this person demonstrates. Let's break down the Push style into its component parts of words, voice and NVC.

Push words

I will start by looking at the types of words people who successfully adopt the Push style tend to use. When you first look at this list you may feel these words sound aggressive. Remember, the voice qualities you use to say these words can have a massive effect in moderating any harshness, and we will focus on this next.

This is not an exhaustive list but merely an indication of a style – you will probably be able to pull many more from your own lexicon.

TABLE 1: PUSH WORDS AND PHRASES

THE WORDS THAT ARE USED	Me; my; I; must; should; will; now; do; need; action; immediately; I'd like; my opinion; I want; I need; my experience tells me; my expert opinion; as I see it; this is so important; don't do that; you must do this; it is essential that this happens; it must happen exactly like this

If we were to put some of these in the context of a sentence it would look like this: 'I need you to do this now', or, 'You must take action on this immediately'. These words and phrases are just simple examples, but they denote the style.

What do you notice about them? Have you noticed that they are very definitive? There is no sense of ambiguity or tentativeness. They are direct and to the point. This typifies the Push style. It is best used when you absolutely need to assert your will in a situation due to urgency or emergency. It is also appropriate for use in situations where people may be contravening safety or legal boundaries.

Push voice

Think back to previous chapters when we discussed the importance of the entire communication package. Just saying the words alone will only get you so far. It is how you say them that really makes the difference. So now we will focus on the Push style voice. Again, I want to draw your attention to the fact that you are not trying to come across as aggressive. It is about being solid and direct.

Let's break this down into the characteristics of an assertive voice.

TABLE 2: PUSH VOICE QUALITIES

HOW THE WORDS ARE USED	Firm tone that is relatively flat; slightly louder than a normal voice but not shouting; slightly deeper; the end of the sentence has a downward inflection; sentences are succinct; appropriate use of pause on key points

If I were to give you a caricature of this, one that would make you giggle but at the same time make a serious point, it would be an Italian American Mafia Boss. Think for a minute about a scene from just about any of the Hollywood Mafia films. The Dons, the big bosses, are always straight to the point and use a minimum amount of drama. The underlings are the ones getting all emotional and passionate about things. The Dons just give instructions. The Don would look the underling straight in the eye and say, 'Go. Take. Fredo. Fishing.' There is no doubt – simply from the delivery of the instruction – that the underling is not being sent to bring home fish for dinner. It's not what they say but how they say it that gets the result they want. It's the measured, deeper tone, clear and succinct, with a definite downward inflection at the end.

Another tool of a strong Push style is the use of silence. Someone who is nervous or less confident always feels the need to fill the space. Someone who is assertive does not feel the need to justify himself or to speak just for the sake of it, he will just speak his truth and be done. The less you say, the more it gets heard.

The Push style is a very succinct and direct style; it is not about talking endlessly and drowning people out. That is called a rant. Less is more with the Push style.

Push NVC

Now let's think about the non-verbal communication that goes along with the Push style. For the assertiveness to succeed you need to consider your entire body, so we are going to work from head to toe and consider each of the elements. These are all aspects we need to consider when we use the Push style.

So looking at the package of NVC for the Push style, you have to make sure that you come over in an authoritative way but not an aggressive way. The idea is that you use your body to create a sense of presence.

Push NVC is shown in the table on the following page.

TABLE 3: PUSH NVC

FACIAL EXPRESSIONS	*Eyes level; neutral expression with the muscles relaxed; forehead unwrinkled and relaxed; no smiling; relaxed cheeks; eyes focused on the left eye but not staring; neutral mouth; head relatively still*
HAND GESTURES	*Hands relatively still resting in front of you on the table or on your legs; if seated then can have fingers interlocked and your elbows sticking out slightly to give the illusion of being bigger; when talking use your hands only to emphasise key points; your hands must be palms down for authority; don't point; have your hands like a blade which you can subtly chop vertically through the air with as you make your key points; use hands sparingly as over-use becomes distracting*
BODY POSITIONING	*If sitting then sit upright with a straight back; your knees should be at 90 degrees to the floor with your feet planted pointing forwards; when you speak in a group situation you need to lean forward; put your hand out in front of you in a blade fashion level with your chest with a slight bend at the elbow and speak at the same time; if standing then stand tall like the oak tree and use your hands sparingly to accentuate key points; you can stand with your hands on your hips for short periods*

In the animal kingdom most animals make themselves bigger if they want to be dominant. However, this can come across as aggressive, so be mindful of this. It is about using your words, body and tone in unison to create a powerful message.

As usual, at the end of this chapter there are some practical exercises. I suggest you practise Push first before moving onto the Pull style. In my experience of teaching people this I always find just focusing on one at a time is more effective.

PRACTICAL EXERCISES

EXERCISE ONE: WORDS

○ Imagine the types of scenarios where you might need to use more Push language. Typically, these will be with people you consider more dominant than you are.

○ Write as many Push sentences as you can relating to each scenario using the types of words listed in Table 1.

EXERCISE TWO: VOICE

○ Choose a person you deem assertive, such as George Clooney, Meryl Streep, Harrison Ford or Hillary Clinton. Listen to how they pronounce their words. Notice the rhythm, the stillness, and the underlying strength of their voice qualities.

○ Take your list of Push statements from exercise one and record yourself on your phone, pronouncing the sentences using the voice qualities outlined in Table 2.

EXERCISE THREE: NVC

○ In a similar style to exercise two, pick someone you find assertive (being sure not to pick someone who is aggressive) and find a video of this person on YouTube. Notice how this person holds him or her self, uses his or her hands, and makes use of his or her entire body to project confidence.

○ Take your list of Push statements from exercise one and say them out loud in front of a mirror. If you are able, record yourself and watch it back. Ask yourself, do the words, voice and body language match? Do you come across as assertive or aggressive? If you feel you come over as aggressive then get some feedback from someone else. It may just be that it feels aggressive to you as this is not your natural style. If it does come over as aggressive, dial your voice tone and posture back a little at a time until you look assertive.

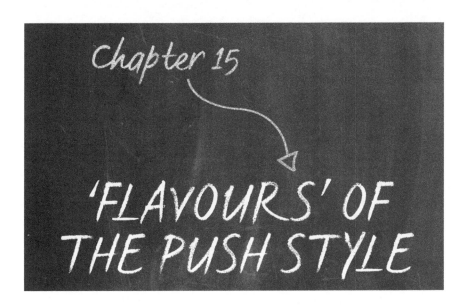

Chapter 15

'FLAVOURS' OF THE PUSH STYLE

You can divide the Push style into Passionate, Fearless and Factual sub-styles.

Within the Push style there are different 'flavours'. While this is not exhaustive, you could divide the Push style into Passionate, Fearless and Factual sub-styles. Let's consider these in a little more depth. These are all Push styles but they are a little more advanced and contextualised. Again, I am explaining them in discrete groups for the purposes of learning.

PASSIONATE STYLE

Let's start with the Passionate style. This style is typified by someone who speaks from the heart, someone who puts passion and energy into the way she talks and the message she is communicating. This style is great for generating enthusiasm and creating energy in others.

There are many examples of people who communicate like this. Someone who does this with a very positive style is Anthony Robbins. If you don't know who he is, Google him and you will probably recognise him immediately. Essentially, he has taken personal development seminars to the next level. There is a movie about him and his seminars called *I am Not Your Guru*. He constructs his presentations in a way that taps right into your emotions and leaves you feeling inspired. I had the good fortune of going to one of his events, and I can honestly say it was one of the best seminars I have been to in my life.

So how does Tony do it? Well, there are a lot of secrets to this. Many are shared throughout this book, however what we are focusing on here is the passion and energy with which he speaks. He challenges your thinking, but in a way that makes you believe you can go the extra steps. He bounces around the stage and booms out his deep voice with varying intonations. One of the stand-out moments of the course I attended was when Tony came down into the audience at 1 am (yes, we were still going) and instigated a water fight with 3000 people. Him against us! His energy and enthusiasm were just staggering.

Okay, this may seem a stretch for the corporate world, but it is more the essence of the style I want you to pick up on rather than the actual example – using passion to enthuse and motivate people. You need to be high energy in your voice, words and animation. It can really lift the mood of others when used appropriately.

FEARLESS STYLE

The next Push style is called the Fearless style. The Fearless style is used when you need to come across as strong, centred and unflustered by distractions. It is, in many ways, the archetypal assertive style. If you were to think of an actor or actress who is the living embodiment of the Fearless style, who would you choose? Don't necessarily think about the person but think about the types of characters he or she tends to play. The man who pops into my head is George Clooney. Okay, he does some of those quirky characters in the Coen Brothers movies, but I'm thinking more of his characters in the *Oceans* films, in *Gravity*, *Up in the Air*, *Michael Clayton* or *Three Kings*. Think about his type of expression when he is delivering a serious message. How does he hold his shoulders? How does he use his hands and posture? There is a stillness and sense of focus when he speaks which has a slight intensity yet it is not threatening. When someone adopts this style when talking to you it is as if you are the only person who exists.

It generates a sense trust and integrity. Some female examples would be Hillary Clinton or Margaret Thatcher.

There is also another element. A Fearless style sets boundaries and is firm about what is right and wrong. Therefore, setting consequences both positive and negative are part of this style. A person being influenced by the Fearless style knows exactly what is in and out of scope and what will happen if he achieves the desired results or does not. A person adopting the Fearless style is not afraid to speak his truth.

FACTUAL STYLE

The final sub-style of the Push style is the Factual style. This is the style that many people reading this book will be most comfortable with. This style is based on logic and facts, and is usually supported with a technical expertise in the given subject. It is a low-energy but very cerebral style. Many of the people I coach fall into this style.

I like to think of this as the Mr Spock style. Do you remember Mr Spock from the original *Star Trek* television series and films? He never showed emotion, and he often said, 'That is illogical, Captain'. In fact, this is probably why Mr Spock and Captain Kirk made such a good team. Captain Kirk was completely Passion style. If I had to broad-brush Captain Kirk's two default solutions to any situation it was to fight or fornicate, whereas Mr Spock was always trying to work out a solution using science and logic.

This style works particularly well if you need to use data and analysis to convince other data-driven or logical people. This style adopts a lower energy with less movement – a calm and factually driven flow of argument. This may entail stages or steps or hard data.

So now that we have looked at some ways to assert yourself, let's have a look at some practical exercises that can help you build this skill further.

PRACTICAL EXERCISES

EXERCISE ONE: PASSIONATE STYLE

- Watch a YouTube clip of someone you identify with as having a passionate style of influence.

- Ask yourself, how does he or she speak and hold him or herself?

- Practise this style in front of the mirror or record yourself and watch it back.

EXERCISE TWO: FEARLESS STYLE

- Again, find a video or an actor or actress who displays this style.

- Consider a conversation you are going to have where you need to influence someone using this style. What consequences, both positive and negative, can you give this person?

EXERCISE THREE: FACTUAL STYLE

- Watch a documentary about something related to applied physics, or a TED Talk on a scientific topic of interest.

- Observe the way this person builds a case for change using facts, figures and logic.

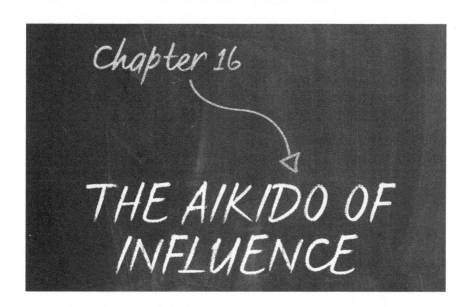

Chapter 16

THE AIKIDO OF INFLUENCE

The Pull style should be communicating that you are open to listening to someone and that you are genuinely interested in what that person has to say.

An *Engaging Executive* needs to have many tools of influence to draw upon. In this chapter we will look at the opposite force to Push, being the Pull style of influence. Are you someone who is always doing the talking? Are you someone who only ever expresses your views without consulting others? If so, this chapter is for you.

WHO IS THE MOST INFLUENTIAL PERSON IN THE ROOM?

It is often easy to assume that the person who talks the longest and the loudest is the more influential person in a room. This is incorrect. You see, statements are easy to reject. I can tell you I want you to do something. You may even agree to do it just to pacify me. Does that mean you will *actually* do it? Possibly. Possibly not. The problem is, if I've just barked an instruction at you, you have not bought into what I'm saying. It is all about what I want and nothing to do with what is important to you.

An interesting thing about the unconscious mind is that it loves questions. In fact, it responds to questions more than it does to statements. A statement can be ignored, while a question has to be processed. That's right, a question cannot go unanswered in the unconscious mind. Every time you receive a question, your mind has to do what is called a transderivational search: it has to search through all your knowledge and experiences to find the answer. Even if you do not open your mouth to provide the answer, you will be forced to process it.

And here is an even more interesting fact: the unconscious mind is more powerful than the most powerful computer. Why? If a computer searches all its databases and cannot find the answer to a question then it comes back blank. The unconscious goes one step further when it can't find an answer: it makes one up. Understanding this is a game changer.

I have spent many years teaching senior and technically minded executives the power of asking questions. For most of them their default style is to always express their opinion (Push). But they nearly always report that once they start to Pull they find out so much more useful information and receive more buy in to ideas in addition to the positional power they assert.

THE PULL STYLE

The Pull style is actually a subtler and more complex form of influence than the Push style. While lesser used, when done well this style has so much more power and the impact is much longer lasting.

A big mistake I see many technically brilliant leaders make is to assume they have to know everything, and that all the ideas have to come from them. As a consequence, all the great ideas of the people that work for the leader are suppressed, or at least underutilised. Steve Jobs made an excellent point when he said, 'It doesn't make sense to hire smart people and then tell them what to do; we hire smart people so they can tell us what to do'. Well, the Pull style is very much aligned with this philosophy. It is about finding out what is in other people's heads and then utilising this either to expand your own thinking or to find something that is important to that person which you can relate back to your objectives. In this way, the Pull style is much less direct, but when it works it gives you 100% alignment between the leader and the follower.

Pull words

In a similar fashion to the chapter on Push, I will identify some of the words that are aligned to the Pull style. Just as the Push style was not to be confused with being aggressive, the Pull style is not to be confused with being passive. It is a non-directive style of influence, and the skill is in getting people to come to their own conclusions. It is most definitely not about sitting silently. It is all about using the energy and enthusiasm of someone else and steering and guiding it with questions. Hence, I call it the Aikido of influence.

TABLE 4: PULL WORDS AND PHRASES

THE WORDS THAT ARE USED	We; us; together; our; suggest; will; how about; can we; shall we; could we; open questions: how, what, where, when, who, why (use why with caution, see below for details); the Pull style also utilises summary and paraphrasing

You will notice from the style of the language that the Pull style is about influencing in a gentle way that puts a degree of control with the other party. In this way the other person can feel a sense of buy in to the decision or direction.

Pull questions

The key skill in using the Pull style is the ability to use open questions. Whenever I teach this to executives they often say, 'Yes, yes ... I know what this means'. But when I subsequently ask them to practise it purposefully within a discussion they frequently struggle. Instead they disguise their statements as questions; for example, 'So, would you agree that we need to sort out this issue first?', or, 'So, do you want to do option A or option B?' These questions are Pull imposters. Of course, you do need to ask clarification questions occasionally, but a whole sequence of them is not successfully using the Pull style – it is doing a soft Push style instead.

There are several examples of Pull imposter questions, such as:

o 'Can you … ?'

o 'Do you … ?'

o 'Could you … ?'

o 'Will you … ?'

o 'Have you … ?'

All of these questions will get you simply a yes or no answer and not a rich and revealing reply.

Another Pull imposter is multiple choice questions: 'So, do you want to do A, B or C?', or, 'Do you think it means A or B?'

Leading questions are also imposters. This is where you suggest what you actually want to happen in the question, so it's not actually a question; for example, 'How much do you enjoy working here?'

Clarification questions are slightly different and are the exception to using closed questions. If you need to get an absolute 'yes' or 'no' before opening up the topic then this is an effective use of a closed question.

The art of the Pull style is to ask a series of questions that steer someone's thoughts but do not impose your own answers. This may be done using a combination of clarification and open questions. Let's imagine you needed to convince a person to work on her people management skills as she wanted to go for a promotion. Here is an example sequence of Pull questions:

o 'So you want to be promoted?' (clarification question)

o 'What makes you want to go down this route?' (open question)

o 'What differences to the way you work can you see at the next level up?' (open question) o 'So, you will need to get results through others?' (clarification question)

o 'How well set up for that are you?' (open question)

o 'So, you are saying you need to work on this?' (clarification question)

o 'What do you need to do to get that experience?' (open question)

o 'What support do you need from me?' (open question)

You will notice the absence of 'why' questions. I am very much against the use of 'why' questions unless it is a completely neutral exchange with no emotions or ego attached. The funny thing about 'why' questions is that they evoke a defensive response. Read the following two questions aloud and see if you can feel the difference. Yes, that's right, *feel* the difference. I want you to connect with how it makes you react. Imagine you have gone in to chat to your boss. Your boss is talking about a project you have been working on, and asks you, 'Why did you do that?'

Okay, now stop and check your reaction. Good.

Now, imagine the same scenario, but this time your boss asks you, 'What made you choose to do that?' Now check your reaction again.

Did you notice a difference?

Most people feel the need to defend or justify their actions when asked a 'why' question. The second question seems to evoke a more rational and less emotional response. This demonstrates the absolute importance of language and how important it is to properly formulate your questions to achieve the desired result.

I am a fan of 'what' and 'how' questions. 'What' questions tend to give you content and 'how' questions tend to get you process answers. I often coach executives to ask just these two types of questions alone when they are practising open questions. It is amazing how much you can find out by just using these.

The key point to remember is that the Pull style is all about asking *and* listening, therefore you should only be talking for about 20% of the time, or even less.

Pull voice

Just as with Push, there is a particular style of speaking that goes with the questions. For the Push style you are wanting to assert yourself, but with the Pull style you create an inviting environment that makes people want to respond to you. This requires a lot of softening of your style.

We will have a look at the voice now and then have a look at the NVC.

TABLE 5: PULL VOICE

HOW THE WORDS ARE USED	A more varied tone; slightly lower in volume; a pinch of curiosity in the tone; use of pause after a question; short and simple questions; slightly softer voice.

If you really wanted to get an idea of this style, think of a really great television or radio interviewer (not a political interviewer, as they tend to use a very challenging style). Think of someone who is trying to open people up and encourage them to contribute. In the UK there was a famous TV interviewer named Michael Parkinson, or 'Parky'. He had a very gentle style of interviewing which was warm and friendly. He would give a little context to the questions and ask them in a curious fashion. There are hours and hours of videos on YouTube of him interviewing people over his decades-long career. They are well worth a look.

Pull NVC

The body language that goes along with the Pull style is much softer than the Push style. It is generally a relaxed style that tends to be more fluid and less formal. Let's have a look at how this works.

TABLE 6: PULL NVC

FACIAL EXPRESSIONS	Soft eyes; a subtle smile; nodding in agreement or to encourage the person to speak; head at a slight tilt to the side to demonstrate listening
HAND GESTURES	Open hand gestures; as you ask a question, open your hands out about shoulder width with palms facing upwards; use an upward palm, horizontal sweeping movement from one side to the other if showing inclusivity to a group; avoid sitting with hands or fingers over the mouth as this can be interpreted as you stopping yourself from talking
BODY POSITIONING	Sit in a slightly laid back position so your back is not at a 90° angle; the hands can be rested on the lap when not being used; you can have a low leg cross or a cross at the knee, but not an ankle on the knee as that can appear defensive

The Pull style should be communicating that you are open to listening to someone and that you are genuinely interested in what she has to say. The purpose of the style is to find out as much as you can about a person's mindset so that you can find out what is important to her. Once you have established this, you can start to ask questions or offer suggestions that can tap into her mindset.

Here is an exercise in which you can practise.

PRACTICAL EXERCISE

EXERCISE: WHAT AND HOW FOR A DAY

○ This exercise is to break you in gently to the art of Pull. Take a meeting you have scheduled for the day and only use 'what' and 'how' questions for the duration of it. You can make statements if needed but try to keep them to a minimum.

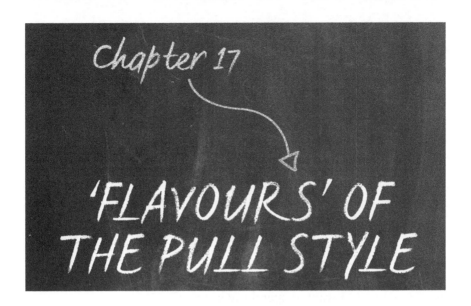

Chapter 17

'FLAVOURS' OF THE PULL STYLE

You can divide the Pull style into Inspirational, Sharing and Challenging sub-styles.

As with the Push style, there are several 'flavours' of Pull style: Inspirational, Sharing and Challenging. Each sub-style has a few unique elements. Again, these are more advanced and nuanced. I would suggest you master the basics of Pull style before moving onto these. Saying that, let's have a look.

INSPIRATIONAL STYLE

This is a high-energy and positive style of influence. It is a style used to open up the mind to possibilities and new ideas. This is a style used when you want to think big, when you need to dream big ideas and create completely new ways of thinking. In essence this is a very upbeat and optimistic style of Pull. The *Oxford English Dictionary* describes inspiration as, 'The process of being mentally stimulated to do or feel something, especially to do something creative'.

This style of Pull means asking the big questions. The tone of voice should be high energy and curious – imagine Dr Martin Luther King giving his 'I Have a Dream' speech. Now, I'm not saying you have to go quite as theatrical as that, but I want you to get a sense of the intonation and energy.

Steve Jobs was also a man who was great at inspiring others, although he wasn't always the easiest person to work for, allegedly. I once heard him ask an amazing Inspirational-style question in an interview: 'If today was the last day of my life, would I want to do what I am about to do today?' Now, think about this question. What does it do to you? It most probably forces you to go deep inside and ask other questions, such as:

o   'What is important to me?'

o   'How would I want to spend my last day?'

o   'What do I still want to do that I haven't done yet?'

And a whole bunch of others, no doubt.

This is the power of the Inspirational style. As a leader, you can set the scene with a vision and then ask Inspirational-style questions to get people to buy in. For example, you can say, 'Imagine a world where anything is possible … what would be the first thing we would do?' The key to these types of questions is that they are about possibilities and not about the current reality. They are about taking thoughts up a level to abstraction and not being stuck in practicality. After all, inspiration is a feeling that comes from within. It is not logical or rational but a feeling of being compelled emotionally to act upon something.

SHARING STYLE

This style is based on the Principle of Reciprocity and on the psychological principle of giving to receive. In other words, you share something about yourself – an experience, something personal – with the sole purpose of getting the other person to open up and share with you. You use your personal experiences to help someone think through a similar issue of his own. You are sharing your experiences and allowing the other person to take from it what he will. Questions can then be used that stimulate thought around the topic. The most important thing to remember is that you are not telling the person what to do. You are giving him a chance to reflect and come to his own conclusions. Your questions can provide a stimulus for this thinking.

I had a particularly powerful experience using this style with a Japanese friend of mine. It is a completely personal example, however it demonstrates the profound impact that a series of well-considered questions has. My friend and I were having coffee. We started talking about our families, and she shared a fact that made me quite shocked and saddened. She told me that she had not spoken to her Father for 13 years. So I asked her, 'What's the story behind not speaking to your Father?' She responded that he had left her Mum for another woman. So I enquired further: 'What made you choose to stop speaking to him?' She shared how in Japanese culture what her Father had done was considered dishonourable, and she had made a conscious decision to cut off her Dad out of respect for her Mother. She positioned it as if her Dad had made a decision to leave her and her Mum together.

I then asked her, 'Has your sister also cut off your Dad?' My friend replied that her sister was still in contact with him. This made me ponder, as I could see that behind the mask of honour and loyalty to her Mum, my friend was hurting. She didn't express this but I could feel it. So I decided to use the Sharing style. I shared with her my own childhood experiences about when my Dad left my Mum for another woman, who is now my lovely Step Mum. I was only six years old at the time. I explained to my friend that despite the fact my Dad leaving hurt me deeply, I was also aware of how much he still loved me and wanted me to be part of his life. I explained that even as a child I realised that my Dad could love me and someone else at the same time. I then asked my friend, 'So, do you think it would be possible for your Dad to love you and his new wife at the same time?' She looked at me and said, 'Yes'. I then asked, 'Do you think you are able to love your Mum and your Dad at the same time?' She responded, 'Yes'. I then asked her, 'How do you think your Dad might be feeling at having lost contact with one of his daughters?'

I could see her eyes welling up, and she started to cry. However, these were not tears of sadness, they were tears of relief. After she regained composure, I asked her, 'So, what are you going to do?' She looked in deep thought for a moment, and then said, 'I'm going to contact my

Dad'. So that day she contacted her Dad for the first time in 13 years. They have been rebuilding their relationship ever since.

I caught up with her a few months afterwards and I asked how it was going with her Dad. She told me that she was still speaking with him regularly. Then she said something that touched my heart. She said, 'Every time I get a message from him, I appreciate you'. This is how powerful questions can be when supported by sharing a personal example. If I had simply said at the start, 'You should stop holding a grudge and make contact with your Dad', I don't think we would have arrived at the same place.

CHALLENGING STYLE

Another way of looking at the Pull style is through the eyes of the Challenging facilitator. This style is used when you really want to help people think differently by directly challenging their beliefs. This is loosely based on the Socratic Method, which is the style of teaching the great Greek philosopher Socrates brought to the world around 400 BC.

The uniqueness of Socrates' teaching style was that he didn't tell his students anything. Instead he used questions to challenge his students' assumptions. The goal of this style is to gain greater knowledge for both the questioner and the answerer.

You do have to be a bit careful when you use this style of influence as it can be a bit confronting. In fact, Socrates was eventually executed because of his constant challenging of the Athenian way of life. The process has been proven in modern studies to make students feel more uncomfortable than just being told what to do. However, the same studies have found this style enhanced a student's ability to acquire knowledge. It works by challenging the assumptions of others, and through a series of questions getting the recipient to think through a problem. It is not a form of debating or arguing for your position. Both parties should learn from this and create new knowledge. So while this style is exclusively question based, you may find yourself using a little bit of Push voice and posture.

The style has a number of principles to it:

o   There are no 'wrong' answers, as 'incorrect' answers put people on the path to the right answers.

o   There are multiple right answers – as this is a Pull style there will be as many answers as there are people you use it on.

o   The role of the challenger is to keep the conversation focused and pull it back in if it goes off topic.

o   The conversation must be kept logical and rational, as this is the basis of reason.

o   Summaries must be used from time to time to help people keep track of the conversation.

Let's have a look at an example of this method in action.

I was in conversation with an executive who was on the cusp of starting his own business and was pondering whether to leave his current corporate job. I asked him about his plans. He told me he was keen to start a coaching business and leave his corporate position. I asked him, 'So what are you doing in your corporate job?' He replied that he helped coach managers in a very niche topic. I asked, 'So what do you want to do with your new business?' He told me that he was going to start a life coaching business, but felt conflicted in that his real passion and track record was connected with the niche of the current job. He felt a sense of loyalty to this firm, and felt he should therefore coach people in an unrelated area. So I asked him, 'Are you passionate about life coaching?' He said, 'To some degree'. I then asked him, 'Are you more passionate about your current niche that you coach within the corporate?' He responded, 'Yes', with absolute certainty. 'So what makes you choose to do something else as your main business?'

He pondered for a moment, and then answered, 'Well, I wouldn't want to compete against my current employer'. So then I asked him the killer question: 'What would happen if you did?' This was the point at which the penny dropped. He looked at me and said, 'I'd probably do really well. I am actually the person my clients "buy", as even within the firm I am a niche within a niche'. I could see his mind suddenly racing as he realised the possibilities.

* * * * *

Of course, all the Pull styles can be used in a coaching context as well as an influencing scenario. We will cover a simple yet powerful model of coaching later in the *Enlighten* stage, in which all of the Pull styles can be embedded. For now, let's have a look at a practical exercise.

PRACTICAL EXERCISE

EXERCISE: PRACTISING PULL STYLES

○ Write a list of questions from as many of the Pull styles as you can. Make sure you cover all of the basic Pull open questions, Inspiring, Sharing and Challenging styles.

○ Now practise saying them out loud in each of the styles: basic Pull, Inspiring, Sharing and Challenging. Record yourself on your phone and listen to it. Does it portray the styles as you understand them?

○ Finally, practise saying the questions out loud in the mirror. Observe your posture, facial expressions and hand gestures. Does this look inviting? Would this make you feel like opening up if you were being asked a question in that way?

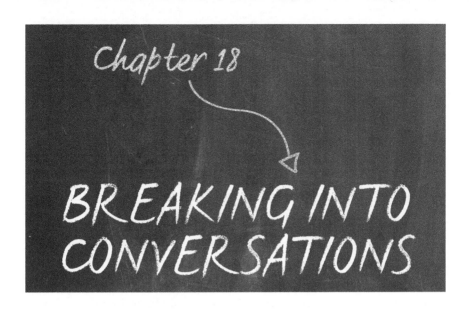

Chapter 18

BREAKING INTO CONVERSATIONS

You can only be influential if others hear your words.

For some, getting a word in edgeways in a group conversation, or even with a very talkative person, is a challenge. This is often a confidence issue: they do not feel their opinion is important. For others, it is the plain and simple fact that they are more introverted, and that by the time they have reflected and processed, the topic has moved on and their point now seems irrelevant.

An *Engaging Executive* will always get her opinions tabled when needed. This chapter is dedicated to showing you how you can get stuck in and have your voice heard. I have to thank a fellow Psychologist and friend, Christian, for many of the great ideas in this chapter. We have worked together for several years, and like all the great people I surround myself with, his ideas have rubbed off on me. I have taught many introverted or less assertive people how to use these techniques, and it has been quite transformational for them.

Ultimately, meetings are an inevitable part of business these days. In client meetings or sales meetings, each person has a role. One side wants something from the other, and there is a challenge to see if they can get it. These types of meetings are clearly defined in terms of who is doing what. However, for many executives life is a series of internal meetings with multiple stakeholders and differing agendas, and in such circumstances it can seem as though the person with the loudest voice gets what she wants. However, I would argue that this isn't always the case: the person who is most *influential* makes the biggest impact. This does not mean hogging the airtime and drowning everyone else out. It means making each point heard and getting buy in.

We started considering the art of influence in the Push and Pull chapters, and will continue in the following chapters. What has not been covered yet is how to insert yourself into a group of talkative people if you are typically more retiring. You can only be influential if others hear your words, so this chapter is all about getting your toe in the door of a conversation so you can work your magic.

MOVING FROM 'LISTENING MODE' TO 'READY TO SPEAK MODE'

As mentioned previously, introverted people tend to think carefully and deeply about things before expressing their thoughts, whereas your classic extrovert will often just think out loud and make course corrections on the fly, or not at all. As a consequence, introverts usually find themselves in Listening mode while extroverts tend to be primed in Ready to Speak mode.

If you tend to be more on the introverted side you need to be able to move between these two modes. This requires a 'mental shift' for our brains, and this takes time – albeit only a second or two – which means the conversation or opportunity to comment may have passed by the time you are ready to speak. Being more consciously focused on being in Ready to Speak mode can help you be ready to put your own point across. This involves shifting your focus at times towards anticipating when a gap in the conversation will occur and how you can find an appropriate time to comment.

Let's have a look at some of the different ways you can achieve this.

The 'can we just go back to ... ' technique

How can you get into a Ready to Speak mode if the ideal opportunity to make your point has already come and gone? I often find my more introverted clients feel the conversation has gotten away from them before they have had time to even consider adding to the discussion. Then they feel it is too late to make their contribution. To that I say, 'bah, humbug' – you have as much right to your views as the extroverts. A simple way to deal with this is to take control of the situation and steer it back to the topic you have now had time to consider. It is as simple as saying, 'I'd just like to go back to the point we discussed earlier. On reflection ... [insert your statement here]'. This technique means you can take the time to consider an issue at your own speed and then comment when you are ready. Don't be afraid to have your points heard.

Using body language as an anchor

We discussed how to create a resource anchor (happy button) in chapter 9: 'Breaking the ice'. Just to remind you, anchoring is where a unique stimulus causes a specific response once that connection has been established. Now we are going to talk about how you can anchor *other people* to respond to a stimulus – you!

The concept of anchoring is derived from another psychological principle known as Classical Conditioning. I'm sure you've heard of the Psychology 101 case study of the Russian Psychologist Pavlov, who conducted a series of experiments on dogs which entailed feeding them and ringing a bell as the food was presented. Each time, the amount of saliva the dogs produced was measured. After presenting the food and ringing the bell simultaneously numerous times, Pavlov discovered that if he just rang the bell and did not present the food, the dogs still salivated. However, if this was repeated too many times with no food appearing, the effect wore off.

We can apply this concept to how you can use your body language as an anchor during group meetings. First of all, you need to establish the correct posture to insert yourself into a conversation. Regardless of whether you are in Pull or Push mode, you will need to adopt a Push style for the interjection, then you can continue Push or swap to Pull once you have the floor. So, assuming a seated position, what is the correct posture? Let's go through it:

1   Make sure you are in the correct starting position: upright with your back at 90°. Your eyes need to be tracking who is speaking. Your arms should be on the table, if there is one, or on your lap, palms down.

2   When you want to interject, in one synchronised movement, lean forward slightly so your head and chest are leaning into the centre of the conversation. As you do this, put out your hand in front of you at chest height, ideally as a flat vertical hand, fingers together, elbow at 90°.

3   As you do the above, it is important that you begin to speak. You must not just lean in and put your hand out and wait for someone to let you speak. So make sure you have something to say or ask. For example, lean in and say, 'There is something I really need to say … ', or, 'There is something I really need to ask the group … ' Make sure you drop your hand once you have started speaking.

4   Once you have made your point or asked your question, it is important you return to the neutral position in step 1. This is the key to this technique, as if you remain leaning forward you can no longer use your body language to indicate you are about to speak.

Interestingly, when you do this a few times within a meeting it becomes anchored by others, and even if you just lean in and put out your hand they will stop and look at you expectantly. After a while you may only need to lean in to get attention, dropping the need for the hand gesture. Just like the bell and the salivating dogs, the body language becomes the anchor for others to allow you into the conversation. Just like the experiment though, if you don't have any value to bring with your interjections the impact will soon wear off.

Other variants of this are nodding and raising your hand slightly, and shaking a finger in a way that communicates your interest and that you have thought of an important additional point. Another effective version is when you agree with someone by saying 'Yes, yes, that is a great point … ', and as people look in your direction, you add your own continuation of the point.

Observing the voice of others and using your voice to get attention

I find it interesting how the tiniest of cues can trigger responses between humans. Many of these cues are out of our conscious awareness; for example, there is that moment at the end of every telephone call when you both just know it is time to end. It can be going great guns before that moment, but then there is a tiny 'nano pause' or a subtle change of tone and you just know that is the end of the call.

If breaking into meetings is a challenge for you then focus intently on identifying the 'cues' of the person speaking that indicate he may be coming to the end of his point; for example, people tend to raise or lower the pitch of their voice when they are completing a point. Once you get your timing right you can easily become aware of when to speak, even if it is just a tiny sliver of opportunity in the conversation.

Another trick you can use is what I call the Politician's Persistence. This is when you have started to speak and someone tries to talk over the top of you. You can repeat the first few words of your point until the other person backs down and allows you to continue. Margaret Thatcher was brilliant at this in the House of Commons. I can't imagine a much more hostile crowd, when half the room is paid to challenge and boo everything you say. She would start her address to the Speaker of the House, and if she was booed or spoken over she would repeat what she had just said, 'Mr Speaker, as I was saying … as I was saying … as I was saying … ' This communicates that you are determined to state your view.

Sometimes the problem is not that you are talked over but that nobody picks up on your point. Being persistent and communicating confidence is essential when this happens. If you are not successful in getting your point across the first time, try again later, otherwise you are communicating to others that your views are not very important.

Using the Interrupt and Repair technique

While interrupting is usually best avoided, there are circumstances when it is required and can be done effectively; for example, if you believe that the person speaking is going off track or dominating the discussion, it is usually acceptable to interrupt.

Interrupting others in certain contexts can be performed respectfully when you engage in 'repair behaviours' as, or after, you interrupt or speak over others. The most common repair behaviour is to apologise for intervening; for example, 'Sorry for interrupting, but I really need to make this point'. This is aligned to one of my favourite expressions in life: it is easier to ask for forgiveness than permission. This approach works as long as you can pull off a genuinely apologetic expression and tone. If you just say, 'I'm sorry', with a stony face and monotone voice, then it will come across as rude.

You can also come back to the other person's point after you have had your say; for example, 'I'm sorry for interrupting – I really need to add something, and then we can come back to your point'. And make sure you do come back to it, to retain credibility and trust.

Of course, another way of interrupting is to just talk over the other person and then apologise once you have finished speaking. You can do this by saying something like, 'I'm sorry I spoke over you. Please continue with your point.'

Be aware of and sensitive to cultural norms around interrupting. For example, in Western society it is less likely to be seen as inappropriate in certain contexts. However, in some cultures, such as some Asian cultures, interrupting can be perceived as causing 'loss of face' and is less likely to be considered fair and reasonable.

So let's look at some exercises that will enable you to practise the techniques in the safety of your own home so that when you use them for real they will be polished.

PRACTICAL EXERCISES

EXERCISE ONE: PICKING THE MOMENT

○ Watch a television show or movie that contains plenty of dialogue. Focus on one person and see if you can anticipate when he or she is going to stop talking. Focus on the facial expressions, the NVC and the tonality. See if you can improve the accuracy of your guessing to the point that you are correct 75% or more of the time.

EXERCISE TWO: BODY LANGUAGE ANCHOR

○ Practise the body language anchor. Practise sitting on your own and leaning in, putting your hand out and speaking all at the same time. Do this until you can do it all in one movement that feels smooth and continuous.

○ Turn on the television again and watch a debate or news interview. Sit upright on a chair and imagine you are sitting opposite the person on the television and the debate is with you. See if you can anticipate when this person will stop talking, then move in with the body language anchor. Practise doing this until you feel comfortable.

Chapter 19

CONTROLLING CONVERSATIONS

The purpose of chunking up is to take the conversation to a higher level of abstraction so it is more difficult to disagree with you.

I have saved the most powerful aspect of influence to last. An *Engaging Executive* will most certainly need this skill in her toolbox. The remaining chapters in the *Guide* part of the book are where I truly believe you will turbocharge your ability to influence; that is, the power to control a conversation.

That's a big claim, isn't it? I mean, how can you control a conversation?

Salespeople and politicians are well versed in this skill. It involves mastering the art of linguistics. An *Engaging Executive* must be an artist when it comes to language. As with other chapters in this book, I am not going to go into great depths about linguistics, but I am going to share with you something that I believe is at the heart of the success of every good public speaker, salesperson, politician and leader of people.

Many years ago I took one of the greatest holidays of my life. I went to Kenya, in Africa. The trip included a hot air balloon ride over the Maasai Mara. It was wonderful floating over the tops of trees, and hovering over lions, elephants and hippos going about their daily business.

I learned something about hot air ballooning that day, too. I always thought that once a balloon took off it was up to Mother Nature where it ended up, as you can't control the direction of the wind. However, this isn't quite true. Through talking to the hot air balloon pilot I discovered that he could actually change direction. He did this by changing the altitude of the balloon. At different altitudes the air currents go in different directions and travel at different speeds, so to change the direction of the balloon he only needed to change the altitude until it started to go the direction he wanted.

This is also what I have realised about language. There are levels to language, and the higher you go the thinner it gets – just like air. The lower you go the more detailed it is. In NLP it is referred to as chunking, and in this chapter I will explain how you can use this to control a conversation like the pilot controlled the hot air balloon.

THE CONCEPT OF CHUNKING

When I first learned the concept of chunking it blew me away.

So what *is* chunking? It is how we group information together, or how we 'chunk' it up or down. If we chunk information *up* then it becomes more information grouped together and this makes it more abstract or thematic. If we chunk information *down* then it makes it more granular and therefore specific. I will first explain the concept of chunking and then we will look at how to use it to control a conversation.

I will use a simple yet powerful example, as a way to explain the concept. So we will start with the word, 'car'.

Chunking down

If we were to chunk down from the word 'car' I could ask you to think of different brands; for example, BMW, Ford and Toyota. If I wanted to chunk down further I would go down a level and start thinking about the models made by each brand. Let's do this with BMW. There are a lot of BMW models these days, but let's pick the 3, 5 and 7 series. Now if you chunk down again we could take the 3 series and list the 318,

328 and M3. From here we could chunk down into colours, optional extras, different interiors and the like.

Now imagine if we had done the same for Ford and Toyota as well. And then what about all the models of all the brands available in Australia? How many variations would we have ended up with under the larger chunk of 'car'? The answer is, *a lot*.

This is important to remember. If you want to find more points of difference then chunk down. Therefore, if you want to be able to find disagreement with what someone is saying then chunk down and you will find more granular points of difference.

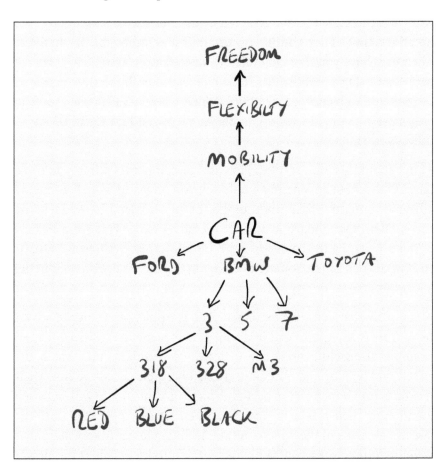

Chunking up

Now let's go the other way and chunk up.

If we start with the object of the car again but this time ask the question, 'What does a car give you?', we might land on something like 'mobility'. If I was to ask you, 'What is the purpose of mobility?', you might say, 'flexibility'. Finally, if I was to ask you, 'What does flexibility give you?', you might say, 'freedom'.

Did you notice that every time I 'chunked up', the meaning became more and more abstract? That is the purpose of chunking up: it takes you to a higher level of abstraction and it is more difficult to disagree with, and therefore is easier to agree with. This is what skillful linguists do all the time. They chunk you up until it is impossible to disagree. Then they have you. For example, if I was asking you to make a choice between having a 'red BMW 318', which was our chunk down ending, or our chunk up ending, 'freedom', which would you choose? You can only have one or the other. Of course, you would go for freedom … unless you *really* like BMWs.

Think about this for a second. How do car companies sell to you these days? Old-school advertising would sell you on features such as engine efficiency, interior space, the number of cup holders. Nowadays, the car is often a secondary feature of the advertising: you see a beautiful family getting in the car and driving off into a picturesque sunset, smiling at each other. You are not buying the car at all. You are buying a lifestyle.

A company that does this extremely well is Apple. My favourite advert of all time is by Apple, and it is called 'Our Signature' (2013). It is an example of absolute brilliance in terms of chunking up. Watch the advert on YouTube and note how effectively Apple show you how their products touch on every aspect and stage of your life … without even mentioning their products. You don't even see an Apple logo until the last five seconds of the advert. Yet the feeling you get from watching it is enough to compel you to buy an Apple product. This is the power of chunking.

Now we can start to look at the process of how to apply it. I am going to talk about this as if you are using the process to chunk someone else up or down. Of course, you can also apply the process to yourself if you wish. So let's start with chunking down.

BASIC CHUNKING DOWN

The purpose of chunking down is to get more granular and uncover details. Some people are naturally chunked up and talk in abstract concepts all the time. Some more skilled linguists may chunk you up on purpose – you can chunk them down, providing you are cognisant of what is happening.

There is basic chunking down and advanced chunking down. Let's look at basic chunking down first. We will cover the rest in the following chapters.

I usually find that due to the nature of the professions my clients work in, they are normally quite good at basic chunking down. They like to get more granular as this plays to their technical knowledge. Perhaps you can relate to this?

Here are some basic chunking down questions:

o 'What is an example of this?'

o 'What specifically?'

o 'What would this look like?'

o 'What is part of this?'

o 'What is the root cause of this?'

o 'What sits underneath this?'

o 'What else?'

Any of these questions will take you down a level of detail and uncover more information. Remember, the goal of chunking someone down is to leave no stone unturned and to find out as much as you can.

Chunking down is also a great tool if you want to disagree with someone. The deeper you dive into the details the more points of difference you can find. If you were looking for a car and I offered to sell you a red BMW 318, the chances of you wanting something that specific are very slim. You could tell me you didn't like the colour red, or the BMW brand, or that the 318 wasn't fast enough. So, if you really want to disagree with someone, chunk him down as much as you can and then find a specific aspect you disagree with.

Okay, so let's give that a practice with some exercises.

PRACTICAL EXERCISES

EXERCISE ONE: CHUNKING UP AND DOWN

○ Take a topic of your choice and write the heading in the middle of a piece of paper. In the same way as the car example on pages 178–179, chunk the topic down as many levels as you can. Then chunk up to see how many levels you can fit in before hitting the most intangible and abstract meaning.

EXERCISE TWO: CONVERSATIONAL CHUNKING DOWN

○ Next time you are having a conversation with someone you know, see how far you can chunk her down by using the chunking down questions. See if you can do this conversationally so that it doesn't feel mechanical. Notice how you can control the conversation in this way.

Chapter 20

ADVANCED CONTROLLING CONVERSATIONS

Our ability to communicate is based on a lot of missing information. This is why using advanced chunking down questions is so important.

In the last chapter we covered the basic stuff when it comes to chunking down. Now let's move on to advanced chunking down. Again, this is derived from NLP and what is called the Meta Model. This is a language pattern that is all about restoring lost information through asking very precise questions.

As a Certified NLP Trainer I have found that teaching this topic can be a bit overwhelming for students due to the complicated labels used to describe the model. So, in this book I am going to give you the simplified and de-jargonised version, which is much more user friendly.

To begin, we'll take a look at the three categories of miscommunication the advanced chunking down questions are looking to uncover. These are Distortions, Generalisations and Deletions. Essentially, all human beings are limited information processors. It is impossible for us to take in all the information presented to us every second and process it all. Therefore, outside of our conscious awareness we are furiously editing. We all do it. In 1974, Tversky & Kahneman published a research paper about the role of heuristics. 'Heu–what–now?', I hear you say.

Heuristics are mental shortcuts, rules of thumb or educated guesses that enable us to speed up decision-making. These guys won a Nobel Prize for this research due to their insights into real-world decision making. I would argue that heuristics is what happens when we delete, distort and generalise. Not only do we delete, distort and generalise when information comes towards us, we also do it when we communicate. As a consequence, it is no surprise there are so many arguments and misunderstandings – our ability to communicate is based on a lot of missing information. This is why using advanced chunking down questions is so important.

Let's take each of the categories and see how to unpack them.

DISTORTIONS AND DISTORTION DESTROYERS

Distortions are where a person distorts the meaning of something to make it mean what it was never meant to mean. Often, this is done completely unintentionally by the listener. In my home country of England, we call this 'getting the wrong end of the stick'. There are four types of Distortion statements:

o Mind Read

o Says Who

o Cause and Effect

o This Means That.

Mind Read statements

This could be claiming to know what is going on in somebody else's head. For example, has anyone ever said to you, 'I know why you are doing that', and then when you have tested him out you realised he was way off the mark? This is a perfect example of a Distortion, as this person has constructed a story in his head that may have little resemblance to the truth.

A great question to ask in such circumstances would be, 'How do you know why I am doing that?' This question unpacks the process of how he arrived at his conclusion, and gives you a chance to correct the

Distortion. This type of question I call a Distortion Destroyer. I will refer to these throughout the chapter as the antidote the various types of statements.

Says Who statements

Another type of Distortion is when someone makes a judgement but with no reference to the source. For example, 'Oh, it's not good form to leave work before 6 pm'. A great Distortion Destroyer response to this would be, 'How do you know it's not good form?' The key point is that you can challenge the assumption inherent in the other person's statement.

Cause and Effect statements

A favourite Distortion of mine is when someone assumes that one thing causes another to happen. I see this a lot with people who like to blame others for how they feel. For example, 'My boss drives me insane'. It could be tempting to agree with the person. However, a more useful Distortion Destroyer question would be, 'What causes you to choose to feel insane?' This one is a bit of an eye opener. You will see the person do a double take when you ask this. What it does is put the cause of the reaction back where it belongs; with the individual, and not an external source. The intention of this type of Distortion Destroyer is to challenge the causal relationship. You will find many types of examples of Cause and Effect statements if you listen to people closely.

This Means That statements

The above type of Distortion is similar to another type I hear a lot, which is when someone puts two things together that have happened simultaneously and assumes they are connected. For example, 'My boss never smiles at me *because* he doesn't like me'. The word to look out for here is 'because'. A great Distortion Destroyer question to disarm this is, 'Have you ever not smiled at someone that you like?' You only need one example and you have immediately destroyed the logic. Again, these types of Distortion are everywhere so keep your ears open for them.

* * * * *

So, in summary, Distortions are when someone has misconstrued the meaning of something, and the Distortion Destroyer questions we have just covered are designed to help re-evaluate the meaning.

GENERALISATIONS AND GENERALISATION DESTROYERS

The world is full of Generalisations. In fact, Generalisations occur every time we open our mouths.

Yes, both of those were Generalisations – I wanted to make it obvious because most people are not aware of how prevalent the use of Generalisations is and the impact they have. As previously touched upon, the human brain is a limited information processor. It would be impossible for even the most intelligent person on the planet not to generalise. Why? Because Generalisations are a mechanism we use for learning and communicating. The entire formalised education system, as well as the experiential process of learning, works on the basis of taking one experience and generalising from it. And when we have two or more similar experiences we are even more prone to generalising a meaning.

This, in many ways, is the benefit of generalisation – it enables us to chunk large amounts of information together and put a label on it. Unfortunately, it can also be the cause of much miscommunication.

A skilled linguist will be able to identify Generalisations and drill deeper into them. There are two main types of Generalisation statements:

o Universal

o Necessity and Possibility.

Universal statements

An easy way to listen out for Generalisations is when you hear words such as 'never', 'no-one', 'always', 'every', 'everyone' and 'nobody'. For example, you may hear someone say, 'That staff member *never* listens to me'. If you don't feel this is a useful mindset, you could ask them, '*Never?* Not even once?' As with the Distortion Destroyer questions that unpack Distortions, if you can find even just one counter example this will normally blow open the Generalisation and people will see it for what it is. These I call Generalisation Destroyers.

If someone says to me, 'You never listen to me' and I feel I have good rapport with this person, I often respond, with a cheeky look in my eye, 'I never listen to you? Not even once? So, how do I know your name?' Of course, I use this sparingly and to make a humorous point.

So what about when people – intentionally or unintentionally – use generalisations on you? For example, someone might be trying to sell you something by saying, 'Of course, it will be *necessary* for you to sign a 12-month contract because *everybody* does it this way. We *always* find this is the most effective approach for our clients.' You could target any of the Generalisations within this statement; for example, 'What would happen if I didn't sign a 12-month contract?', or, 'Has there ever been anyone who didn't do that but still got great results?'

Necessity and Possibility statements

Words such as 'should', 'shouldn't', 'must', 'mustn't' and 'necessary' indicate supposed necessity. 'I *should* get this document finished before I leave tonight' can be countered with a Generalisation Destroyer. A question I use frequently when I hear people talk about 'shoulds' and 'shouldn'ts' is, 'What is the worst thing that could happen if you didn't?' I often find that once people stop and truly ponder the question they suddenly have a realisation that the world is not going to end if they don't get their document finished that night.

In regards to possibility, words to listen out for include 'can', 'can't', 'will', 'won't', 'may', 'may not', 'possible' or 'impossible'. 'I can't tell my client that she is taking the wrong approach' could be countered with a Generalisation Destroyer such as, 'What would happen if you did?'

＊ ＊ ＊ ＊ ＊

In summary, Generalisations can be damaging as they hide a lot of sweeping assumptions that may well be unfounded. As you can see, Generalisations are everywhere, so we need to be on our guard. If you are not on your guard they will be able to use this against you. If you are switched on right now you will be asking the question, 'Who are "they"?' Well, this is what we are going to talk about next.

DELETIONS AND DELETION DESTROYERS

Deletions are another consequence of us being limited information processors. Deletion occurs when we selectively pay attention to certain aspects of our experience and not others. We then overlook or omit other aspects of our experiences. Without Deletion, we would be faced with much too much information to handle with our conscious mind. So in a way, Deletion is necessary for our sanity. Unfortunately, it can also lead to miscommunication and assumption, as upon hearing a sentence containing a Deletion our minds will plug the gap with our own content.

As a skilled linguist you need to be on the lookout for Deletions, and use Deletion Destroyer questions to chunk people down to recover the lost information. In many ways, a Deletion is less visible as it is normally contained within a word you may well accept at face value.

Deletion statements often contain:

o   verbs that require clarification

o   Monster Nouns

o   Meaningless Comparison statements

o   Missing Persons statements.

Verbs that require clarification

Some examples of verbs that require clarification are 'success', 'failure', 'perform', 'develop' and 'produce'. So if someone was to say, 'How can you guarantee us a successful outcome?', your Deletion Destroyer response could be, 'What would success look like to you?' Or if someone said, 'This project has been a failure', you could respond, 'How specifically has it been a failure?' You may well find that it was only one aspect that was deemed a failure, and in fact there were many successful aspects that have been deleted.

Monster Nouns

When it comes to Monster Nouns, this is where a fluid and ongoing process has been turned into a noun. As a consequence, something which is inherently complex is drastically simplified by turning it into a single word. Thus, misunderstandings as to the precise meaning are common. Some examples of Monster Nouns are 'training', 'profit', 'communication', 'manage' and 'leadership'. I had an interesting learning with a boss who used to manage me years ago. I had a team of consultants reporting to me at the time. My boss said he wanted me to take a more active role in *managing* the team. That was about as specific as his instructions got. So I took it upon myself to book in one-to-one catch ups, coaching sessions and training events.

After several months my boss took me aside and asked me why I hadn't been managing the team more as he had requested. He was a very process-orientated person and I, being a Psychologist by training, was a very people-focused person. It turned out that what he saw as *managing* was actually to keep closer checks on their timesheets. Neither of us was categorically right or wrong, we just had very different interpretations of the word 'manage'. I had always associated great managers with those who took an interest in me and who helped nurture and develop me as a person. Ultimately though, it was my responsibility to chunk down my boss and understand specifically what he wanted from me. This is the problem caused by using Monster Nouns, so be mindful to unpack them whenever you hear them.

Meaningless Comparison statements

Also be on the lookout for Deletion statements that contain labels that are only relevant as comparisons; these contain words such as 'good', 'bad', 'effective', 'ineffective', 'expensive', 'better', 'worse', 'happy' and 'sad'. What is missing here is the source of the comparison. For example, I was selling a training programme to a client once, and she said, 'It's very expensive'. My response was, 'Compared to what?' She said, 'To other training programmes', to which I answered, 'Do you know how they stack up to my programme in terms of the content, delivery and results?' She wasn't able to answer this question, and so price quickly became a non-issue.

Missing Persons statements

Finally, we have Deletion statements where the person who made the statement is not mentioned. Don't you just love those statements that start, 'You know what *they* say … ?' My first response is always, 'Who are "they"?' I very rarely receive a coherent answer, which then takes any power away from the statement. Another I frequently hear is 'the business'; for example, 'Let's feed that back to the business', or, 'What I am hearing from the business is … ' This is a massive deletion, because unless the 'business' is made up of a collective consciousness reminiscent of the 'Borg', what we are actually talking about is an individual stakeholder, or at best, a stakeholder group. So remember to ask questions that unpack who the mysterious 'they' group are.

✳ ✳ ✳ ✳ ✳

In summary, Deletions are dangerous because they mask a lot of missing information. If in doubt, chunk down to uncover the detail.

Remember, we can chunk down by asking basic probing questions, which will give us more detail. We also have advanced chunking down which is divided into three main categories: Distortion Destroyers, Generalisation Destroyers and Deletion Destroyers. Use these to reveal the hidden or misconstrued information in your daily communication and the world will suddenly look different. Let's practise with some exercises.

PRACTICAL EXERCISES

EXERCISE ONE: DISTORTION DESTROYERS

○ Next time you hear someone using a Distortion –
  for example, 'My boss drives me insane' – ask him a
  Distortion Destroyer question such as, 'What causes
  you to choose to feel insane?' See if it makes the
  person rethink the situation.

EXERCISE TWO: GENERALISATION DESTROYERS

○ Next time you hear someone using a generalisation –
  for example, 'My staff never listen to me' – ask her
  a Generalisation Destroyer question such as, 'Never?
  Not even once?' See if it makes the person rethink
  the situation.

EXERCISE THREE: DELETION DESTROYERS

○ Next time you hear someone using a deletion –
  for example, 'This project was a failure' – ask him a
  Deletion Destroyer question such as, 'How specifically
  has it been a failure?' See if it makes the person
  rethink the situation.

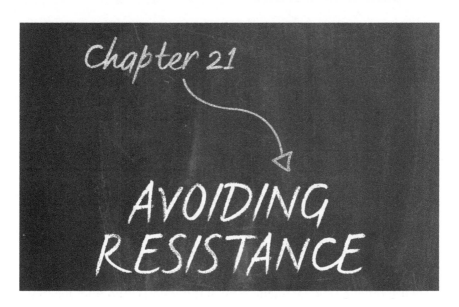

Chapter 21

AVOIDING RESISTANCE

Avoiding resistance is definitely a trait of an Engaging Executive. It is also a powerful way of finding out what is really important to people.

Now that we have fully explored chunking down, we can start to look at how to chunk up. This is one of my favourite topics when it comes to linguistics. Once you have read this you will see the hidden structure of language used by politicians in just about every campaign. Avoiding resistance is definitely a trait of an *Engaging Executive*. It is also a powerful way of finding out what is really important to people.

CHUNKING UP

Chunking up is the art of abstraction. As we have already discovered, when the human brain doesn't have enough information, it fills in the blanks. Even more important, it fills in the blanks in ways that fit with what we already believe.

An *Engaging Executive* can use chunking up to sell concepts to others and remove resistance. Let's take a well-known example from the election campaign that brought Barack Obama into office. In 2007 Obama was travelling the country giving speech after speech. He was so successful as a speaker that some people suggested he was using covert hypnosis during his speeches to win over the masses.

Whether or not he really did is not the issue. What matters for us is that he used some beautifully crafted language that was chunking up at its best. One famous line from his campaign speech goes like this: 'America is in trouble … we need change … and … that is why I will be your next President'. Let's stop a second and ponder why this is such a beautifully constructed sentence and how it works.

If you are not American just imagine your own country in this sentence. Now reflect on the statement: 'America is in trouble'. If you were listening to this statement, do you think you could find one thing about your country that troubled you? Who can't, right? I bet if you had a room full of people each would have their own unique answer, yet each person would be nodding along. Now consider the next part, 'we need change'. Thinking about your own country – do you think you could find one thing you would like to change? I bet you could. Do you think if you were in a room full of people they would all be thinking the exact same thought as you? Nope. I bet they would all be nodding though. And here is the clincher. As you have agreed to the first two elements, you are now primed to accept the suggestion that he should be your next President. It is almost as if he has earned the right due to the first two ambiguous statements.

This is the power of chunking up, and this is why *Engaging Executives* need to be skilled linguists.

Did you see what I did there?

Thank You for Smoking

As some homework, I want you to watch the film *Thank You for Smoking* (2005). It is an amazing demonstration of the power of language. The film is a light-hearted fiction about a man named Nick, who represents a tobacco company as a lobbyist. The film is full of mindboggling examples of how he defends tobacco even in the face of solid anti-smoking evidence. There is a notable scene where he teaches his son how to win an argument. He does this by getting his son to argue for his favourite flavour of ice-cream, chocolate. Nick picks vanilla. I'm not going to ruin it for you by detailing the conversation, but it will blow your mind. If you don't watch the whole movie, at least look up this scene on YouTube – search for 'Thank you for smoking ice-cream argument'. You will see in that one-minute clip everything I have explained to you regarding chunking up. You will see how Nick chunks his son up to abstraction and wins the argument about which ice-cream is the best. (Okay, here's a spoiler … the best flavour is 'Liberty'. You'll just have to watch the scene …)

Chunking someone up by asking questions

You can chunk up using abstract statements or you can chunk someone else up by asking questions. We will be spending more time on how you can chunk up using statements later. For now, we will examine how to chunk someone up by asking questions.

The goal of asking chunking up questions is always to find out the higher meaning of what someone has said to you. Often when I speak to people I am aware that the request they present to me is not actually what they want, it is more a single representation of what they want. By using chunking up questions you can help to identify what is really important to someone. Here are some useful chunking up questions:

o 'What is important about this?'

o 'What is the purpose?'

o 'What does this give you?'

o 'What is the goal of doing this?'

o 'What are you trying to achieve?'

o 'What outcome are you looking for?'

Any of these questions should take you up a level of abstraction.

As a consultant I found these types of question very handy. As a less experienced consultant I would ask clients what they wanted me to do, and I would take their answers at face value. Sometimes clients would tell me later that they did not get the result they wanted, even though I gave them exactly what they had asked for. This is when I started to use chunking up questions to find out the problem behind the problem. If a client asked for a specific solution, I would ask, 'What are you trying to achieve?', or, 'What is the purpose of doing this?' Most of the time I would discover that by asking the chunking up questions I would uncover the *real* desired outcome, and that the solution the client had initially asked for was not actually the best tool for the job.

Let's put this into practice with some exercises.

PRACTICAL EXERCISE

EXERCISE ONE: BASIC CHUNKING UP

○ Start with your own job title and chunk yourself up. Use the chunking questions on page 197. See how many levels you can chunk up before you reach the highest level of abstraction.

○ Once you are comfortable with chunking conceptually, see if you can successfully chunk someone up conversationally to find out what is driving her need.

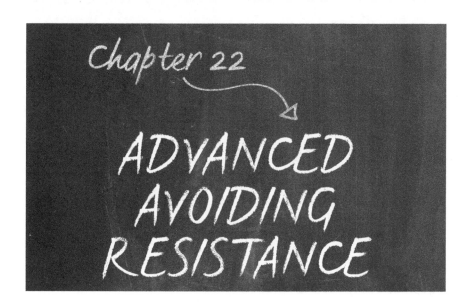

Chapter 22

ADVANCED AVOIDING RESISTANCE

When we are intentionally chunking people up we can use ambiguity to our advantage.

This chapter is the mirror image opposite of the 'Advanced controlling conversations' chapter. Whereas in that chapter we were looking to uncover Distortions, Generalisations and Deletions, now we are looking to create them. This is advanced chunking up. 'Why are we looking to create them?' you may be asking. Because the person who controls the chunk size controls the conversation. And an *Engaging Executive* knows when to use ambiguous language – like Barack Obama did – to create agreement.

The language patterns we are going to consider now were derived from modelling the language patterns of the most famous hypnotherapist of all time, Milton Erickson. Again, these language patterns are taken from NLP and are awash with jargon, so I will attempt to simplify it into a more user-friendly format. The Milton Model is a rich and beautifully crafted set of language patterns. I will only talk about the patterns that I have personally found most useful. As these language patterns are the reverse of advanced chunking down, some of the same labels have been used. Just think about this as being the reverse side of the same coin. In advanced chunking down we used questions to uncover the ambiguity. In advanced chunking up we use statements loaded with ambiguity.

DISTORTION STATEMENTS

So we know that Distortions are when meaning has been twisted by the receiver, either intentionally or unintentionally. When we are intentionally chunking people up we can use this ambiguity to our advantage.

Cause and Effect statements

Let's imagine that you needed to convince someone to do something. One way we can do this is to put together two things in a way that makes them seem linked by causality. This is called using Cause and Effect statements. The person chunking up makes a statement that implies one thing causes another. The statement may be technically untrue, or there may be no direct link between the one thing and the other. However, structuring the sentence in this way makes it sound highly plausible. For example, 'People become rich *because* they worked hard at school', or, 'Getting a promotion *makes* you happier'. The active ingredient here is the italicised word in each sentence. The highly regarded Psychologist Dr Robert Cialdini in his book *Influence: science and practice* (2008) quoted numerous experiments testing strategies of influence. He discovered that merely using the word 'because' after asking a favour from a stranger increased the chances of acceptance to 94%. It didn't even matter if the reason that came after the word 'because' was trivial. The trick to using any of the chunking up language is for it to sound plausible but not specific. In this way, the conscious mind just accepts it and you are 'putting one past the goal keeper'. The great thing is, because you are reading this one chapter alone you will improve your ability to influence. Sorry ... I couldn't resist that cheeky Cause and Effect statement.

This means That statements

Another kind of chunking up distortion I love to use is to equate two things together. In other words, you are suggesting that one thing means another thing. This type of distortion is not saying one thing causes another, like above, but suggests that if one thing is true the other will also be. For example, 'If you are feeling a little bit confused *it means* you are starting to learn something new.' Another example is, 'The fact you want to become better with people *means* you will.' How about, 'America is in trouble. We need change. That is why I'm going to be your next President.'

These types of statements can be very powerful, and when used fluently can be very influential. The trick is to start with something that appears true to the listener and then suggest it 'means' something that you want it to mean. This will often be taken at face value.

Assumption statements

Really skilled linguists know how to use Assumption statements well. This is where you construct a sentence that has several inbuilt assumptions. Normally the assumptions are placed in the sentence in such a way that they are accepted, as the focus has been placed elsewhere. For example, '*As you are starting to understand* the concept of Distortions, the next topic will be easier'. The statement presupposes that you are starting to understand Distortions and focuses your mind on the next topic. As you are now thinking about the next topic, you have assumed you will ultimately learn how to use Distortions.

Several years ago I was looking to rent a new apartment. I had been searching high and low, and I was starting to think that I was never going to find something I actually liked. Then I found the perfect place. Unfortunately it was an open house viewing and there was another couple that was also interested. I was absolutely certain that I wanted that apartment, as it was head and shoulders above anything else I had seen. The problem was, so did the guy from the other couple. There was only one thing for it. I had to use all of my learned powers of influence to seal the deal.

I'm a great tenant. I always pay my rent on time and take good care of the place where I am living. However, I knew that explaining this to the agent in front of the other guy wouldn't really give me any leverage as he would just say the same thing. So I embarked on my plan. First,

I built rapport with the agent by talking about common interests. I used Matching and the Rapport Triangle, as discussed in the *Network* section of this book. However, the guy I was competing with cottoned on to my strategy and started to befriend the agent as well. I continued with the rapport building until the end of the showing, and then the agent asked if either of us were interested. We both said yes at the same time.

We followed him down to his car and he gave us the application forms. I could see at this point that my rival's girlfriend was starting to become impatient about getting to the next viewing. He gave me a stern look as he could see that I wasn't in a hurry. As he turned his back and walked towards his girlfriend, I made my move. I turned to the agent and unleashed my carefully crafted assumption statement. I said, 'I really like this apartment. How can *we* make sure *I get it*?' He paused for a second, and then said, 'Simple, just fill out the form and have it to me by tomorrow'. So I said, 'And if I do that, I will have the apartment?' To which he replied, 'Absolutely'.

I did end up getting the apartment, and I put it all down to the assumption statement. There were two assumptions built into the statement. The first was 'we' were working as a team. The second was that I was going to 'get it'.

GENERALISATION STATEMENTS

As you will recall, Generalisations are when we take something specific and extrapolate it to many things. There are many types of Generalisations that can be used to chunk someone up.

Necessity and Possibility statements

In a reverse way to advanced chunking down, we can use Necessity and Possibility statements to do this. This time you use them to make suggestions hold more weight. For example, 'You *must* be aware that this is the best way forward'. This statement leans on the word 'must' and has the effect of making the listener feel he should be aware of something. You *must* be aware that by reading this book your ability to influence others *should* only get better. Another example is, 'You *should* practise using chunking language every day'. This type of statement has the effect of making the listener feel she needs to do something. Of course, you *should* have worked that out by now for yourself. Both of these examples are Necessity statements as they make the recipient feel it's a necessity to do something.

A Possibility statement would be similar but phrased around how possible something is, such as, 'You *can* become more engaging and influential with practice'. These statements are very helpful when you want to enable someone to do something. For example, you may want to motivate a member of your team to do something that she has never done before. You could do this by saying something like, 'You *can* trust yourself as you *will* do the best you can'. Both the italicised words have the effect of giving permission to the person and making the task seem more possible.

Universal statements

The next category of Generalisations always has the impact of convincing everyone, and it never fails. These are called Universal statements, and I just used three in the previous sentence, including 'always', 'everyone' and 'never'. These statements have huge power as they have the impact of generalising massively. For example, if you were to say, '*Everyone* knows the importance of developing good relationships', it makes you feel part of the crowd and collective wisdom. The tendency is to then agree with the statement. That is because *everyone* has a tendency to be swayed by the majority. Dr Robert Cialdini in his book *Influence: science and practice* (2008) talks about the power of social proof. This is the linguistic equivalent, and in business we hear these types of generalisations *all the time*.

So by now you probably get the picture about how to use universal statements and their power in *every* conversation and with *anyone* you speak with.

DELETION STATEMENTS

When using Deletions to chunk up we are taking advantage of the ambiguity inherent in a statement to make arguments that are hard to come back against. This is the skill of being 'artfully vague'.

Abstraction statements

The first of these I call Abstraction statements. These types of statements are rife in the corporate world, and they are typified by any statement that utilises Monster Nouns, as covered earlier. For example, 'Let's do *business*'.

What does that even mean? Business is a complex process with almost countless parts yet we talk about it as a simple noun. A skilled linguist will take advantage of this and use the ambiguity to gain agreement by forming arguments laden with Abstraction statements.

How do you know an Abstraction statement when you hear one? When I was learning NLP there was a beautiful phrase that I remember to this day: 'If you cannot put it in a wheel barrow' then it is an abstraction statement; in other words, if you cannot touch it or feel it. This is because it is, in fact, a complex process given a simple label. For example, 'You are gaining new *insights* as you read this book' is probably hard to disagree with, yet everyone reading this book may gain different insights. The vagueness of the word 'insights' makes this difficult to disagree with. How about, 'Reading this book will help you improve your *communication* skills'. It is hard to know what this actually means, yet this entire book is about communication and so the statement's ambiguity is hard to disprove.

This is the power of using abstraction statements. Knowing when to use them to resist push back is a core *skill*. I know … I did it again.

Comparison statements

Another form of Deletion for chunking up is Comparison statements. This is when you make comparisons but purposely omit what you are actually comparing to. Examples of the words to form such comparisons are 'better', 'best', 'harder', 'faster', 'stronger', 'improved', 'more', 'less', 'very', 'bigger', 'smaller', 'brighter', 'louder', 'healthier', 'superior', 'smarter' and 'enhanced'.

An example of this in a sentence is, 'Once you have mastered chunking up you are going to enjoy it *more*.' More than what? Or, 'You are a *better* manager than you were *before*.' Better than what? When before? As you can see, sooner or later you will be clearer on what chunking up statements mean and be able to write better ones than those shown here.

So how many comparison words did you find in that last sentence?

Comparison statements are effective because they have the impact of making the listener accept the judgement when it is not actually based on anything tangible or evidence based. It is even more powerful if you put a number in the mix. For example, 'If you work with us you will achieve *better results by 20%'*. Based on what? Better than what? What is meant by 'results'?

Now that I have explained these types of statements, pay attention next time you watch an advert or read any marketing literature.

Missing Persons statements

The final type of chunking up deletion I will share with you I call Missing Persons statements. People love Missing Persons statements because they are wonderful for giving blanket descriptions, which is what they want.

In that last statement the words 'people' and 'they' are the missing persons. Who are these 'people'? Have you noticed how many times 'they' get involved? Other examples of such Missing Persons statements are 'employers', 'men', 'women', 'bosses', 'staff' – the list goes on.

In the advanced chunking down statements we looked at how to drill down into these types of statements. When using these same statements to influence it lends weight to an argument by making it appear that there is a generalised view held by many people. By using statements such as, 'You know what *they* say … ?', or, 'Many *people* tend to agree … ' you are creating an imaginary collective of people who are all of the same mind. *People* are influenced by the majority position. Dr Robert Cialdini (2008) talks about the power of being influenced by the modal group behaviour. So *Missing Persons statements* can be a powerful way of influencing our *bosses*, *staff* and *clients*.

USING ADVANCED CHUNKING IN THE REAL WORLD

This may all sound a little abstract, so let me give you an example of how I used advanced chunking up to manage a real-life disagreement. Once upon a time I was rolling out a mentoring program for a large public service organisation. I was asked to come in for a couple of hours and talk to the mentors about the skills of a mentor and to set them on the right path.

The room was filled with very senior managers, some of whom had volunteered and some of whom had been 'volunteered'. As a consequence, I had to win the crowd over as I had a lot of folded arms and frowns facing me. I started by giving an overview of the High Potential (HiPo) Program the organisation was running. I gave an overview of the selection process. It was clear that some of them were looking to vent, so we were sucked down a wormhole of discussing the merits of the selection process and whether the right people were on the program.

Considering the mentoring stage was the last component of the HiPo program that was well underway, it seemed futile to spend too much precious time on the debate, but the conversation started to go around in circles. This was a classic situation of 'shutting the barn door after the horse has bolted'. So I thought about how I could quash the debate, and I decided to reframe the conversation by using chunking up language. I said, 'I am sure if we each had it our *own way* we would have picked *different* people to be in the *HiPo* pool. I'm *sure* we all know of *someone* who deserved a place on the *program* that didn't get in.' At this point many people in the room started to nod. So I continued, 'In fact, I *can't* think of one *organisation* I have *worked* with that was *universally happy* with the choices of *people* in their *top talent* program'. At this point people started to loosen up and nod in agreement. 'So *that is why* we need to focus on why we are here today. On how can we *help* those *people* who *are* on the program. On how *we can help* these people to make the most of their *careers*. On how you *can best use* your vast experience for the *greater good* of the *organisation*.'

At that point the noise stopped, and everyone got on board.

This is power of chunking up and using abstract language. If you keep your language vague enough it is virtually impossible to disagree with what you are saying, and it takes the wind out of people's sails.

* * * * *

This has been another big chapter. Remember, practice makes perfect, so let's now turn to some exercises that will allow you to hone your skills.

PRACTICAL EXERCISES

EXERCISE ONE: ADVANCED CHUNKING UP

See how many statements you can write down in the
context of your working environment in relation to each
of the following:

- Cause and Effect statements
- This Means That statements
- Assumption statements
- Necessity and Possibility statements
- Universal statements
- Abstraction statements
- Comparison statements
- Missing Persons statements.

EXERCISE TWO: TRIALLING YOUR STATEMENTS

- Using your statements prepared above, see if you can
  start to drop them into conversations. Observe to see
  if you get a reaction to them or whether they are
  accepted at face value.

- If you find yourself in a disagreement, try using
  advanced chunking up statements to reach an
  agreement.

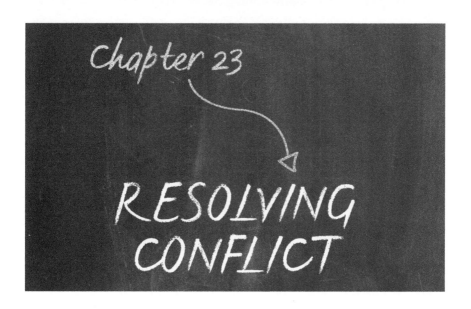

Chapter 23

RESOLVING CONFLICT

What is the problem behind the problem that needs to be solved?

Once you have a good grip on chunking up and down, you will be able to recognise the levels as you listen to a conversation. As we have previously discussed, chunking down gets you into the detail and chunking up gets you into the abstract. An *Engaging Executive* is able to identify when to chunk up and when to chunk down. When you can do this you will be able to guide conversations effortlessly.

There is a great NLP model that uses both chunking up and down to resolve conflict. There are times in your career when you will be at loggerheads with someone. Sometimes it will be imperative that you achieve what you want at the other person's cost. However, if this is your predominant style you may find that you end up burning all your bridges. The Conflict Resolution Model has been designed to help facilitate win–win outcomes.

THE CONFLICT RESOLUTION MODEL

Let me be clear: this model is not a negotiation model for winning. It is a model to help both people move to an amicable solution. For it to work, both parties need to be able to move from their starting point.

In mediation, skilled mediators know that chunking up will always lead to gaining agreement. The more abstract you get the harder it is to disagree. The model works by leveraging the principle that once you chunk up high enough you will ultimately find that people want the same things. Once you get to this higher level need, you can seek agreement on how best to achieve it in a mutually beneficial way.

The model also works on the assumption that, in the vast majority of cases, people do *not* want what they originally ask for. Most of the time people really want what this thing gives them. For example, a young man asks his parents for a motorbike for his 18th birthday. He may say he wants a nice shiny new motorbike but what he *really* wants is what it gives him. This could be a sense of freedom to travel anywhere. It could be a sense of identity as one of the 'cool kids'. Or it could be the longing for something that marks him out as an adult and not a child anymore. I talk about this example with some level of authority as this was me at 18.

Now, hypothetically, there could have been other alternatives to a motorbike that would have achieved the same things. If my parents had been so opposed to a motorbike that they bought me a sports car instead then I am pretty sure I would have been just as happy. A sports car would have given me freedom, made me feel cool and marked me out as an adult. So remember, the secret of this model is to find out what a person *really* wants. In other words, what is the problem behind the problem that needs to be solved?

The model can be broken down into five simple steps. Let's have a look:

Step 1: Identify what each person wants

Step 2: Diplomatically state your opposing agendas

Step 3: Explore what each person ultimately wants

Step 4: Celebrate any mutual goals or agendas

Step 5: Find a mutually beneficial way of achieving the goal

1. Identify what each person wants

Before you can come to a mutually beneficial agreement you need to clearly understand what the other person wants. You will need to explore this, but only so far as gaining clarity. Ensure you do not get bamboozled by an Abstraction statement; in other words, something so nebulous you do not understand what it really is. If you think this is happening, you might ask, 'Tell me more about this'. However, you should not attempt to drill into this too specifically as this will have the effect of entrenching the person in his position. The last thing you should do at this stage is to ask a 'why' question.

2. Diplomatically state your opposing agendas

Once you have a clear understanding of what the other person wants, you will need to diplomatically state your own agenda, goal or desired outcome. The last thing you should do at this stage is to use the phrase, 'I disagree', or, 'No … ' In fact, the secret is to use the exact opposite.

Agreement Frames

There are three magical phrases that can smooth away the initial disagreement and set you up for a productive conversation. In NLP these are called Agreement Frames. At first they may seem counterintuitive, however they are actually very clever and extremely effective.

The first is, 'I agree'. You are probably saying to yourself, 'What? I don't *want* to agree'. But the trick is to agree to something, anything, even just a tiny part of what has just been said. Hearing someone say 'I agree' has a soothing effect. Hearing someone say 'I disagree' has a bristling effect. Even if you can't agree on even some small aspect, you can 'agree that this is an important issue and we need to sort it out'.

The second phrase is 'I respect … '. You can respect many things about an opposing position without taking it on. 'I respect the fact you have brought this to me', and, 'I respect the points you have made' are just two examples.

The third magic phrase is 'I appreciate … '. Again, you can appreciate a lot of things. You can 'appreciate that this is a difficult situation', or, 'appreciate your argument has some merit'.

The big 'I' statement to avoid at this moment is 'I understand'. This phrase can really backfire. It assumes you know everything about what is going on for the other person. While this is completely fine to use in a conceptual or academic conversation, when there are strong emotions involved it is best to steer clear of this one.

So that covers the 'diplomatically' aspect of step 2. Now you put forth what you would like out of the situation. You have used, 'I agree', 'I respect', or, 'I appreciate' to open the door. Once you have done this you need to put a full stop in the sentence, pause and then introduce what you want.

Whatever you do, don't say the words 'but', 'however', 'on the other hand', or any derivative of these. For example, if you say, 'I agree that this is an important issue and that we need to sort it out, but … ', then whatever you have said before the 'but' is negated. 'However' has the same effect. I say to my clients, if you are going to say 'however' you might as well say 'what-*eva*'. A better way of approaching this would be something like, 'I agree that this is an important issue and that we need to sort it out. (Pause.) Another aspect we need to consider is … '

It is essential that you both state your position clearly so that each of you is clear on the other person's position.

3. Explore what each person ultimately wants

The key element of this step is to really understand what the drivers are of the other person's goal. As discussed earlier, what we ask for is often a representation of what we want but not *actually* the thing that we really want. This is where our good friend, chunking up, comes to our aid. Any of the previously mentioned chunking up questions will work here.

For example:

o 'What is important to you about this?'

o 'What does this give you?'

o 'What is the purpose of that?'

o 'What does this mean to you?'

The trick is to make the question sound conversational and not like an interrogation. Only ask one chunking up question at a time, and then discuss it a little before moving to the next chunking up question.

There is something magical about the rule of three here. If you can chunk up the person three times, chances are you will get to the driver; in other words, the highest level of need. Each time you successfully chunk up the person you will get to something that is an even higher level of abstraction. This is where you are likely to find agreement with what you want. Examples of this abstract level could include 'recognition', 'efficiency', 'for the greater good', 'being valued' and 'profits'.

4. Celebrate any mutual goals or agendas

During this stage it is important for you to be on the lookout for something you can agree with. When you find it you need to acknowledge it and bank it overtly. For example, you could say something like, 'I completely agree that [efficiency] is important to the business'. Achieving efficiency, in this example, will now form a mutually agreeable goal, which you will leverage to find a win–win solution.

There is another magical phrase to use here: 'So if we can find a way of achieving [efficiency] that is mutually beneficial, will you agree to do it?' At this point you should not receive any push back – that is, if you have found the most important higher order goal. If you have not, you must keep going until you do. This is the goal that will allow you to move to the next step.

This stage is really important, and you must make it absolutely clear to the other party that you are on the same page as her here. This will be an anchor point for when you start to work your way down to a mutually beneficial agreement.

5. Find a mutually beneficial way of achieving the goal

What goes up must come down. This is where we begin the process of chunking down. This next step can be the trickiest. This is the stage where you require the most patience and tenacity. Once you have reached the peak of the abstract and mutually agreeable goal, you then need to work your way down and gradually get to a point of agreement on something tangible, so this is the stage of the model that is likely to yield the most false starts and dead ends as one or the other of you disapproves of the solution. When this happens, just remember to go back and re-acknowledge the mutually agreeable goal in step 4.

There are two main ways you can come down: you can make suggestions or you can ask questions. My preferred path is to chunk down slowly with questions. You can do this in stages by saying something like, 'So what categories of solution can we explore?', and, 'So what are some examples of these?' Once you get down to a level that is more tangible you can start to make suggestions.

The key at this step is to try to not end up where you started. The point of this model is that you end up somewhere completely different to the two starting positions but in a place that is mutually agreeable.

AN EXAMPLE OF THE CONFLICT RESOLUTION MODEL

To demonstrate this model I will use a fairly straightforward example. In reality, this model can be used for much bigger disagreements or conflicts.

So the scene is a common one: a staff member asks for something from his manager but the manager is not in a position to give it to him.

The conversation might go something like this:

> **Staff member:** 'Hello boss, thanks for seeing me. There has been something I have been wanting to ask you for some time. Can I have a pay rise?'

> **Boss:** 'I appreciate you coming to me with this. I respect that it must have taken some courage. You say you want a pay rise. At the moment we are in a salary freeze across the entire organisation, and that is not something I have much control over. Tell me. What is important to you about getting a pay rise?'

> **Staff member:** 'Well, as you know, I'm always the first at the office and I'm always the last to leave. I'm always at the top of the performance tables too. I feel I need to be rewarded for working so hard.'

Boss: 'Okay, I agree you have worked very hard. So what does being rewarded mean to you?'

Staff member: 'It shows me that you value me and appreciate the contribution I make to the organisation.'

Boss: 'I respect that you want to feel valued. Everyone should be recognised for the contribution they make. So if we can find a way to recognise you in a way that is mutually beneficial, would this be okay?'

Staff member: 'Yes, as long as it is meaningful to me.'

Once you have agreement at the highest level, you can start chunking down again to find another solution that you can both agree on.

Boss: 'Okay, so what types of things would show you that you are valued?'

From this point the scenario could go a number of different ways. The key is to find something that is meaningful to this staff member and also something that the organisation can provide. Stop for a moment and put yourself in the situation of the boss. If you had to be creative and come up with a bunch of ideas right now that could show how valued this staff member was but that didn't involve a salary increase, what would you suggest?

Stop reading and do this now. I'll wait.

Okay, so what did you come up with? You could have had things such as time off, flexi-time, a change of job title, commendations, special projects, more responsibility, and further education and training.

This model will only work if both parties are willing and able to move from their initial positions. If this staff member had wanted to get a mortgage and the only way to do so was to get a pay rise then this model would not have been relevant. Saying that, it is amazing how many times I have realised that what was first asked for was not what someone actually wanted. It was merely a representation.

* * * * *

Okay, time to practise the model with some exercises.

For more information and resources on the
GUIDE stage, go to www.engagingexec.com.au

PRACTICAL EXERCISES

EXERCISE ONE: PRACTISE AGREEMENT FRAMES.

○ Next time you get into a disagreement with someone, practise using the Agreement Frames: 'I agree', 'I respect' and 'I appreciate'. Observe the difference compared to remaining combative.

EXERCISE TWO: PRACTISE THE CONFLICT RESOLUTION MODEL

○ Next time you end up in a dispute with someone and you want different things, see if you can employ the Conflict Resolution Model. Remember to chunk up to an overarching outcome that you both want, before chunking back down to the solution.

ACKNOWLEDGE

Part V

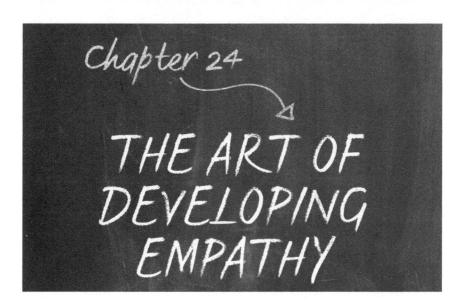

THE ART OF DEVELOPING EMPATHY

A valuable lesson I have learned in life is do not try to use logic to beat emotion … it almost never works.

We are all influenced by our emotions (unless you are a Vulcan). If you doubt that we are all in touch with our emotions, just think back to the action movies you have watched over the years. Have you ever winced at a scene where someone gets shot by a laser gun in a science fiction movie? Probably not. It was too removed from reality. Now recall one of those scenes where there is a graphic and realistic fight, one where the movements and reactions are something you can relate to – those visceral scenes where you can almost feel it, blow for blow. Why can you sense the pain? You are not there. It's because you are connecting with someone else's pain. The Oscar-winning film *The Revenant* is also a great example of this phenomenon. The scene where Leonardo DiCaprio is attacked by a bear is absolutely harrowing.

It is important for an *Engaging Executive* to develop and demonstrate empathy. If you only use the skills developed up to this stage in the book you will come across as personable, interesting, influential but potentially self-centred, unless of course you can also recognise, understand and appreciate what is going on for others.

LOGIC VS EMOTIONS

I have coached numerous executives who have declared, 'I don't have time for emotional people'. But a failure to pick up on emotions is not only a wasted channel of communication, it is also a fast track to having disengaged staff and disgruntled peers or bosses. From coaching over 1000 executives, I have noticed a distinctive pattern: those who can trade in both logic and emotions have the greatest traction within their organisation and get better organisational results.

Often task-focused managers steer clear of anyone they deem 'emotional' as they don't understand them and see them as irrational. However, the 'irrational' behaviour is usually a cumulative effect that may well have been exacerbated – or even caused – by that manager. In a misguided attempt to remedy the situation, the task-minded manager uses a logical argument to clear things up. But a valuable lesson I have learned in life is do not try to use logic to beat emotion … it almost never works. Being cold, dispassionate and logical in the face of someone who is emotionally upset is just about the worst thing you can do.

So what should you do? The answer is you should use empathy.

We will start this chapter with an explanation of what empathy is. Then we will look at how to develop it and make use of it. I will give you some tips on how to develop basic empathy in this chapter and then a more advanced empathy process in the next.

WHAT IS EMPATHY?

Empathy is the capacity to understand or feel what another being is experiencing from within the other being's frame of reference; that is, the capacity to place oneself in another's position (Bellet & Maloney, 1991). This is where the phrase 'standing in someone else's shoes' comes from.

Empathy has both internal and external components. First of all, you must have self-awareness to have empathy. If you have no clue about your own feelings then it is highly unlikely you are going to understand how others feel. You need to be able to listen to your own inner feelings and your self-dialogue. You need to be able to label your own experiences and emotions.

Then you need to be able to understand what is going on for someone else. You need to be able to pick up on the emotions of others or get on the same 'wavelength' as them. This involves getting in touch with the other person's feelings and, yes, standing in his shoes. When you can really get into the other person's mindset and emotions you are able to start seeing the world through his eyes.

Empathy is different to sympathy. Imagine you are walking down the street and you see a homeless person looking dishevelled and cold, so you give him some money. Would this be empathy? The simple answer is no. That would be sympathy or pity. You are feeling sorry for him – that is different to feeling empathy. If you were to sit down next to him and start talking to him to understand how he came to be like this and how he felt about the world and his place in it, this would be empathy.

DEVELOPING BASIC EMPATHY

The benefits of developing and employing empathy are:

o   it builds trust and respect

o   it enables disputants to release their emotions

o   it reduces tensions

o   it encourages the surfacing of information

o   it creates a safe environment that is conducive to collaborative problem solving.

The good news is empathy is a skill that can be learned.

There are three key stages to developing empathy: identification, understanding and reaction:

o   **Identification** is being observant of the subtle differences in someone else's behaviour. For example, are there minute changes in the person's facial expressions or tone of voice? Is the person's eye contact slightly less engaged? Is the person saying certain words but the rest of the non-verbal communication seems incongruent?

o **Understanding** is when you gently start to ask questions and put yourself in the other person's shoes. How can you get to understand the situation from her perspective and take out your own view on the matter?

o **Reaction** is how you then change your baseline behaviour to relate to that person and understand and join her emotional space.

Let's have a look at each of these.

Identification

The ability to identify how someone is feeling in any given moment is a gift. It is like having a sixth sense. When you can chat with someone and gauge how he is reacting to your message, it gives you an amazing ability to course correct so that what you are trying to communicate is received in the way you intended.

In NLP, this ability is called sensory acuity. It is the ability to sharpen your senses to observe and identify tiny moment-to-moment changes in a person's behaviour. These are likely to be quite minor deviations from the person's own baseline of behaviour.

When learning this technique it can be useful to practise on someone you already know well. You do not need to be an empathy expert to spot a change in behaviour. If someone walks past you cursing under her breath and then slams a door, this is an obvious change in behaviour (unless this is a person who is just angry all the time!). But we are looking for very subtle changes in behaviour. For example, a while back I was running a number of training events at the same venue. I had made an effort to develop rapport with all the staff there. One of them, Maria, set up the refreshments for my courses. We often had a joke and a chat about life. As a consequence, I was very aware of her baseline behaviour.

I was running a group session when she popped her head around the door to ask me a question. Within a nano-second and from across a decent-sized room I could spot she was not her normal self. Before she could ask me anything, I said, 'Hello Maria, do you have a cold?' She responded, 'Yes ... how did you know?' The interesting thing is *I don't know* how I knew. It just came to me. This is due to years of practising my sensory acuity. Sometimes I surprise my course participants because I can tell from their expressions that they want to ask me a question, so I say, 'Dave, what do you want to ask?' I nearly always receive a pleasantly surprised look followed by a question. I only know this because I have observed and banked their default expression and therefore I can notice differences.

Changes to look for

Here are some things you can observe, and then look for any differences moment to moment:

o **Changes in skin colour** – look out for more or less redness on the person's face or neck.

o **Changes in the facial muscles** – look out for asymmetry in the person's face, such as an eyebrow or cheek raised slightly.

o **Changes in the shape of the eyes** – this is the biggest tell for me; I tend to look out for small changes in the shape of the eyes as the muscles contract, even the slightest of squints.

o **Changes in the direction of the eyes** – look out for whether a person starts looking away from you differently to before.

o **Changes to breathing speed** – observe if the person is breathing more deeply and slowly, or if he is breathing more quickly and more shallowly from the chest.

o **Changes to posture** – observe any changes to posture, such as leaning toward or away from you, or crossing of arms or legs.

o **Changes to the voice** – listen out for changes in tone, volume, pauses and pace.

With the above you will note that I have not attempted to give a prescriptive definition as to what each means. I am not a big fan of '101 body language tips', and instead believe you have to look at groupings of patterns to understand meaning. The key point is that you start to look out for changes. You need to reach a point where you can notice slight variations in behaviour that indicate something has changed for the person you are interacting with. Once you are cognisant of someone changing her verbal and non-verbal communication you can move to the next step, which is to understand it.

Understanding

The goal of this stage is to really get into the mindset of what the other person is thinking. There are a number of steps that can really help you do this. Let's look at these one at a time.

Park your own perspective

This can be very challenging, yet it is essential. You must completely stop seeing the situation through your own values and beliefs about the world and truly look through the other person's eyes. You can always come back to your model of the world later. It is okay to accept that other people have different ways of looking at the world, and that the world is not black and white. You must be willing to let go of your ego, especially if you are involved in the situation. Empathy is not about 'winning' or being 'right'. It is about showing an appreciation for the way another person sees the situation.

Immerse yourself in the other person's world

Now that you have stopped trying to see the situation through your own lens, you need to step into the world of the other person. Actively imagine you were him. How would he be feeling right now? What are all the ways in which his version of the story could be true? Don't rush to give solutions. This is not the time. This is the time to be in his space with him and allow him to talk.

Use questions to find out more

As well as listening attentively and holding off your own judgements, there is an active element to this stage; that is, asking the right questions. These are questions designed to open up the other person, not to shut her down or lead her to where you want to go. Any kind of open question will do the job here: 'how', 'what', 'when', 'who' and 'where'. (We already discussed in chapter 16 the negative impact of 'why' questions with emotive topics.) In the *Guide* segment of the book we covered how to ask really good open questions using the Pull style.

This would be effective here. The goal is to completely allow the person to express herself.

Reaction

This is where the first two stages above come together to influence your response. Your reaction should be calibrated to how the other person is responding, and this leads us to the concept of Pacing and Leading, which is derived from NLP. Doctors Brinkman and Kirschner label this concept as 'blending and redirecting' in their book *Dealing with People You Can't Stand* (2012). This is also related to 'energy matching', and it is one of the most powerful methods I have ever learned for empathising with someone at an unconscious level. In other words, it is not so much about what you *say* but what you *do*. It requires you to consider all aspects of your non-verbal communication, and the biggest component is the energy you use. Pacing and Leading is when you observe a person's overall energy and demeanour and then adjust yours – from your baseline – to meet it. If you believe this person is in an 'unresourceful' state you may decide to match him for a while, known as *pacing*, before *leading* him out by slowly changing your own energy level.

You might be asking yourself, 'Why on earth would I want to match someone else's unresourceful energy?' The answer is best illustrated with a simple example. I am sure that at some point in your life you have felt down in the dumps. You know, bleak, low energy, or even sad. Use your powers of empathy and get into that mental space right now, just for a few seconds.

Are you there? Now imagine that your good friend has just walked into the room and has seen you like this. Your friend has a very positive intent of trying to cheer you up and get you to a happy place. So your good friend decides to come over, slap you on the back, and with the biggest smile and most energetic voice shouts, 'Cheer up!'

Stop and consider, right now, how this would make you feel. I am guessing the answer is not 'cheerful'. I will also suggest that you may be feeling somewhat annoyed, quite possibly frustrated, or even combative. Hang on a moment, though. This well-meaning friend was trying to cheer you up, so why has it backfired? The answer is, he was not empathising with you in a way that respected your feelings in that moment.

So let's consider a parallel universe where your friend comes over and uses a completely different approach. Let's just empathise with *him* for a second. He is having a great day and feeling good about the world. He then turns a corner and sees you hunched at your desk, with your head buried in your hands, your eyes looking downwards, and you are breathing slowly and deeply. He suddenly realises that you are in a bad way. He parks his own happiness for a moment and observes your general low energy and mood. He decides to sit down next to you and quietly asks, 'What's up, buddy?' You look up and see he has a concerned expression on his face, and he is also leaning forward on the desk with his head slightly tilted. You respond to him in a low-energy way, reflective of your mood, and he matches the energy, tone and pace of your voice. You start to feel that he gets you and the mood you are in right now.

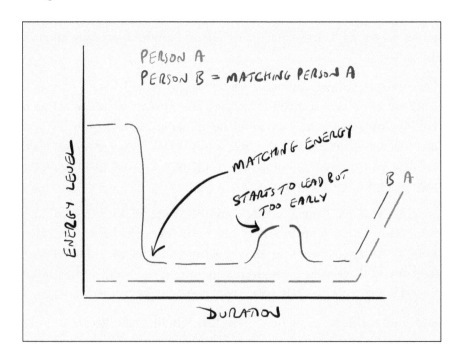

As you talk further over the following minutes, you feel he has started to slightly lift the energy of his voice and the speed at which he is talking. Not that much, but enough to bring you along and start to take you a small step away from your starting point. You continue to talk, and periodically – at appropriate moments – your friend keeps upping the energy bit by bit, until you are both communicating normally (at your baseline).

This is Pacing and Leading, and it works miracles when developing empathy with someone who is in a different emotional space to you. The key ingredient is to match someone's energy, *not* his emotion. You may choose a slightly more productive emotion if you are trying to lead the person out of a less productive one, but the energy must be matched.

Sometimes when you attempt to lead people out of their unresourceful state you may find they do not follow you. This is because you have tried to lead them prematurely. All you need to do if this happens is to go back to the energy level you were at before and stay there a little longer, and then try again. Remember, you can only move at the speed the other person wants to go. The purpose of this process is to stay in empathy with the person and at the same time lead him to a more productive place.

* * * * *

Okay, so let's look at some fun exercises you can use to practise your new skills on others.

PRACTICAL EXERCISES

EXERCISE ONE: CALIBRATION EXERCISE

This exercise is designed to develop your sensory acuity. You need a willing volunteer. It might help if you already have some rapport with this person so that you can explain the purpose of the exercise and have him play along. It might also help if you ask someone who is quite emotionally expressive and not someone more stoic.

o The first part of the exercise is where you explain the rules to the volunteer. You will ask him to imagine someone that he really enjoys being around, someone who brings joy to his life. He mustn't tell you who it is. As he does this, ask him to hold the thought for 10 seconds and ask him not to deliberately show any emotions. Study his face for 10 seconds and bank it in your memory.

o Part two of the exercise is to ask him to think of a person he really dislikes. Get him to repeat this for 10 seconds and memorise the differences.

o Part three of the exercise is to ask your volunteer to randomly think of the person he likes or the person he dislikes for 10 seconds, but he is not allowed to tell you which he is thinking about until after you guess.

See how many you can get right in a row.

EXERCISE TWO: WALK A MILE IN ANOTHER PERSON'S SHOES

Not literally, however I do want you to pick someone at random, someone who you know pretty well. I want you to imagine what it is like to be her. What are the challenges in this person's life? What are the joys? How does this person regard herself relative to others around her? Spend about a minute really getting into the mindset of someone else, and remember to look through her eyes and not label her with your own judgements.

EXERCISE THREE: PACING AND LEADING

Find someone for a non-critical conversation where you can practise your skills. Try to find someone who is in a different state to you: more or less energetic. For example, someone who is demotivated or bored, or someone who is bouncing around with joy. Get into the same energy, and see if you can hold that energy for a few minutes before you gradually try to change the energy level. See if you can make them follow your lead.

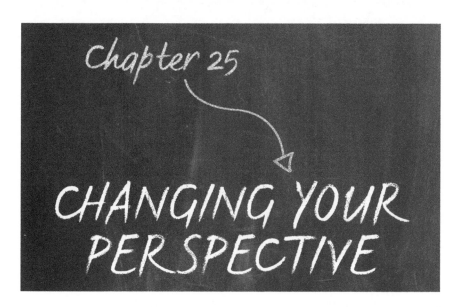

Chapter 25

CHANGING YOUR PERSPECTIVE

The process in this chapter works by enabling the deepest level of empathy and by getting you to think about how best to manage a situation.

The previous chapter would have given you pretty much all you need to get by with regard to developing basic empathy skills. This chapter is for those of you who would like to take it to the next level.

I am not going to cover any more about what empathy is in this chapter, I am just going to share with you a process I have found to be amazingly powerful in resolving interpersonal conflicts. It works by enabling the deepest level of empathy, and by getting you to think about how best to manage a situation. The process is also useful if you are helping someone else to see her way through an interpersonal situation. I have used this many times to coach others in times when empathy is a must.

PERCEPTUAL POSITIONS

This process is derived from NLP, and it is known as Perceptual Positions. I have used it many times in my personal and professional life, and it has now become somewhat second nature to me. The process involves thinking through a situation from three different perspectives, one at a time. The process works best when applied to one-to-one situations, however the process can be used when considering groups.

The three perspectives are called positions one, two and three. These positions are described below.

The most enlightening part of this process is that it helps you look at any given situation through three unique lenses. While all three lenses come from your own imagination, it is surprising how revealing the process can be. I have known people to come to profound realisations using this method. Some have even shed a tear as these have happened.

Let's look at each position before going on to discuss how to use them.

Position one

This is when you are considering what *you* want so that you can assert *your* needs on the situation and enforce your own boundaries. Some people only ever see through the lens of position one and live most of their lives like this. I have met some executives in my time who would fit this category, only ever fighting for what they can get, even if it means stepping on others. When taken to the extreme, position one can result in very pig-headed or selfish behaviour. You might get what you want – but for how long? What is the collateral damage caused along the way?

Position two

This is when you are considering the perspective of *someone else*. This position is where your advanced empathy happens. Some people can live too much of their lives here too. My gorgeous aunty is one such person. All her life she has put others before herself. She would give away her last penny if someone else needed it. The problem with position two is that when taken to the extreme it can result in someone who has no sense of self and who is generous to a fault. Ultimately, this person could get taken advantage of.

Position three

This is when you are considering the situation from an *objective and detached perspective*, taking no side in the matter. This is really helpful when you need to detach yourself from the emotions and give impartial advice. Some people are very impartial all the time. While this can be useful, when taken to the extreme it can result in someone who is disconnected and numb to the world, someone who is detached from everyone and everything, having no joy in life.

* * * * *

As you can see, each position has its own pros and cons. There is no best position to be in. In order to develop empathy though, you must embrace all three, even if you have a dominant position.

HOW TO GET INTO EACH POSITION

Now that we understand what each position is, I will describe how to get into the mindset of each. It is important that you fully immerse yourself in each position and think only through the lens of that position. For the sake of learning each position, think of a mild interpersonal disagreement you have had in the past. Do not pick a 'biggy' for this practice, as what I am about to show you is not the full process. That will come next, after I have taught you how to get into the mindset of each position.

Getting into position one

In this position you are imagining the situation by looking out of your own eyes, feeling what you feel and hearing what you hear. This is your own view of the situation as you experience it. You are fully in the problem situation and living it as if it is happening right now. The goal is to imagine everything from your own selfish perspective – at this stage you are not to consider anyone else's needs other than your own.

Getting into position two

This is the perceptual position of the other person. In this position you imagine you are looking out of her eyes back at you. (This is all imagination, by the way.) It is most important that you do not imagine looking through your own eyes at the other person. You *become* this person. It's about walking, seeing, hearing, feeling, thinking in another person's shoes, and you must completely and utterly imagine the situation from this person's perspective. There is no aspect of *you* in this perspective, only this person's needs and wants. When you adopt the second position you would speak to yourself (position one) and address yourself as 'you' or by your name.

Getting into position three

From the third position, you are like an interested but not directly involved observer of the other two positions. Imagine you are like a camera on the wall, just passively observing with no emotional connection to the situation. It is a useful position for gathering information and noticing the relationship dynamics going on between positions one and two. In the third position, if you were to refer to the first or second positions you would use third-person pronouns such as 'he' or 'she'. You can also use the names of the people involved.

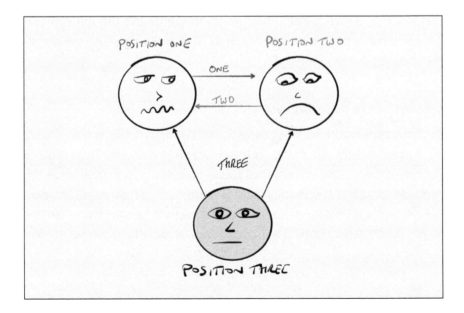

HOW TO COMPLETE THE PERCEPTUAL POSITIONS PROCESS

This is a step-by-step guide that should be used in conjunction with the above instructions on how to get into each position:

1   I find it most powerful if you can physically separate the three positions by either standing or sitting in three different locations, one for each of the positions. These positions should only be one or two physical steps away from each other.

2   Next, practise getting into the mindset of each position. You are not yet undertaking the process: this is just getting you into the headspace. Do this by standing or sitting in each spot from step 1. Take only one position at a time, and stand or sit in the respective spot. Take your time with this, getting a full visual, sound and feeling representation of what it's like to be in each position. Start in position one. Imagine yourself looking at position two and seeing the 'other' person. Once you have done this, mentally distract yourself so you can let any emotions go, then move to position two and repeat the process, this time looking back at your imaginary self. Distract yourself again, then move to position three and repeat.

3   Clear your mind again, then fully put yourself into position one by standing or sitting at the position one spot. Follow the instructions 'How to get into each position' above. Once you are fully into this mindset, verbalise what you see the person in position two doing and what you need and want to happen from the situation. Speak from the head and heart and don't edit yourself. When you are done, jot down whatever came up for you.

4   Clear your mind again, and then move into the position two spot and get fully into this mindset. Once in this mindset, speak from the head and heart of position two as if you were this person talking to you about the situation. What are your needs as this person? When you are done, jot down whatever came up.

5　Clear your mind again, and then move into the position three spot and get fully into this mindset. Imagine you are looking back at the interaction between position one and two. Once in this mindset, observe what is going on between positions one and two as if they were two complete strangers to you. Be 100% objective, and do not pick sides of the argument. That is not your role in this position. Your role is to imagine you are the coach of position one. What advice would you give position one on how to handle the situation, now that you (in position three) have seen it from both sides? Remember, you cannot give advice to position two … this person is not really there. When you are done, jot down whatever came up for you.

6　After the process, go and do the things you told yourself to do. Take action only as long as your own advice will repair the situation and not damage it further.

This process is best learned by reviewing a situation that has happened in the past. It can also be used to prepare for upcoming meetings. Once this process has been practised and internalised, you will find you can even do it 'on the fly' with live situations.

This is a powerful process, yet not one that comes naturally to most. So let us now look at how you can practise this process with some exercises.

*For more information and resources on the
ACKNOWLEDGE stage, go to www.engagingexec.com.au*

PRACTICAL EXERCISES

EXERCISE ONE: LIST SOME EMOTIONAL SITUATIONS

○ Write a list of challenging emotional situations from your past. Write them down as they come to you. Once you have written down as many as you can, order them in terms of emotional impact, starting with those that were the most painful or awkward.

EXERCISE TWO: PRACTISE PERCEPTUAL POSITIONS

○ Take the top three and start on the third-ranked situation. Work your way through the Perceptual Positions process and see what insights you can gain by looking at this old encounter through different eyes.

○ Work your way through the second-ranked situation, and then through the first.

GLOW

Part VI

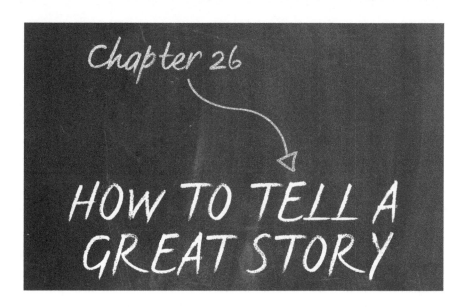

Chapter 26

HOW TO TELL A GREAT STORY

If you want to truly be an Engaging Executive you need to be able to tell an engaging story and be entertaining.

Now that we have worked on how to *En-trance*, *Network*, *Guide* and *Acknowledge*, it is time to focus on how to be entertaining; that is, how to *Glow* and light up a room. You know how to start a conversation, build rapport, influence the decisions and empathise. If you do everything by the book up to this stage, you will be getting into longer and more frequent social interactions. If you want to truly be an *Engaging Executive* you need to be able to tell an engaging story and be entertaining.

There are some very good reasons to be entertaining, and the better you become at telling stories the more you will be able to engage others. You may not have a job whereby you need to tell stories regularly, but the ability to tell a good story is still hugely valuable.

The art of storytelling goes back to the beginning of language. Before writing it was the only way humans could pass down learning from one generation to the next. Nowadays it is a powerful business tool. When you think about those people you find most engaging, what do you notice about them? Most probably, many of things that we have considered in this book. You may also have noticed their ability to tell a good tale and to use humour appropriately.

Now, when I talk about telling stories, I do not mean the kind that start with 'once upon a time'. It could be stories of a difficult business deal, or a great project, or an important experience you once had that gave you a key learning.

This chapter is about how to construct a good story, and then how to tell it really well.

THE STORY OF HOW I DISCOVERED STORIES

Have you noticed how some people are great at telling stories? They seem to know how to structure them and how to reveal each part of the story in a way that keeps you enthralled. Everyone enjoys a good story when told well. It takes you to another place and time, and gives your imagination free reign. We are going to uncover the secret structure of how to do this.

This process was a massive learning for me when I started to date again after seven years of being in a relationship. I went on a lot of dates that were not great, and I know I had a lot to do with that. For a start, I had no idea what to talk about, so I would turn up and cross my fingers and hope that I would 'hit it off' with the 'lucky lady'.

Most of the time I died on my feet, and the more times I died the more I dreaded going on dates. I was a bit confused, as I knew when I was in a training room I could tell training-related stories all day long. Why didn't the same magic happen on dates?

I eventually made the connection between what I did so well when I ran training courses and what was missing in my dates. In a training environment I had cues such as familiar topics or recurring questions from participants that would trigger my stories. On a date, I had no such structure. This is the same as when people talk to strangers of any kind, business or social. You wrack your brains to think of stuff on the spot, run out of things to say, and then freeze up. For many of us, social gatherings, networking events or even business lunches and dinners mean that we need to have prolonged exposure to people we don't know and don't know much about.

Having a few stories up your sleeve is a way to avoid those awkward silences. It is also a skill that makes you easy to remember and demonstrates you can add social value.

CONVERSATIONAL BUILDING BLOCKS

When I had my 'a-ha' moment, I also realised the key to telling engaging stories was not trying to be highly creative every time I opened my mouth. It was actually being able to tell the same story until I became really well versed in telling it. It is like a 'set piece' in soccer: the team has practised a particular shot 100 times and knows the sequence of passes before the shot on goal.

Most people put themselves under a lot of pressure by trying to come up with new and interesting conversations with each person they meet. This is unnecessary. What you want to do instead is be able to have the same conversation 100 times until you become an expert in it. Create a series of stories or topics you can talk about without thinking; these are what I call Conversational Building Blocks. Once you have created a big enough repertoire of building blocks you will be able to engage in interesting conversations for hours.

Brainstorming and mind mapping your topics

The first thing you need to do to build up your library of Conversational Building Blocks is brainstorm all the topics you can think of, and then start to fill them out with as much detail as you can. You can use whatever you like as long as you are passionate about it; for example, travel, sports, films, arts, television, books, your origins, what you do for fun, your career, your goals, or your dream job. It really is limitless. (At the end of this chapter there are some exercises to help you get started with this. You might wish to do these now. Then we will talk about how to structure them.)

I use a concept called mind mapping to get the topics out of my head and on paper. If you have not used mind maps before, you should try them. Mind mapping was created by Tony Buzan, and it has been used in NASA, among other places, to enhance creative thinking. There are plenty of YouTube videos about how to mind map, and there are many software programs that can help. There is nothing like a good mind map to help me come up with content. I even mind mapped the content of this book before writing it.

The Short Story Rule

If you just did the mind mapping exercise you would now have a few topics on the table. So how do we make them interesting?

When I was working in outplacement I would help people prepare for job interviews. A good candidate will always know what it is they want to say before the interview. A good interview response is a mini story explaining something that happened, how you dealt with it, and the outcome.

Every story needs a beginning, middle and end. This I refer to as the Short Story Rule. I frequently hear people telling me what I think will be a great story, so I get curious, I pay attention, I look engaged, and then the 'story' just seems to finish without a proper ending.

Always think of the end before beginning. Every time I tell a tale, in my mind I will race through to the end and make sure there *is* actually an end. And this is why rehearsed or considered stories tend to work best – you already *know* the end.

Let's have a look at one of my default stories as an example. At the age of 41 I decided to go skiing for the first time in my life. My mate Stu and I packed up our gear and headed off to Thredbo Ski Resort. Stu was an expert skier, having grown up in New Zealand. I was a keen motorcyclist and so the principle of leaning into corners was very familiar to me. I knew I was going to be a natural. I mean … what could go wrong?

I had decided to wear my motorcycle suit as it passed as a ski suit on a quick glance, but it had a secret weapon. It was fully fitted with motorcycle armour on the elbows, knees, hips and back. The thought of falling down on fluffy snow was about as intimidating as a kitten in pyjamas. I was Iron Man.

On day one of the trip I booked into a beginner lesson, and after two hours we had only just touched on the basics. I thought to myself, 'If it takes two hours to learn this as a group then I'm not going to get very far in three days'. I decided the whole process was too slow, so I asked Stu to teach me. We spent an hour on the baby slopes, and I pretty much got the hang of parallel skiing and doing those sideways stops that make the snow spray everywhere.

I said to Stu, 'Let's go up to the green slopes'. So off we went, my confidence growing all the time. On the green slopes my progress continued. Yes, I fell down a few times, but with my suit of armour on I was indestructible. After a few runs I shouted to Stu, 'To the blue runs!', and off we went.

Now this was starting to get a little scary, and I could feel it in my stomach. There were little jumps and some steep inclines for a novice, but on I went. Yes, I fell down some more, but in my armour I was fine. I just brushed myself off and carried on.

It was getting late in the afternoon and my goal was to get to the black runs on my first day. I said to Stu, 'One more run and then off to the black runs'. However, I never made it down that one more run. On my last blue run I gathered such momentum that my legs started weaving independently until, at an uncontrollable speed, my skis crossed, dug into the snow and catapulted me into the air. Down I crashed onto my shoulder to the sound of a loud 'crack'! I lay there in agony until the ski patrol came and pumped me full of drugs, before sledding me down the mountain to the hospital, where I had a titanium plate inserted in my collar bone.

It turns out snow isn't that soft.

As you can see, my story had a beginning, middle and end.

Notice how I gave some context first. The beginning is all about setting the scene and introducing the characters. This would include who you were with, where you were, and any other factors relevant to the story.

The middle is the meat of the story. This is where you take the audience on a journey and build the scene. You need to describe what is happening so that it conjures up vivid imagery for the audience. You need to gradually build up the interest in the story by putting the protagonist up against an obstacle or antagonist. In the case of my skiing story, the protagonist was me and the obstacle was the mountain.

Finally, the end is where the threads of the story come together and you hit the audience with the punch line. I like to think of the punch line first before telling a story, especially if it is one I am telling off the cuff or for the first time. In my story the punch line was me cracking my collar bone after thinking I was indestructible.

In the diagram below I have presented the stages of the Short Story Rule. You will see that the secret to the art of storytelling is to build the anticipation all the way to the end.

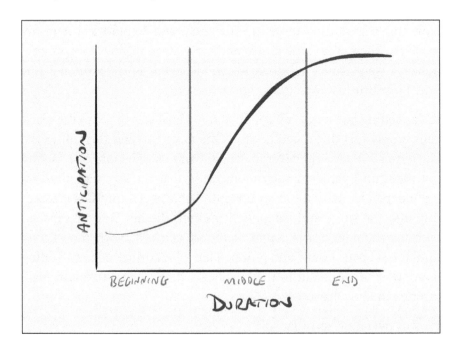

VAKOG!

No, it's not a Russian swear word (at least, that I know of). Let's have a look at VAKOG.

If we want to get beyond facts and opinions in the Rapport Triangle then we need to tap into the emotions. You can tap into the senses as you tell your stories by using VAKOG. This stands for:

o **V**isual (what you see)

o **A**uditory (what you hear)

o **K**inesthetic (what you feel)

o **O**lfactory (what you smell)

o **G**ustatory (what you taste).

Think about how to build these in as you construct a story. For example, when I tell people about why I love to ride motorbikes I throw in as many VAKOG words as I can. I say, 'I love to get up on a sunny Sunday morning, put on my full leather race suit and head up the Old Pacific Highway. What's great about riding a motorbike is you can smell the changing scenery as you pass through the wooded areas and pass the sea. You can feel and hear the wind rushing through your helmet and touching your face. I lean my bike over as far as I can, trying to touch my knee on the tarmac. One wrong move will send me out of control and into a tree, so my heart is pounding and my focus is intense. For 45 minutes, time stands still as only that moment in time exists, corner to corner, side to side. That feeling of mortality and being in the moment is why I love motorbikes.'

Or I could just say, 'Yeah, I go motorbike riding on Sundays. I really enjoy it.'

Which version do you like better?

Don't just say the words. *Feel* the words. Express yourself as if you are there in the story – act out the emotions as if you are living them again.

SHARING YOUR INNER DIALOGUE

Another great tip when story telling is to give the listener the inner dialogue that was going through your head at that time so they can relive the moment with you. This is a learning that came to me when I worked as a Corporate Psychologist. I was at a company conference and I was asked to speak about one of my ideas. At the end of the presentation, my Managing Director said, 'I have finally worked out why Duncan is so interesting to listen to … he shares his inner dialogue as he describes something'.

Letting people into your thought processes is like letting someone see behind the stage of a show. Of course, you need to be selective about what you share. I'm not suggesting you should share every thought, just every now and then. Do this with the phrase, ' … and I thought to myself … '. For example, 'So I was walking into a crowded room one day and I thought to myself, *"I wonder who is going to be the easiest person to talk to first … "*. I spotted a gentleman standing on his own looking shy, and I started to speak to him.' This personalises a story and makes it feel like you are sharing more about who you are.

INTRODUCING YOUR STORIES

How should you introduce your stories? If you were to just come out with a random story without positioning it then the story may fall flat. You need to somehow link it to the topic on hand. For example, with my skiing accident story I wouldn't just randomly start telling it. This is a story I choose to pull out whenever I am discussing topics such as skiing, accidents, stupid decisions, over-confidence or having metal plates in your body.

Another way you can introduce your stories is to lead with a loaded question. Ask a question about what you want to talk about of the person you are talking to. Allow her to answer. Show genuine interest in her response, and then see what happens. For example, 'So, have you been skiing before?' Normally, once a person has finished answering she will respond by asking you the same question … cue your prepared masterpiece.

* * * * *

Okay, so let's get the ball rolling on your storytelling with some practical exercises.

PRACTICAL EXERCISES

EXERCISE ONE: BRAINSTORMING AND MIND MAPPING

○ Brainstorm some topics that could make Conversational Building Blocks. Don't filter it at this stage, just write down as many as you can. Come up with at least 10. Then take a piece of paper, a tablet or a computer and mind map the topics you think would make great stories.

EXERCISE TWO: THE SHORT STORY RULE

○ Take one of the topics you came up with in exercise one and apply the Short Story Rule to it. What is the beginning of the story? Where does the scene begin? Where were you? Who was there?

○ What is the middle of the story? Fill out the details. Make the listeners feel they are there.

○ How can you add some VAKOG language?

○ How can you add some inner dialogue?

○ What is the end of the story? What is the twist in the tale? What is the punch line? What was the big realisation?

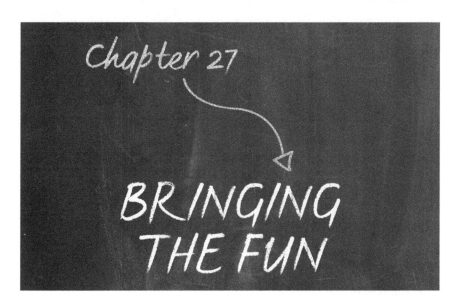

Chapter 27

BRINGING THE FUN

'A sense of humor is part of the art of leadership, of getting along with people, of getting things done.'

Dwight D. Eisenhower

While it is not the role of the *Engaging Executive* to be the funny person of the office, if the US President is onboard with the importance of humour then you should be too. Now we are going to look at humour and its important role in the workplace, and then I will share some tips on how you can enhance your own sense of humour.

HUMOUR IN THE WORKPLACE

As a consultant, I have been allowed to nose around hundreds, if not thousands, of organisations, both public and private sector. I can gain an immediate feel for an organisation as I walk around. Some of that is projected by the decor, some by the way the office has been structured, but the aspect I notice most is how people relate to each other. Is it super formal and deathly silence, or is there warmth to it? Do people interact for reasons other than pure business? Is there friendly banter? If you consider that most people spend five days of their week at work and two days at home, the place you spend a large part of your life is going to have a massive effect on you.

I am a big believer in building the 'social fabric' of an organisation. This means creating a sense of connection between people, whereby the process of interaction is enjoyable. Now I'm not talking happy-clappy tree hugging here; I am talking about simple pleasantries that have a big impact on how you and the people around you feel at work. Using humour is one of the quickest and most powerful ways of doing this.

The importance of having fun at work

Researchers Dr Lee Berk and Dr Stanley Tan at the Loma Linda University in California have researched the benefits of laughter and found amazing results. Laughing:

o   lowers blood pressure

o   reduces stress hormone levels

o   improves cardiac health

o   boosts T cells

o   triggers the release of endorphins

o   produces a general sense of wellbeing

o   gives you a free abdominal workout.

In other studies, doctors have found that people who have a positive outlook on life tend to fight diseases better than people who tend to be more negative. Psychologists Mesmer Magnus, Glew and Viswesvaran – in 'A meta-analysis of positive humor in the workplace' (*Journal of Managerial Psychology*, 2012) – state that employee good humour is associated with enhanced work performance, satisfaction, workgroup cohesion, health and coping effectiveness, as well as decreased burnout and stress. And they found that a supervisor using humour leads to enhanced subordinate work performance and satisfaction, improved perception of supervisor performance and satisfaction with the supervisor, and better workgroup cohesion, as well as reduced work withdrawal. So there is definitely a medical and psychological case for being entertaining and humorous at work.

Andrew Tarvin is an award-winning speaker, bestselling author, and international humourist who has done a TED Talk or two. He has an awesome webpage called '30 benefits of humour at work', all backed by research and real-world examples. It is a great read, and I am going to cherry pick some of my favourites that I have personal experience of in the workplace.

The first is that humour gets people to listen you – this is almost a no brainer. Would you rather listen to someone who is flat and serious (unless that is appropriate for the situation), or would you rather listen to someone who brings a bit of humour to the message? There is a fine balance, however, as you still need to be taken seriously. When you make people laugh, even periodically, it releases the neurotransmitter dopamine, which serves as a reward for the brain as it creates a sense of euphoria. Humour also reduces cortisol – the stress hormone – and releases endorphins. So, you make people laugh, their own reaction makes them feel great, and they associate that feeling with you. That is what I call a win–win.

Another benefit is that humour increases the likeability of the speaker, for many of the same reasons as above. And when you make a room of people laugh it elevates your social value; the fact everyone is laughing means that they all share a common liking of the person that made them laugh and this acts as social proof that you are a 'good guy or girl'.

HOW TO BRING THE FUN

Let's now consider the how of being more humorous. This is going to be class 101, not a complete guide on how to be funny. There are some great books, videos and courses out there on how to be funny, so if this chapter tickles your funny bone I would highly recommend having a look at those.

Take yourself less seriously

I actually did a course on how to be a stand-up comedian a few years ago. It was fascinating to understand that, just like everything else we have unpacked in this book, humour also has a structure. At the end of the course we had to perform a 15-minute set at an actual comedy club. It was one of the most terrifying things I have ever done in my life. Doing presentations or training sessions and popping in the odd joke when people are not expecting it is relatively easy, as no-one assumes you will be funny. However, when you go up on stage in a comedy club it is like you have a big sign over your head saying, 'Hey everybody, look at me, I think I'm hilarious'. It takes a lot of living up to. But you don't need to be a stand-up comedian to add humour to a situation. In fact, humour is best delivered when it is not expected as it has more impact. But you must begin by lightening up and realising that you are not perfect. Not taking yourself too seriously is the first step in being able to inject humour into a situation.

For some of my clients I have actually recommended they take a course in comedy or some other area that will get them out of their own heads. Often people are so conscious of saying something wrong and looking silly that they hold themselves back and don't express themselves at all. I had a wonderful client who worked in professional services. He was always so proper and polite, and social etiquette was of the utmost importance to him. The problem was, if he made the slightest faux pas he was mortified, and would ruminate on the event for days. There was one time he recounted to me when he had to meet someone in the reception of his large corporate offices. He had never met this person before and, being the gentleman he was, he wanted to ensure that his first impression was flawless. So into the reception area he came. He identified his target sitting down, and approached her. He said, 'You must be Jane … how lovely to meet you', only to find out it wasn't Jane at all. Now, this has happened to most of us, but this was enough for him to feel complete and utter embarrassment, and caused him great distress.

His problem was that he took himself way too seriously, so he was always on the lookout for what could embarrass him or give a bad impression. I set a task for him that was a game changer: to research improvisation classes. If you are not familiar with improvisation – or 'improv' – it is a type of acting class but you have no script, minimal structure, no right or wrong, and you just make up stuff as you go. It is a group activity, and it forces you to think on your feet and get out of your head. One minute you might be acting like a tree, then a farm animal, then telling a random part of a story, then opening an imaginary gift. The point was for this lawyer to make a complete and utter fool of himself in a safe environment and to learn to laugh at himself.

He absolutely loved it, and he learned to see life with a bit of humour.

10 tips for becoming more humorous

In Larry Wilde's book *Treasury of Laughter* he outlines 10 tips for becoming more humorous:

1 Become familiar with humour classics.

2 Review books on comedy technique.

3 Watch comedians at work.

4 Listen to comedy recordings.

5 Practise gestures before a mirror.

6 Take acting classes.

7 Join a dance class.

8 Get voice training.

9 Read a joke book 15 minutes every day.

10 Seek guidance from a pro.

I think even if you were to do just a few of these you would gain great benefit, and have a cracking time in the process. There are also some great videos on YouTube that will instruct you on how to be more humorous. These are well worth a watch.

Telling jokes well

While I am not trying to position myself as a comedy coach, there are some simple tips you can put into place when telling a joke. Just like when we discussed how to build a story, a joke requires a beginning, middle and end, so make sure you have all three parts, especially the punch line. I can't count the number of times I have listened to someone tell a joke and at the end they say, 'Oh, wait … what was the punch line again?'

A joke essentially uses misdirection. The art of telling a good joke is first provide the setup. A setup is when you give the listener an expectation of what will happen. At this stage you need to give the listener all the context she needs to understand the punch line. The setup should take about 10 to 20 seconds. You then deliver the punch line in a way that shatters that expectation. This causes incongruence, which is the source of the humour. For example, Jimmy Carr is one of my favourite stand-up comics. He is famous for his quick-fire one liners. One joke of his I recall goes, 'I went to a Hollywood party for the rich and famous recently and Brad Pitt was there. People say, you should never meet your heroes. But I think Brad handled it really well.' The 'rule of three' applies to telling jokes – same, same, different. This sets up misdirection perfectly.

My final tip is to laugh at your own jokes first. One of my friends pointed this out to me once. He was actually talking to someone else about being funny, then turned to me and said, 'Do what Duncan does and laugh at the end of your joke'. I didn't realise that I did this but he caught me fair and square – I do. Now, if you tell a terrible joke and laugh at the end this clearly is not going to help. However, if you tell a half-decent joke and laugh at the end it acts like a cue for everyone else to laugh. It seems to have a very positive effect. This is why TV producers use canned laughter. It has been scientifically proven to make people laugh louder and longer.

✳ ✳ ✳ ✳ ✳

So let's have a look at some practical ways you can work on developing your humour with the following exercises.

PRACTICAL EXERCISES

EXERCISE ONE: DO SOME RESEARCH AND TAKE ACTION

- Go online right now and research any of the following that you may be interested in:
  - books on comedy writing
  - YouTube clips on how to be funny
  - courses on stand-up comedy
  - courses on improvisation.
- Take action on at least one of these items – today!

EXERCISE TWO: WRITE OR LEARN SOME JOKES

- Write some jokes, or learn them from books or videos.
- Practise saying a joke out loud until you can deliver it fluently and get the timing right.
- Deliver your joke to someone to see if it gets the reaction you want.

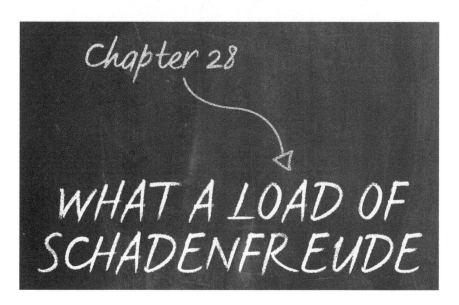

Chapter 28

WHAT A LOAD OF SCHADENFREUDE

We can always see the doom and gloom if we look for the doom and gloom but if we look for the funny side then suddenly the whole situation changes.

In the previous chapter we looked at some activities you could do to take yourself less seriously and lighten up. In this chapter we will extend this by looking at a psychological principle that seems universal across humans: schadenfreude. The best way to take yourself less seriously is to talk about times when you took yourself too seriously. Look for the humour in a bad situation, and uncover the irony and absurdity of life. We can always see the doom and gloom if we look for the doom and gloom but if we look for the funny side then suddenly the whole situation changes.

THE CONTENT REFRAME

Share your embarrassing moments and laugh at yourself. This is called a Content Reframe, and it is where you look for a different meaning within the same situation. If you start with the question of 'what is comical about this?' then you will immediately start to look for it. This will help improve your mood and the mood of those around you. Find ways to turn your trials and tribulations into Conversational Building

Blocks. I often find the worse situations make the funniest stories once you reframe them. This works on the principle of 'schadenfreude', which is the pleasure derived by someone from another person's misfortune. If you have ever seen the TV shows *The Office* or *Extras* by Ricky Gervais, he is an absolute master at creating schadenfreude.

I am going to demonstrate the principle by recalling a travel story. While painful at the time, I started telling the story within 12 hours of being back and found that people took great pleasure in my tragedy. My misery was causing other people joy. So here is the tale. See if you can detect the Short Story Rule and the use of VAKOG.

AHHHH ... PARIS

I once had the most dreadful weekend away in Paris. It really was the most terrible cluster of mishaps I could imagine, and it felt like it had been scripted by Ricky Gervais. It started with me and my girlfriend (at the time) deciding to go on a romantic trip to Paris, the city of love. Being UK based at the time we booked a package deal via LastMinute.com. It included a return train ticket via Eurostar and two nights at a hotel placed right next to Montmartre. From the website it looked boutique and perfectly placed for enjoying the wonders of Paris.

Off we set on the train from London with our bags, rocketing underneath the English Channel. When we surfaced, the sky was dark grey and the rain was coming sideways. The doors of the train opened and an icy wind hit us in the face. Hmmmmm ... not the best start, but never mind. So we jumped in a taxi and gave the driver the hotel address. This was before the days of smartphones, so we were a bit at the mercy of the professional drivers to get around. After what seemed like an age, we arrived at the hotel. We walked in and went to the check-in desk. The French receptionist asked for our passports, and being the custodian I pulled them out of the pocket that I always keep them in, and handed them over. We were then given the key and instructed where our rooms were.

So up the stairs we trundled, carrying our own cases. When we opened the door to our room it was like walking into a museum of derelict furniture. Everything looked dirty and tired. The bed sagged so much in the middle it could have passed for a hammock. The bathroom was disgusting and the shower head had broken off. 'I'm not having this,' I said to my girlfriend in my finest English accent, and off to reception I went. I explained the situation to the receptionist who had taken our passports, only for her to look at me blankly as if I had requested a ticket to Mars. Reluctantly she grabbed another key and thrust it in my hand. So off we went again and trundled up even more steps to our room, still carrying our cases.

The new room was exactly the same – but worse. The bed was more sunken than a pirate chest and this time the bathroom had blood splattered on the wall. So we trundled back down to reception again. This time the receptionist rolled her eyes and tutted as if I was being a complete dandy. Again, she chucked another key at me and off we went. This room was pretty similar to the first, but by now we realised that this was the standard of the place and we would have to make do.

The rest of the weekend followed suit. Every meal we had was awful. We must have managed to find the lowest rated restaurants in Paris by random bad luck. It rained non-stop and was freezing. Pretty much everything we planned had a twist in the tail, but that was nothing compared to what happened when we tried to end this godforsaken trip.

On the last day we couldn't wait to go home. As I checked out of the hotel I informed them that I would be making a complaint to LastMinute.com and walked out feeling righteous and vindicated. We jumped in a taxi and headed back to the station. We got there in less than 10 minutes and it cost less than half of the taxi ride to the hotel, at which point I realised that the driver who took us there had completely ripped us off and taken us on an undisclosed tour of the backstreets of Paris!

We arrived in good time and so I suggested to my girlfriend that we check in and then have a last drink in Paris. So off we went to the international check-in desk. I put my hand inside my normal passport pocket and … nothing was there. What? I checked again. Nothing. I checked all my pockets, then my bag, then my case. My girlfriend asked me what was wrong as I frantically frisked myself. I explained that the passports were missing – and then it dawned on me. I had left them at the hotel!

I checked my watch, and I had just enough time to get there and back if I got an honest taxi driver. So I left my girlfriend with the luggage and raced off into the street and jumped in a taxi. I got to the hotel quick sharp and raced in, sweating and puffing.

'I left our passports here, can I have them back please?' The receptionist from hell gave me the death stare from hell.

'No,' she said in her French accent, as she looked at me intensely.

'What?' I responded with a somewhat agitated tone.

'We don't have your passports,' she retorted.

'You *do*,' I demanded, 'Don't play games with me just because I said I was going to make a complaint.'

She gave me another death stare and again replied, 'We don't have your passports.'

I was absolutely livid, but the more I insisted she give them to me the more she insisted she didn't have them. I thought to myself, *think Duncan, think*. I decided the best course of action was to get back to the international terminal and report our passports as stolen in the hope they could give us temporary ones.

As I got back to the terminal, I saw my girlfriend standing there in tears. She looked terrified. While I was away, two Frenchmen had started harassing her and trying to lead her away. She had resisted, but no-one had come to help her.

So now I had no passports and a distraught girlfriend. I tried my best to console her and I gave her a big hug. As I hugged her I felt something familiar in her coat pocket. I put my hand in the pocket and pulled out our passports.

'What the hell is this?' I said, immediately losing all compassion for my poor girlfriend's situation.

'Oh … yeah,' she said, 'the receptionist gave them back to me when we checked in.'

In that moment I experienced every emotion ever identified by humanity. It was like I was having an out-of-body experience. Then I snapped myself back into reality and checked my watch. We had exactly five minutes before check-in closed: 'Come on! Let's run.'

So with our heavy cases we ran as fast as we could to the elevator that would take us up to the departure level. We jumped into the lift, followed by an absolutely stunning looking girl and her equally impressive rugby-shirted boyfriend. This guy was built like a tank and could barely squeeze his shoulders into the lift. The girl looked like she had just walked off a catwalk. My girlfriend and I backed up against the wall of the elevator to make room.

Just as the doors were about to close this rather drunk looking Frenchman staggered towards the lift. The rugby guy kept the door open for him. As the drunkard staggered into the lift, he caught his shoe on the edge of the lift door and lost his balance. Of course, he reached out to save himself, and it just happened that the nearest thing to hand was the catwalk model's chest. The rugby guy didn't take too kindly to this, and a fight ensued right in front of us. It was not pretty, and my girlfriend and I did what little we could to dodge the blows. Unfortunately the buttons of the lift were all on the other side of the fight.

After a minute of wrestling and screaming the fight broke up and the Frenchman left rather worse for wear. I checked my watch … one minute left. As we reached the check-in desk the clock ticked over and they shut the gates. No amount of pleading or begging could open the gates and we watched as the train slowly pulled away from the station.

Just to top off the trip, we found out the tickets were not flexible and so we needed to book two new tickets at full price … which cost more than the original weekend away in the first place.

And that was the tale of my trip to Paris – the city of pain.

* * * * *

If you enjoyed reading that tale, you now understand the principle of schadenfreude. I have told this story many times and it has now formed one of my Conversational Building Blocks whenever I hear someone talking about Paris or nightmare trips.

How many schadenfreude tales do you have to tell? Use the following exercises to get a few ideas down using the principles of storytelling and humour we have already looked at in previous chapters.

For more information and resources on the GLOW stage, go to www.engagingexec.com.au

PRACTICAL EXERCISES

EXERCISE ONE: MIND MAPPING NIGHTMARE SITUATIONS

o Mind map as many nightmare experiences as you can remember. Don't think about the whole story at this point, just note it down.

EXERCISE TWO: CREATE A SCHADENFREUDE STORY

o Now think through each one using the Short Story Rule – does it have a beginning, a middle and an end?

o How can you bring VAKOG language to the story?

o How can you reframe the tragedy to be funny using the principle of schadenfreude?

ENLIGHTEN

Part VII

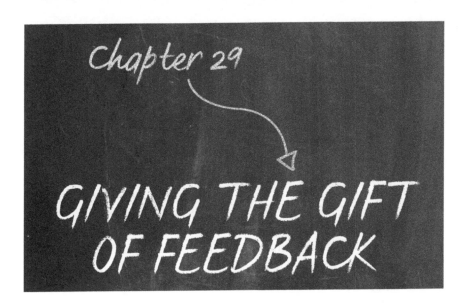

Chapter 29

GIVING THE GIFT OF FEEDBACK

As a manager or leader of people it is your role to pass on your observations and wisdoms to the next generations.

As we move into the final stage of the ENGAGE model it is important to consider that up to this point we have been focusing on developing your own skills. This is a lifelong journey for all of us, but the best people managers I have ever worked for, and with, are also exceptional at bringing the best out of others. An *Engaging Executive* thinks beyond just herself. Learning is a process and it never ends until we end. No-one ever wakes up one morning, looks herself up and down in the mirror and says, 'By Jove, I think today is the day. It is … I'm fully developed! There's not a single thing I can improve upon.'

As a manager or leader of people it is your role to pass on your observations and wisdoms to the next generations or those who are not as skilled in a particular area as you are. This is how society improves, and this is how organisations progress. It is our responsibility to help others grow and develop. This transfer of learning is what makes the human race stand out above all others.

This part of the book is about the *Enlighten* stage of the model. It is about how to give feedback, to coach and to mentor. In my opinion, these are the most powerful techniques when it comes to developing

273

people. They also require you to draw on the skills you have learned within this book.

So let's start with feedback, why it is important and how to do it well.

THE FUNCTION OF FEEDBACK

If I was to ask a room full of people, 'Would you like your boss to only give you mindless encouragement rather than what you really need to hear to improve?', how many of them do you think would say yes? Not many, I bet. Almost everybody likes to hear the truth about his performance.

Saying that, nobody likes to receive 'negative feedback' because it damages the ego, so the trick is to not have feedback seen as a negative but as developmental. It is all about how well it is framed and delivered. It also depends on whether the term 'feedback' comes with a sense of dread or not. If the only times you ever hear the phrase 'I'd like to give you some feedback' it is followed up by something negative then the culture of 'feedback' in your organisation is poor.

Feedback needs to be balanced and well considered. The purpose of feedback is to make the future more productive. It is about focusing on the solution, not the problem. It is also about creating an environment where people are open to feedback at an individual, team and organisational level. According to PwC, nearly 60% of respondents to a survey reported they would like feedback on a daily or weekly basis. This number increased to 72% for employees under age 30. So people do actually want to hear the feedback, but are you brave enough to give it to them?

I read an interesting study on www.forbes.com on the impact of giving honest feedback. The study had a sample of almost 23,000 leaders. In terms of the ability to give honest feedback, those who ranked at the bottom 10% received staff engagement scores that averaged 25%. In contrast, those in the top 10% for giving honest feedback had staff who ranked at the 77th percentile in terms of engagement. While there may have been other factors at play here, the message is fairly clear – people want honest feedback.

The same article also revealed that in a different study of nearly 52,000 leaders there was a trend related to how much people asked for feedback. Those who ranked at the bottom 10% in asking for feedback were rated at the 15th percentile in overall leadership effectiveness. However, leaders who ranked within the top 10% of asking for feedback were rated at the 86th percentile in leadership effectiveness.

The conclusion we can take is that feedback is essential for our growth. Feedback is one of the most effective ways of calibrating your behaviour in the absence of hard metrics. The other benefit of asking for feedback is that it role models good behaviour. If you are always dishing out feedback yet never on the receiving end, that most probably means one of three things: that you haven't been asking. Or, people are not comfortable giving it to you, for whatever reason. Or finally, it could just mean you have the 'Mary Poppins Effect' – you are practically perfect in every way …

TOP TIPS ON HOW TO BETTER GIVE AND RECEIVE FEEDBACK

Now that we have built the case for giving and receiving feedback, let's turn to some practical tips on how to do just that.

Ultimately, you need to be just as good at receiving feedback as you are at giving it. If you easily dish out feedback but get all sensitive when you receive it then you will not have any credibility. Therefore, see these tips as the complete package of how to do the feedback process well.

Tip #1: See it as a gift

There is a saying that goes, 'Feedback is a gift'. It might not always feel like it, but it absolutely is if you approach it with the right intent and delivery. So first, let's talk about being in the right mindset to receive feedback. Once you can take feedback comfortably, even graciously, from others you will be able to deliver feedback much better yourself. This is because you will have no fear of it.

I learned a fantastic analogy for feedback over 15 years ago. It has always stuck with me, and I use it on all my leadership development programmes. I call it the Christmas Analogy. At Christmas time, in most Western societies, we give presents to each other. Sometimes you receive a gift that is so perfect, you eagerly accept it and put it to use right away. Sometimes you receive a gift that is practical but not immediately useable, so you save it for later. And there are, of course, some occasions when you receive a gift and you think to yourself, 'What on earth possessed you to give me this junk?' You know it's going in the bin the second you open it.

Receiving feedback is no different. Like a gift, when you receive the feedback you should always thank the person for giving it to you, then decide what you are going to do with it: use it now, use it later, or chuck it away.

Tip #2: Don't take it personally

When I first learned about NLP, one of the most life-changing components of the programme was called 'useful fictions'. It was essentially a list of beliefs which, if you chose to adopt them, would change your life.

How would they change your life? It is simply that everything you believe about the world is a lie that you tell yourself. There are good lies and bad lies. The good lies are the ones that make you feel empowered and confident to do something. The bad lies are those that niggle at you, causing you to doubt yourself and tell yourself you are unable or not good enough.

These lies are your belief system. Beliefs are not the truth, but we act as if they are. I always say to my clients, if you are going to lie to yourself about the world, then tell yourself the good kind of lies. One such lie, or useful fiction, is this:

There is no such thing as failure, only feedback.

If you were to open up the minds of the world's elite, those people who have reached the top of whichever field you like, you will find this belief. You see, people with a winning mindset don't know what failure is. The word does not exist in their vocabulary. Instead, to them the world is a massive experiment. Everything they do is a 'test and measure' process. They look at life like an engineer does. An engineer builds a system and then tests it to see if it produces the result she desires. If it doesn't, the engineer will take a look at the aspect that did not produce the right result, tinker with it, and test again. At no point does she pull out a hanky and start to get emotional about it.

Tip #3: Catch people doing things right

One of main reasons why people dislike feedback is that most of the time it is used to tell people they are doing something 'wrong'. Feedback should not just be corrective, it should also point out what people are doing well. I like to refer to this as 'catching people doing something right'. In psychological studies it has been shown that negative feedback comes associated with negative emotions and can actually result in people revising their goals downwards to avoid the pain. However, positive feedback is associated with more positive emotional rewards and leads to higher effectiveness and a revision of goals upwards. But, I am not talking about giving meaningless or false praise. It has to be useful and specific. I used to have a manager who said 'good job' to everything I ever did. Sometimes I felt he would have said it if I tied my shoelaces in his presence. That's not helpful at all, because if somebody hears 'good job' any time they do *anything*, they actually have no way to discern when they've truly done something well.

An argument I tend to hear a lot from my clients is, 'Well, they are just doing their job. Why should I praise them for that?' This goes back to the points made above. If the feedback is genuine, specific and positive, it leads to an increase in effectiveness. There is only so far the 'I'm only going to tell you when you have screwed up' school of management will get you. It certainly won't make you an *Engaging Executive*.

Tip #4: Find the value for the person

Sometimes the trick to giving really great feedback that leads to behavioural change is as simple as finding out what is of value to the individual. This can then be leveraged. I've had many memorable feedback discussions over my career. One of them happened in Adelaide during my first year in Australia. I was asked to provide 360-degree feedback to a gentleman who clearly didn't want to be there. He was in his late 50s, Canadian, silver haired with a ponytail, and he wore a paisley shirt. I started the session using my normal patter, but about 10 minutes in I realised this guy was just playing along and not really taking it seriously. I stopped and I said to him, 'You're not really into this, are you?' He looked me square in the eye and said in his drawn-out Canadian accent, 'This is just a buuunch of well-structured buuullllls#@t'. I chuckled, and said with a slight tone of sarcasm, 'Why don't you tell me what you *really* think?'

I closed the report and slid it away from him. I knew that if I was to gain any traction in the session I would have to find the value in it for him. So I asked him, 'So, what is going on for you right now?' He explained how he had less than a year in the job before retirement. He had been working in Learning & Development, and was actually quite passionate about leadership programmes. I asked him, 'So what kind of legacy do you want to leave on this organisation? Or do you just want to disappear as if you had never existed?' He seemed to wake up when I asked him this. I could see the cogs turning in his mind. He then became very passionate, and started telling me how there was this leadership programme he had designed that he really wanted to get up and running as his swansong. The challenge was he was being met with some resistance from his peers and bosses, and he didn't know why. At that point I looked over at the 360-report that had been completed by his peers and manager. I patted the report and I said, 'Hmmmmm … I wonder if there may be any answers in here?'

He looked up with a glint of curiosity in his eyes and said, 'Yeah, there probably is. Let's take a look.' It turned into a highly productive session with plenty of action points, which he took away with relish.

Tip #5: Give timely and precise feedback

As you can probably tell, I am a huge believer in giving useful feedback. You may also be able to tell from this chapter that there is a skill to doing so.

I was once conducting a leadership programme in a large public sector organisation. As part of this training there was an accreditation process. After I had completed the training and the assessment, there were a few people who had just missed the mark. I had a lot of very specific information I could provide that would have informed each person how best to improve. The organisation was very hierarchical, so the feedback had to come from the big boss and not me. I did question this, but I was given a clear message that this was the way it was always done and 'people were fine with it'. The feedback I gave to their supervisor was passed to the big boss, who then gave feedback to the internal team. Unfortunately, there was a negative side effect to this approach.

After the assessment I went back to carry on working on the project, and I just happened to keep bumping into the internal team members who had not made the cut. I observed a high degree of awkwardness from them. Normally I was greeted with smiles and friendly comments, but now those individuals looked at the floor as they passed me. This went on for a few days, and then I started to feel uncomfortable. I made a decision to visit each of them to investigate.

It transpired that by the time the feedback had gone up the chain and then back down the chain it had lost a lot of its specificity. It had been distilled down to a near pass/fail message. This, combined with the time the feedback process had taken, had left them feeling confused and disenfranchised. One even explained how he had gone from being a huge advocate of the programme to a naysayer. So I sat with each of these people and shared the more specific feedback, which appeased them greatly. The feedback was now useful to them, rather than just making them feel as though they hadn't measured up.

This is the difference between giving general and specific feedback.

Tip #6: Use a simple formula

This last tip I am going to share with you is a simple model I have used for over a decade to provide feedback. I have used it both as a specific formula and as a general model if I am to have a more conversational style of feedback. Regardless of whether or not you use the actual words, if you were to keep in mind the structure you would undoubtedly craft your feedback more effectively.

Before I explain the feedback formula I want to tell you what it is *not*. There is a similar model of feedback called the 'feedback sandwich'. This is where you give some positive feedback, then the negative, and then end on the positive. I am not a big fan of this model. I think it dilutes the feedback and gives people an opt-out clause to drown the constructive feedback with loads of overinflated positives. In Australia, where I do much of my work these days, it is frequently referred to as a 's@#t sandwich'. While this is not a term I would suggest you use, it does kinda tell you a lot about how it is perceived.

The model I use has three modes, each with a different intent.

What worked

This is where you start with the positives that you have noticed. These must be genuine, and must be the elements that I refer to as 'the difference that makes the difference'. In other words, what are the active ingredients of what you saw that led to success or would have achieved the right result? Keep this clear and simple.

What didn't work

This is where you give the constructive feedback. You point out what you observed that will not lead to the desired result. Again, you need to curate your feedback here, particularly if you see a large gap between where the person is now and where he needs to be.

People often make the mistake of including everything they noticed instead of the active ingredients only. If someone needs development in an area you can help by focusing on one to three specific things. There is something magic about the number three – the unconscious mind loves it. Think about this yourself. If you see one of those 'how to' guides and it says 'three things you need to do to … ' versus '10 things you need to do to … ', which one do you think will be more accessible? Three things to hold in your head is realistic – 10, on the other hand? Well, unless you are Rainman.

In the future

This stage is about next steps. The person should know and understand what he needs to *keep* doing and *stop* doing. He needs to know what to do next. Often feedback starts with what didn't work and ends with what didn't work. All this does is make people feel deficient. The most important part of feedback is focusing on the solution. How can you take this person to the next level? This is why my training programmes have loads of opportunities to practise the next step.

✳ ✳ ✳ ✳ ✳

So, these are my top tips for giving great feedback. Remember to start with yourself and start asking for more feedback from others. Then remember to balance your feedback and catch people doing things right. Finally, use the feedback formula and this way you will capture all of the essential components. Try out the exercises at the end of this chapter to hone your feedback skills.

PRACTICAL EXERCISES

EXERCISE ONE: ASKING FOR FEEDBACK

○ Be brave and go and ask some people you know to give you feedback on how you are at work. Ask this person to use the feedback formula: what worked, what didn't work, and what they would like you to do in the future. Remember the Christmas Analogy as you receive the feedback.

EXERCISE TWO: CATCH SOMEONE DOING SOMETHING RIGHT

○ As you go about your day, be on the lookout for someone doing her job well. It may be someone you work with, or it may be someone outside of your place of work. Pay her a compliment on what it is that this person is doing well. Be specific.
Do not give any negative feedback, only positive.
See the reaction this has.

EXERCISE THREE: USE THE FORMULA

○ If you manage people or if you have people who report to you on a project basis, give them some feedback. Pick the right moment and use the feedback formula. Get into a regular habit of giving feedback – don't make it a once-a-year occasion that is tied to performance reviews.

Chapter 30

HELPING OTHERS GROW

The gift of the coach is to challenge the thinking of the coachee and break him out of the problem box that he has found himself in.

So we arrive at the final chapter of the ENGAGE model. This chapter is all about how to bring out the best in others and help them grow. This is the ultimate goal of a true *Engaging Executive*.

I'm very fortunate that in my role I get to hear a lot of wise sages speak. I used to work on a public service leadership development programme that would have some of the most senior members of the public service conduct Q&A sessions. One very inspirational leader who held a high position in the Australian Taxation Office used to say that for an organisation to grow the leaders must enable their teams to work at the leaders' own level. This is the only way that the leaders can free up their time to focus on the level above them, which in turn enables their bosses to do the same.

The most effective way to achieve this is via feedback, coaching and mentoring. This creates autonomy, not dependency. However, knowing when to give feedback, coach or mentor will depend on the stage of development of your staff.

So how do you know when a staff member is ready to receive each?

SITUATIONAL LEADERSHIP THEORY

In the first part of this chapter I am going to outline a leadership model that has some very intuitive benefits. In 2000, when I did my Bachelor of Science thesis I realised that the number of different and competing models published every year on leadership alone is mind boggling. What I am not going to do here is outline the most 'cutting edge', flavour-of-the-month leadership theory. Instead, I am going to do what I have done in the rest of the book and outline a model that is highly pragmatic and easy to operationalise. My weapon of choice, from the million and one theories, is the Hersey–Blanchard Situational Leadership Theory (SLT). It has two main components, being leadership style and the maturity level of those being led.

This can be drawn as a grid, shown below.

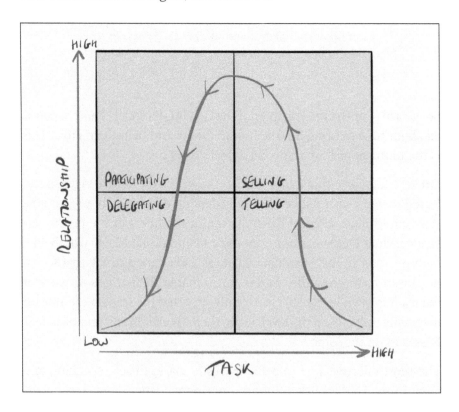

According to Hershey and Blanchard, a situational leader does not adhere to a certain theory or trait. A situational leader identifies the needs of the individual performing a task and adapts her leadership behaviour to maximise that individual's performance. The fundamental assumption of the situational leadership theory is that there is no single 'best' style of leadership. Effective leadership is task-relevant, and the most successful leaders are those who adapt their leadership style to the maturity of the individual or group they are attempting to lead or influence. Effective leadership varies not only with the person or group being influenced – it also depends on the task, job or function that needs to be accomplished.

The theory can therefore aid us in understanding which style of leadership is required in different circumstances. SLT fits very nicely with the theme of behavioural flexibility being presented throughout this book.

The SLT styles

There are four styles that correspond to the diagram opposite. Following is a description of each.

Telling

This is a high task-oriented and low relationship-oriented leadership style. It is used when staff members are at the lowest readiness level and so they're unable or unwilling to perform the task, for whatever reason. This is a directive style where leaders make the decisions, provide lots of direction, clearly communicate expectations, clarify roles, explain how to improve, and monitor performance closely. Communication with this style is largely one-way and task specific.

This style is most effective when a staff member is new to an organisation or task. It is also more aligned to managing underperformance. This is a very transactional style of leadership and only appropriate for people who fall into this category. It is most aligned to a Push style of communication. Unfortunately, many managers and leaders have this as their default style, regardless of the people they are managing.

Selling

This is high task-oriented and high relationship-oriented leadership. This style is most appropriate when a staff member is not yet capable of performing the task, but is willing. With this style, leaders must continue to make decisions, communicate expectations, and direct behaviour, however this is a more communicative style in which the leader must engage in two-way communication and seek ideas and suggestions as to what is needed for success. In this style the leader is still in charge but uses influence instead of authority to guide the staff member. While guiding the work being done this style also reinforces the staff member's willingness to do it. Many of the tools in the *Guide* section of this book align to this style.

Participating

This involves low amounts of task-oriented and high amounts of relationship-oriented behaviour. At this level a staff member can do the task but requires support as he works more independently. Therefore, in this style minimal direction is needed, with too much direction being perceived by the staff member as micromanagement.

This level is about providing support to build staff confidence and focusing on the relationship. Day-to-day decisions should be delegated to the staff member, with the leader acting more as a coach. The content in this chapter is most aligned with this style of leadership.

Delegating

This is where the control shifts from the leader to the staff member and the leader steps out of the picture. The leader becomes involved in dividing up and allocating the tasks, but the emphasis is on monitoring rather than doing. With this style the staff member chooses when and how the leader will be involved after the task has been assigned. With this level of staff maturity the leader could take more of a mentor role as the staff member is both capable and willing to do the task. Leaders must remember not to step away completely though as this could be perceived as a lack of interest or an abdication. Feedback is still important at this stage.

This style of leadership is most aligned to mentoring, which is touched on at the end of this chapter.

✳ ✳ ✳ ✳ ✳

Now that we have looked at the different styles of leadership, let's look at how we can adopt a more coaching style of leadership that would be appropriate for more experienced staff.

WHAT IS COACHING?

This may sound like a dumb question, because everyone knows what coaching is, don't they? Or do they?

I am often surprised when I talk to leaders about coaching. There are some very differing views on what coaching means. So let me be clear: when I speak of coaching I am referring to a particular style of coaching. If you are already 'coaching' someone in a different way to this, that is coaching too – it just isn't what this chapter is about.

Let me illustrate this with an example. Often when I ask people, 'So, what is coaching?', I get the response, 'When you show someone how to do something'. In the world of sports coaching, this may well be right. I have had several tennis coaches over the years. They have been great at teaching me form and tactics. However, notice that I used the word 'teach'. This is really what this style of learning is: teaching. If you don't know anything at all about a topic or skill then you need to be taught. This is more aligned to the telling style of situational leadership theory. Saying that, I am sure when Stefan Edberg was coaching Roger Federer he wasn't teaching him form on his backhand. It would have been a much more cerebral kind of coaching. I would imagine it would have been helping Federer understand how to change his game and adapt his style as he aged gracefully.

When I speak of coaching it is what I classify as 'non-directive coaching'. This will be the focus for the remainder of this chapter. From this point, when I refer to coaching I am talking about this non-directive style.

The purpose of coaching

With non-directive coaching you are helping people come to their own realisations. You transcend the teaching mode, and instead help people learn for themselves. In fact, what you are really doing is teaching people to think. We have all heard the wise maxim of:

> *Give a man a fish, and you feed him for a day.*
> *Teach a man to fish, and you feed him for a lifetime.*

This is the very essence of non-directive coaching. As we saw earlier, this style is not for everyone. It requires a strong will to learn, and a reasonable skill for the task in the coachee. For example, if I had a staff member who was completely demotivated and inexperienced for an assignment, no amount of coaching would get her where I wanted her to go. If I had a super eager Junior Doctor who was learning neurosurgery for the first time, no amount of coaching would help him either. If I was lying on the operating table about to be put under and I heard the Chief Surgeon say, 'So, where do you think you need to cut first?', I would be off that table in a flash.

Coaching, in my sense of the word, is when you have someone with a high will and a reasonably high skill level, someone who is able to marry experiences or ideas, which he may not yet have appreciated, with the goal in hand. The gift of the coach is to challenge the thinking of the coachee and break him out of the problem box that he has found himself in. Referring back to the *Guide* section of this book, coaching is very much a Pull style. In fact, many of the questioning techniques outlined in that chapter will help you become an exceptionally good coach.

Some people argue that coaching takes too long and that it is easier just to tell people what to do, or worse, do it yourself. Well, if you think coaching is about getting a job done fast, you are missing the point. Coaching is all about lifting your staff to the next level, so that in the fullness of time you will be able to step away from them and let them get on with it. This does mean putting in some time and effort beforehand. Remember, Rome wasn't built in a day. Coaching requires patience. Coaching requires you to use your experience and wisdom to craft clever, thought-provoking questions that enlighten a person.

Finally, coaching requires you to allow people to make mistakes and learn from them. 'What!?!' I hear you scream. Not cataclysmic mistakes. Just the level that it takes to realise there is a better way, or a quicker way. The key is that the coachee comes to the realisation herself.

HOW TO STRUCTURE A COACHING SESSION

As with much of the content in this book, there is more than one way to skin a cat.

I have come across numerous coaching frameworks in my profession, and each has its own benefits. Some are quite basic and some are very complicated. Again, I come back to the principle of the minimum effective dose. Some books are entirely about one particular technique. This is not my goal here. I want to give you something that you can learn quickly and something that can get amazing results. For this I am going to lean on one of the most widely used and acknowledged coaching frameworks, the GROW model by Sir John Whitmore. This man has an interesting past, including being a 2nd Baronet, a racing driver, a sports psychologist, a business coach and a bestselling author. You could say he knows a thing or two.

The GROW model

The most beautiful thing about the GROW model is its simplicity. It's made up of just four intuitive stages which work wonders. As a Psychologist and NLP Master Coach I have been taught many mind-boggling frameworks for helping people come to realisations, yet 95% of the time the simple GROW model will do the job and do it well.

Here is what the acronym stands for:

G = Goal – the purpose of the Goal stage is to help your coachee clearly define what it is she is trying to achieve.

R = Reality – this stage of the model is about establishing, testing and challenging the way the coachee is thinking about the situation.

O = Options – at this stage of the model you are encouraging solution generation via brainstorming and creative questioning.

W = What next – the final step of the model is to put together an action plan that has all the elements of a mini project plan.

While the model is presented in a linear format, you may find yourself moving back to some of the previous steps if new information comes to light. For example, if you discover more obstacles in the Reality stage, you may choose to go back and redefine the goal.

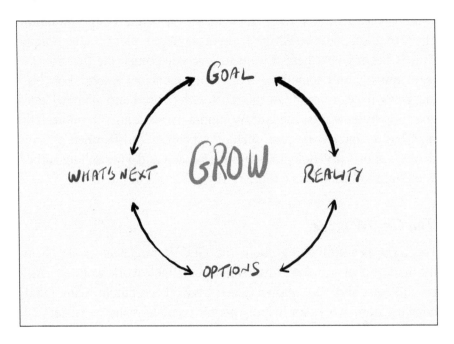

Let's consider each stage of the model.

Goal

It is amazing how many times I have coaching sessions with someone who is not actually that clear on what he wants. Without a clear goal, the conversation just turns into a nice chat.

Coaching is a conversation with a purpose. Sometimes you may need to spend a while exploring the goal before it truly becomes clear. This may mean delving into the Reality stage of the model and circling back if you cannot find clarity easily. The goal needs to be something that is clear, concise and very specific. Most of the time people will give you something very nebulous. For example, when I coach people on soft skills they often say, 'I want to improve my communication'. This is not a clear and specific goal. Does this person mean written or face-to-face communication? Is this person talking about pushing or pulling? Is this person talking about being more engaging? Is this person talking more about actively listening or developing empathy? You get the gist, right? A goal needs to be very clear to both you and the coachee before you begin.

Another element of the goal stage is to test the goal to ensure it is realistic. Sometimes people set goals that are way beyond their resources or timescales. While we need a goal to be stretching, we are not looking for mission impossible.

It is also a good idea to chunk up a little using the technique from the *Guide* part of the book. If you are finding it difficult to clarify the goal then ask some questions to chunk up to the purpose of the goal.

Some example questions you can use for establishing the goal are:

o 'What is your goal?'

o 'So what is it you want to achieve?'

o 'What is your objective?'

o 'What specifically would you like to achieve?'

o 'Why is this goal important to you?'

o 'What would you like to happen that is not happening now?'

o 'When you achieve this, what would it look like?'

o 'How realistic is this goal?'

o 'What will achieving this goal give you?'

o 'What is the purpose of achieving this goal?'

Reality

In my opinion, this is the most important stage of the coaching process. Why? Well, let's imagine you go to your boss and ask him to help you with a problem. You have no idea what to do, which is why you have gone to your boss. He puts on his coaching hat and asks you, 'So, what do *you* think you should do?' You would probably look back at your boss in despair for asking such a stupid question.

Therefore, it is essential at the Reality stage to loosen the coachee's grip on the problem. You need to establish what the coachee believes is the current situation, including what he has and hasn't tried to do. What are the factors involved in the scenario? Who is involved in the scenario?

Once you have established the facts as your coachee sees them, you need to challenge them. The purpose of coaching is to help someone realise that she has all the answers within herself, she just doesn't know it yet. Think about this for a second. Has there ever been a time in your life when you thought a task was unachievable? Of course. Now, have you ever had a time when you actually managed to achieve the unachievable? If the answer is yes then you will now have a different belief about that task. If you were to attempt it again, you would come at it with an entirely different perspective.

I often like to talk about Roger Bannister to make this point. If you are a bit light on sporting history, Roger Bannister was the first man to break the four-minute mile. What made this unbelievable was the hype that surrounded the feat at the time he was attempting to achieve it. Doctors were saying it was impossible – the demands on the human body were so great that he would have a heart attack. Psychologists were saying the pain would be so much he would pass out on the track. He proved them all wrong on 6 May 1954. But what happened next was even more amazing. An athlete named John Landy came along and broke Bannister's record a mere 46 days later.

So what happened? Did humans suddenly evolve to be faster after hundreds of thousands of years in just over a month? Or could it be that once the myth of the unbreakable four-minute mile had been dispelled, people actually approached the task differently? This is the purpose of the Reality stage: only once you have dispelled the myth that the task cannot be done can you move onto generating options.

Let's have a look at some of the questions you can ask in the Reality stage:

o   'Tell me what's happening?'

o   'Who else is involved?'

o   'Where is this happening?'

o   'When does this happen?'

o   'Is there ever a time that it doesn't happen?'

o   'What are the factors we need to consider here?'

o   'What have you tried so far?'

o   'What haven't you tried so far?'

o   'What is the problem?'

o   'What is the problem not?'

o   'How do you know your perception is accurate?'

o   'What would happen if it wasn't accurate?'

o   'Is there any other way the situation could be different to how you perceive it to be?' (This is not an Options question, it is to challenge assumptions.)

Options

For many coachees, finding options for going forward will be the most challenging part of the process. As the coach you will need to be very patient – there will be a temptation for you to jump in and tell the coachee what to do. I see this almost every time I teach someone how to coach. The other big temptation is to try to steer the coachee to exactly what you thought he should do in the first place. This is not really coaching in the non-directive sense, more steering with leading questions.

The purpose of the Options stage is to create an environment where the coachee can brainstorm and test ideas while feeling safe to do so.

The slightest frustration or criticism at this point will most probably lead to the coachee regressing into a state of dependency. The real trick in mastering the Options stage is to ask questions that really open up a coachee's model of the world. It starts at the Reality stage, and this is where you kick it up a gear. As a rule of thumb, you should attempt to find a minimum of three options. This is because one is necessity, two is a dilemma and three is a choice.

Let's have a look at some Options questions:

o 'What else could you try?'

o 'What ideas do you have so far?'

o 'What haven't you attempted to do yet?'

o 'Who do you know that does this well? What does he do?'

o 'What could you do to change the situation?'

These are typical Options questions. Sometimes they will yield great results. However, if that fails you will need to go to the Advanced Options questions:

o 'I know you can't think of any other ways to solve the problem, but imagine that you could. Humour me and pretend you did know – what would you say?'

o 'If you were King/CEO/President/God [insert all-powerful entity of your choice that is appropriate for your coachee] for the day, what would you do?'

o 'If you could invite any three people into this room, dead or alive, real or fictitious, who would they be?' Wait for the answer and write down the answers. You then say, 'So what would [person no. 1] do in this situation?' Explore the answer. 'What would [person no. 2] do in this situation?' Explore the answer. 'Finally, what would [person no. 3] do in this situation?'

The magical quality of these questions is their ability to suspend reality. Often we are stuck inside the problem and we need something to stimulate our thinking from another angle. By taking a different perceptual position, your coachee may well find a new angle on a situation. For example, imagine I was to present you with a problem and ask you to solve it. Now imagine I was to ask you to imagine how your Mum would solve the problem. Do you think you would both come up with the same solution? Of course not. However, the act of imagining what your Mum would have done breaks you out of your own way of looking at the problem.

What next

The final stage of the model is all about planning what to do next. Some Coaches like to sift through the options in the Options stage of the model. I prefer to evaluate options during the What next phase. This is done by looking at the pros and cons of each option and working out which one is the most effective and actionable.

This stage is also about establishing the level of commitment to the action plan. If the commitment is any less than 10 out of 10 then you should explore what would need to happen to make it a 10. During this stage you also need to establish any obstacles and any support required to counteract these. Once this has been done you can move into looking at timeframes, milestones and measurement.

A typical oversight at the What next phase is to overlook the measurement aspect of the goal. If a goal cannot be measured, how do you know you have achieved it? Goals can be in the form of metrics or feedback from others.

My final tip would be to set 'check in' times with your coachee around the milestones and final measurements. This is especially important if you are doing an ongoing series of coaching sessions.

Questions you can use at this point include:

o 'What are the pros and cons of each of the options?'

o 'Which option will give you the best result with the least effort?'

o 'What obstacles do you foresee?'

o 'What support will you require to overcome the obstacles?'

o 'When are you going to start?'

o 'What are the milestones along the way?'

o 'What is the timeline for this goal?'

o 'How committed are you to this goal on a scale of 1 to 10?'

o 'What needs to happen to make you a 10 out of 10?'

* * * * *

That's ACE!

Another useful acronym to consider when coaching is ACE: Acceptance, Clarity and Energy. If you have successfully conducted a GROW model coaching session then your coachee should be on board with the goal. Ideally, coaching is only ever conducted with a person who has accepted the problem as a problem. If I was managing the performance of someone who did not believe he had done anything wrong then coaching would not be a good tool for the job. You can't exactly say to someone, 'Sit down, I'm gunna coach the hell out of you'. To be a coachee you need to be the one asking for help.

Clarity is what should be achieved especially in the Goal and What next stages of the GROW model. If a coachee is in any way confused as to what to do next, the coaching session has not done its job. That's why I detest the line, 'Go away and have a think about it'. This is just plain lazy on the side of the coach, unless you have specified certain avenues to explore and report back. Energy should be present in the coachee in the form of excitement. If you have truly helped him to think through the situation from another perspective and come up with a plan that did not exist before, there should be some obvious momentum.

MENTORING – ANOTHER OPTION

I'm often asked what the difference between coaching and mentoring is. The simplest answer is this. A Coach does not need to be an expert in the relevant topic. A Mentor normally does have a strong body of expert knowledge or experience in the relevant topic. A Coach can be of any age or level of experience (theoretically), whereas a Mentor is normally two levels or more above the mentee.

The role of a Mentor

The role of a Mentor is to espouse wisdom from a position of experience. The term 'Mentor' is derived from the story of Homer's *Odyssey*. Odysseus, king of Ithaca, had to leave his son to fight in the Trojan War, and entrusted the care of his household to a man named Mentor, who serves as teacher and overseer. I'm not going to discuss mentoring in depth, as many of the skills in this book will enable you to be a splendid Mentor. This short section is just to position mentoring as another role that can be performed in the *Enlighten* stage of the ENGAGE model.

I have both had Mentors and been a Mentor to others in my career. It is a very rewarding process, and I have often learned as much from the Mentee as he or she has learned from me. Whereas a Coach will not usually give ideas or suggestions, a Mentor is expected to do this. However, this is done in more of a soft Push style, making suggestions and helping the Mentee to think through issues. The purpose of mentoring is to inspire and enlighten, however it is not a classic teacher role. It is all about taking the Mentee's thinking to another level.

Another role of a Mentor is to create networks for the Mentee. This will require making introductions to other significant players that can be useful. You will need to have worked on your own skills from the *Network* section of this book to do this well.

Matching Mentor and Mentee

Having helped a number of organisations set up and run mentoring programmes, I have made several realisations. It is important that both the Mentee and Mentor have a say in who should be the Mentor. I have found the process of doing this on paper to be very problematic; in other words, looking at someone's background and experience and making a paper match. Mentoring works best when there is a mutual desire for the relationship. I often advise my clients who are looking for a Mentor that it is like dating: you have to identify who you are keen on and then ask this person on a date. Most of the time people are delighted to be asked if they would like to be Mentors. It is very flattering.

When I have set up mentoring programmes with multiple Mentors and Mentees I have actually used a speed-dating type setup. I use a large room with seats in a circle. There are pairs of seats, one for the Mentor and one for the Mentee. The Mentors stay seated and the Mentees move around, one position at a time after a fixed time. After each rotation, I ask both the Mentors and Mentees to complete a Mentor Matching Form where they make comments about their interaction. At the end of all the rotations, I ask both Mentors and Mentees to order their choices. The entire experience is dynamic and fun.

It's not just a coffee catch up

When becoming a Mentor it is important to have an objective. Again, I have seen Mentoring sessions turn into coffee catch ups that go nowhere and then fizzle out. I always advise that the first session is a planning session, and that there should be an agreed number of sessions that the Mentor and Mentee contract to keep. This can be revised on an ongoing basis. In the same way as coaching, the Mentee should be required to set goals for between the sessions and to be accountable for completing the tasks agreed with the Mentor.

✳ ✳ ✳ ✳ ✳

The role of Mentor is very gratifying and self-assuring. You will find out more about yourself, and realise that you have learned a thing or two as you have progressed through your career. You will also come to realise that sometimes the most rewarding feeling is not from showing that you are the expert in the room; it is from helping others grow by sharing your wisdom. It is this care for others and this removal of ego that will help to make you an *Engaging Executive*.

Let's have a look at some practical exercises.

***For more information and resources on the
ENLIGHTEN stage, go to www.engagingexec.com.au***

PRACTICAL EXERCISES

EXERCISE ONE: WHICH STYLE OF LEADERSHIP?

○ Draw out the situational leadership theory grid and plot your staff or project team in each of the segments. Which of them needs which type of style? Which is your natural style of leadership? Which of your team would benefit from a different style to the one you use as your default?

EXERCISE TWO: GO AND GROW SOMEONE

○ Find someone who is willing to be coached by you. It is most important that this person volunteers and is not doing it under duress. Establish what the person would like coaching on, and then use the GROW model. If you feel the topic requires more than one coaching session then agree on this with your volunteer – agree to meet as many times as required.

EXERCISE THREE: BE A MENTOR

○ Find out if there is a Mentoring scheme where you work. If not, position yourself as a Mentor looking for a Mentee. Remember, your role is to help this person navigate the complexities of your field or organisation. Agree on six sessions to begin with and meet once per month for an hour. Agree on actions for the Mentee to complete after each session. Review them at the beginning of each subsequent session.

CONCLUSION

Part VIII

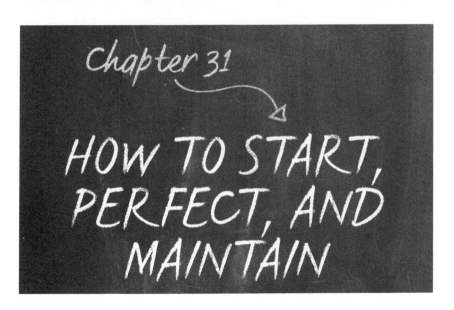

Chapter 31

HOW TO START, PERFECT, AND MAINTAIN

Soft skills are not linear, and 2 plus 2 does not always equal 4 when it comes to this art. Patience, persistence and continuous self-review are the keys.

Having reached this far in the book, I would hope you have started to at least play with the many tools and techniques contained within. For some, sheer willpower alone will be enough to get you started. However, for many, you will be hit by the niggling doubts and inner chat that keeps telling you, 'not this time, but next time'. Having seen too many executives learn new soft skills and then fail to employ them, I know exactly the difference between those who do and those who don't go on to become *Engaging Executives*. It is our old friend, fear of failure.

Those who go on to become *Engaging Executives* are those who are willing to get out of their comfort zone and make mistakes. They are the ones who will try something new from this book and impartially observe the outcome. If they achieve the outcome they want, they will repeat the same process. If they don't, they will tinker with it and try again. Remember, failure is our friend. Embrace it and learn from it. Soft skills are not linear, and 2 plus 2 does not always equal 4 when it comes to this art. Patience, persistence and continuous self-review are the keys.

THREE INGREDIENTS

Having immersed myself in the world of personal development for the past 20 years I can tell you emphatically the three ingredients to making a permanent change to your behaviour. First, you need to find someone who is better at the target skill than you are. Secondly, you need to immerse yourself in an environment that forces you to utilise the new skill. Finally, you need to embrace repetition.

Let's look at each of these.

Finding people better than you

The quality of the people you surround yourself with sets a ceiling on your learning. If you surround yourself with people who make you feel comfortable at the level you operate at now you will never get better. However, if you can spend time with those who can do something better than you, it will raise your own standard. It is like when I first started learning tennis. I was hopeless – I mean, so hopeless that if the ball went over the net and landed anywhere in the court I was pleased. I would play with people who were equally as bad because it made me feel good about myself. In fact, if I 'won' I felt on top of the world. But it was all a lie. I was lying to myself that I was good at something.

After a while, I joined a tennis club and I soon realised my true level. In my mind I thought I was an intermediate player. That is until I met someone who said he was 'okay', and so I decided to challenge him to a match. It became apparent after just one game that his version of 'okay' and my version of 'okay' were very different. Being in the presence of someone far more skilled than me made me work harder and learn from my mistakes, of which there were many. After many months of practising, I finally beat him.

Guess what I did next? That's right, I looked for someone better than him. This is how we grow and develop.

Even more powerful than this is getting a coach. The most talented people on the planet all have coaches. Presidents, sporting legends, millionaire business people – all have coaches. Even great actors need Directors to bring out their genius. It is important to have someone you trust who can push you and provide feedback. Even when I wrote this book I had a writing coach and an editor. Remember, you do not need to bang your head against a brick wall when learning. Find someone who has already made the mistakes and allow this person to help you accelerate through the learning process.

Immersing yourself

Find likeminded people who are willing to practise with you. When working on their own I have found people will often read an instructive book like this one and do nothing with it. They will not live up to their full potential because it can be hard to be self-motivated. So, find yourself an accountability buddy, someone who can keep you accountable to your goals. When I was learning to date women again after a seven-year break, I found a group of guys who were trying to learn the same skills. We would go out every Thursday and Friday night and socialise together while practising talking to women. Even when we made spectacular blunders we had a good laugh about it and then gave each other feedback. We acted as our own support group. The mere thought that we were not alone was a great incentive to push harder and learn from our own and each other's mistakes.

Rinse and repeat

Repetition is the mother of all learning. Everything I have ever successfully mastered in my life has come down to three simple words: practice, practice, practice. There is a principle made famous by author Malcolm Gladwell, known as '10,000 hours leads to mastery'. This was based on the original work of Anders Ericsson, who is a psychologist and scientific researcher from Florida State University. His conclusion from multiple decades of study is that talent is not innate. When you see someone who is great at something we often assume 'she must be a natural'. However, according to Ericsson, there are two factors that lead to excellence in any skill. One is the amount of time spent (this is where the principle of 10,000 hours comes from). The other is how you use those 10,000 hours. Just the time alone does not lead to mastery. Most of us in our thirties or forties have been driving for at least 10 years, which usually adds up to at least 10,000 hours of driving time. However, that does not make us Michael Schumacher. Mastery comes from the discipline of taking one tiny aspect of the skill and focusing intensely on learning, reviewing and perfecting it before moving on to the next component. This is what perfects a skillset.

So, as you go forth and start your journey towards becoming an *Engaging Executive*, make sure you do three things:

o   Find someone better than you and spend time with them.

o   Immerse yourself in an environment where you can learn.

o   Practise, practise, practise.

WHERE TO FROM HERE?

If you have enjoyed reading this book and have found the tips and techniques useful, you may be interested in further services of *The Engaging Executive* coaching and training company. I appreciate that sometimes it is easier to learn soft skills in an environment that is safe. This is why my programmes are built around the concept of the 'behavioural sandbox'. This is an environment in which you can practise and try out new behaviours without fear of getting it wrong. You can push the envelope and receive feedback on when you are pushing too hard or not pushing hard enough. Sometimes trying out these new behaviours in the real world can be a bit daunting. It is not always clear if you have mastered the technique or not, as there is no-one to give you feedback.

The Engaging Executive runs a highly interactive programme that embeds the concepts of this book. The programme goes beyond being educational to being transformational. It is designed around the 70:20:10 principle of learning and extends over 12 weeks. The programme is not for everyone: it is only for those who have reached a point of realisation that only by enhancing their influence, interpersonal and communication skills will they achieve more in their life and career. It is only for those who are devoted to pushing outside of their comfort zone to get to the next level. It is only for those who want to build a network with people who are likeminded. The entire programme is the perfect balance of challenge and support.

All *Engaging Executive* programmes are run by highly experienced and qualified coaches and facilitators. In addition to our flagship programme, *The Engaging Executive* offers executive coaching sessions on how to develop the skills discussed in this book, if you are unable to attend the full programme.

I am also available for keynote speaking events, and can design a custom package to discuss any of the themes in this book.

If you would like to find out more about our programmes, coaching or keynote speaking events you can contact me at:

o www.engagingexec.com.au

o duncan@engagingexec.com.au

ABOUT
DUNCAN FISH

Duncan's mission is to help people feel confident and skilled in the art of communication, whether this is business or social. He takes great pleasure from seeing people make personal breakthroughs and the ongoing success that superlative communication skills brings his clients. Duncan's ultimate driver is to help people free themselves from their self-imposed prisons, especially when it comes to soft skills. Your life is a reflection of what you believe you can and can't do. He knows this because he has been there.

Duncan Fish, C.Psychol AFBPsS, M.Sc, B.Sc. is an Associate Fellow of the British Psychological Society (BPS), a Chartered Occupational Psychologist (BPS UK), and a Registered Practitioner Psychologist (HCPC UK). Duncan was initially educated in Psychology with an M.Sc. in Organisational Psychology from the University of Manchester Institute of Science and Technology (UMIST) and a B.Sc (Hons) in Psychology from the University of London. Feeling that traditional Psychology only held some of the answers to human interaction, he studied Neuro Linguistic Programming (NLP) at the Practitioner, Master Practitioner and Certified Trainer levels. He is also a certified Hypnotherapist.

Having made massive personal breakthroughs with his own social challenges, Duncan felt there was one final obstacle he needed to address: his fear of talking to strangers. This took him down an unexpected path, culminating in him adding Dating Coaching to his skillset.

Duncan has worked with hundreds of corporations and government departments located in over 20 countries. He works with a wide portfolio of clients around Australia, New Zealand and Asia.

Check out his LinkedIn profile and follow his blogs on:

o   https://au.linkedin.com/in/duncanfish

Printed in Australia
AUHW010450120919
317189AU00012B/152

9 780994 584304